PLUTARCH'S HISTORICAL METHODS

PLUTARCH'S HISTORICAL METHODS

An Analysis of the
Mulierum Virtutes

PHILIP A. STADTER

1965
HARVARD UNIVERSITY PRESS
Cambridge, Massachusetts

© Copyright 1965 by the President and Fellows of Harvard College

All rights reserved

Distributed in Great Britain by Oxford University Press, London

Publication of this book has been aided
by a grant from the Ford Foundation

Library of Congress Catalog Card Number 65-13850

Printed in Great Britain

For
L. A. C.

PREFACE

Plutarch's fascinating collection of anecdotes of women's deeds, the *Mulierum Virtutes*, has not been studied as a unit since M. Dinse in 1863 defended by stylistic comparison its Plutarchian authorship. Evidently there is a need for a study of the short histories which Plutarch incorporated in this work, not only individually, but as part of a greater whole, which taken together express the interests and method of Plutarch. In this commentary I have analyzed each story of the *Mulierum Virtutes*, considering its setting in Greek history and giving special emphasis to the investigation of the source of Plutarch's account. With the help of this inquiry and by constant consideration of all of Plutarch's historical writings, I have come to certain conclusions concerning Plutarch as a writer of biographies and other treatises based on historical materials. These conclusions shed some light on the perplexing question of the role played by Plutarch's writings in the reconstruction of Greek history, especially for the period before Herodotus.

No attempt has been made to improve the text of the treatise, an occupation for which neither training nor inclination serve me. The text used is that of W. Nachstädt's Teubner edition of the *Moralia*, vol. II (Leipzig, 1935). It occurred to me to publish the Greek text together with the commentary, but the added expense of reprinting a text readily available in two editions outweighed any gain in convenience for the reader.

I owe a special debt of gratitude to Prof. Herbert Bloch of Harvard University for his constant encouragement and criticism during the course of my work. I wish also to thank Prof. A. E. Raubitschek, who read the first drafts of several sections of this study, and helped resolve various difficulties, Prof. Sterling Dow for discussion of a number of historical questions, and Mr. G. L. Huxley for allowing me to read the proofs of his book *Early Sparta* (Cambridge, Massachusetts, 1962) before publication. Professors Henry R. Immerwahr and Kenneth Reckford kindly read through the manuscripts and freely offered suggestions and criticisms. Any errors therefore must be ascribed to a certain wilfulness of the author, not to a lack of good will on the part of friends and critics.

P. A. S.

Chapel Hill
February 1964

CONTENTS

I INTRODUCTION 1

II THE *Mulierum Virtutes* AND POLYAENUS' *Strategemata* 13

III COMMENTARY 30

IV PLUTARCH'S INTEREST IN HISTORY 125

BIBLIOGRAPHY 143

INDEX 147

PLUTARCH'S HISTORICAL METHODS

ABBREVIATIONS

The full titles of the Greek histories of Beloch, Bengston, and Busolt will be found in the bibliography.

BCH—*Bulletin de correspondance hellénique.*
BLund—*Bulletin de la société royale de lettres de Lund.*
Busolt-Swoboda—Georg Busolt and Heinrich Swoboda, *Griechische Staatskunde*[3]. 2 vols. Munich 1920-1926.
CIL—*Corpus Inscriptionum Latinarum.*
CP—*Classical Philology.*
CQ—*Classical Quarterly.*
CW—*Classical Weekly.*
FHG—Müller, *Fragmenta Historicorum Graecorum.*
FGrHist—Jacoby, *Fragmente der griechischen Historiker* (citations give the number assigned the author by Jacoby, and the number of the fragment [F] or testimony [T]).
HSCP—*Harvard Studies in Classical Philology.*
IG—*Inscriptiones Graecae.*
JHS—*Journal of Hellenic Studies.*
RE—Pauly-Wissowa-Kroll, *Real-Encyclopädie der klassischen Altertumswissenschaft.* (For Ziegler, *RE*, see Ziegler.)
REA—*Revue des études anciennes.*
REG—*Revue des études grecques.*
RhMus—*Rheinisches Museum für Philologie.*
RivFC—*Rivista di filologia e d'istruzione classica.*
SBBerlin—*Sitzungsberichte der . . . Akademie zu Berlin.*
SBMunich—*Sitzungsberichte der . . . Akademie zu München.*
Schmid-Stählin—Wilhelm Schmidt and Otto Stählin, *Geschichte der griechischen Literatur.* 2 parts in 7 vols. 1920-1948.
SEG—*Supplementum Epigraphicum Graecum.*
SIG[3]—Dittenberger, *Sylloge Inscriptionum Graecarum*[3].
TAPA—*Transactions of the American Philological Association.*
Tod, *GHI*—Marcus N. Tod, *Greek Historical Inscriptions.*
Ziegler, *RE*—Konrat Ziegler, *RE* s.v. Plutarchos 2, XXI 1 (1951) 636-962. Published separately as *Plutarchos von Chaironeia*, Stuttgart 1949.

I

INTRODUCTION

Plutarch states at the beginning of his work that the *Mulierum Virtutes* (*Gunaikôn aretai*) was written for his friend Clea, a priestess at Delphi, to demonstrate that the virtue of men and women is the same.[1] As his argument, he presents a series of examples of virtue in women: twenty-seven historical or semihistorical accounts of Greek and barbarian women, ranging in time from Bellerophon to the Mithridatic wars, and in location from Salmantica in central Spain to the Persian royal city, Pasargadae. They have not been arranged chronologically, but are divided between deeds done by groups of women and by individuals. The division is marked by a transition sentence at the end of the fifteenth story (253 E). These accounts are of interest for the historical information they furnish, and especially for the opportunity they provide to study Plutarch's handling of isolated historical anecdotes, set apart from the mass of material which surrounds such anecdotes in the *Lives* and obscures their form and treatment. A study of the *Mulierum Virtutes*, therefore, provides a clearer understanding of the materials used by Plutarch in his historical accounts, where he found them, and how he treated them.

There has been no reasonable challenge to Plutarch's authorship of this work.[2] The *Mulierum Virtutes* has been accepted as

---

[1] 242 F: *mian einai kai tên autên andros te kai gunaikos aretên*.
[2] M. Dinse, *De libello Plutarchi Gunaikôn aretai inscripto* (Berlin 1863), demonstrated at length that there is no significant difference in style between this and other works of Plutarch. His conclusion is confirmed by the special studies of G. E. Benseler, *De hiatu in oratoribus Atticis* . . . (Freiburg 1841) 442–444; Burkhard Weissenberger, *Die Sprache Plutarchs von Chaeronea und die pseudoplutarchischen Schriften* (Würzburger Diss., Straubing 1895) 63–64, quoted by Dryoff, *Jahresbericht* 108 (1901) 29; and Alfred Hein, *De optativi apud Plutarchum usu* (Diss. Breslau 1914), who does not discuss the *Mulierum Virtutes*, but by his silence shows that he believes it genuine. The objection of C. G. Cobet that

authentic and praised by all those who have concerned themselves with Plutarch.[3]

Although the *Mulierum Virtutes* cannot be dated exactly, it must belong to the latter part of Plutarch's life. The reference in 244 B to the life of Daiphantus is of no help, for we have no evidence for the date of that lost work. The narrative of Camma (*Mul. Virt.* 20) suggests, however, that it is of the same period as the *Amatorius*, where Camma's story is also told in some detail (768 B–D). The *Amatorius* is dated by R. Flacelière to the last decade of Plutarch's life (ca. A.D. 115–125).[4]

Plutarch's dedication of *Mulierum Virtutes* to Clea suggests the same late date.[5] Clea, to whom Plutarch also dedicated the *De Iside*, was a leader (*archêis*) of the Dionysian Thyiad at Delphi (*De Iside* 364 E) and active in the cult of Isis and Osiris (*De Iside* 351 E, 364 E). She is probably identical with Flavia Clea, the *archêis* who made a dedication to Matidia II, the aunt of Antoninus Pius,[6] and the Flavia Clea who dedicated a statue of her mother Memmia Eurydice to Apollo.[7] Since the dedication to Matidia was made in the reign of Antoninus Pius

---

it was too elegantly written to be Plutarchian (*Mnemosyne* 4 [1855] 240 *et alibi*) was later retracted (*Collectanea Critica* [Leiden 1878] 491–492).

[3] See R. Volkmann, *Leben, Schriften und Philosophie des Plutarch von Chaeronea* (Berlin 1869) I, 188; J. J. Hartman, *De Plutarcho scriptore et philosopho* (Leiden 1916), 127–129; Schmid-Stählin II⁶ 1, 514; Ziegler, *RE* 859. The hesitation expressed by F. W. Walbank, *Oxford Classical Dictionary* s.v. Plutarch, 707, "Of various collections of anecdotes and apophthegms claimed for P., *De mulierum virtutibus* ... may be genuine: many are spurious," is prompted by a false association of the *Mulierum Virtutes* with the *Apophthegmata Laconica* and *Apophthegmata regum et imperatorum*, which were probably not published by Plutarch.

[4] *Dialogue sur l'amour* (Annales de l'Université de Lyons, 3e ser., Lettres, fasc. 21, Paris 1952) 10–13. See Castiglioni, *Gnomon* 24 (1952) 17. T. Sinko, *Rozprawy Wydzialu Filologicznego* (Polska Akademia Umiejętności) 67,5 (1947) 18–19 argues unconvincingly for a date soon after the death of Domitian, and therefore dates the *Mulierum Virtutes* to the same period.

[5] See the notices on Clea of Ziegler, *RE* 677, and T. Renoirte, *Les "Conseils politiques" de Plutarque* (Louvain 1951) 137–138.

[6] J. Jannoray, *BCH* 70 (1946) 254–259.

[7] Pomtow, *Klio* 17 (1921) 169 = *SEG* I, 159. The inscription is dated by Pomtow ca. A.D. 100, but by Jannoray (above, n. 6, p. 256 n. 4) to the latter part of the reign of Hadrian. However, the dedication is probably to be dated earlier than Jannoray suggests, before the *De Iside* was written, for it omits the title *archêis* used in that work.

(A.D. 138–161), and Plutarch died ca. A.D. 125,[8] it is most likely that Plutarch dedicated these two works to Clea no more than ten years before he died.[9]

Many Greeks had expressed themselves on the proper excellence of women before Plutarch.[10] He showed his awareness of this tradition by his reference in his introduction (242 E) to the opinions of Thucydides and Gorgias on the subject. Men then as today found in women every manner of evil: the opinions of Homer's Agamemnon[11] or Semonides[12] are illustrative. The classic statement of the misogynist position, incorporated into a general view on man's situation, is Hesiod's myth of Pandora: woman is an evil contrived by Zeus to punish men.[13] Classical Greece was a man's world, and notable women such as Artemisia or Aspasia the exceptions who proved the rule. With the new interest of the Sophists in man, however, the traditional conception of woman was also re-examined. Socrates suggested that woman, although weaker, had the same nature and *arête* as man, and could be educated by her husband.[14] This principle was accepted by his pupils Antisthenes[15] and Plato and by most subsequent philosophers, but was interpreted in various ways. Plato believed that it meant that women must become as much like men as

[8] See Ziegler, *RE* 640–641 and J. Jannoray, *REA* 47 (1945), 256–257.

[9] Ziegler, *RE* 716, who does not mention these inscriptions, says only that the *De Iside* must be dated after Plutarch became a priest at Delphi (ca. A.D. 95–100). It is considered a late work of Plutarch by R. Hirzel, *Der Dialog* (Leipzig 1895) II, 217–218, and Schmid-Stählin II⁶ 1, 513. Ziegler does not attempt to date the *Mulierum Virtutes*.

[10] On Greek attitudes toward women see A. W. Gomme, "The Position of Women in Athens in the Fifth and Fourth Centuries," *CP* 20 (1925) 1–25, reprinted in *Essays in Greek History and Literature* (Oxford 1937) 89–115; L. A. Post, "Woman's Place in Menander's Athens," *TAPA* 71 (1940) 420–459; H. D. F. Kitto, *The Greeks* (Hammondsworth, Middlesex [Penguin Books] 1951) 219–235; Joseph Vogt, "Von der Gleichwertigkeit der Geschlecter in der bürgerlichen Gesellschaft der Griechen," Akadamie von Mainz, *Abhandlungen der geistes-sozialwissenschaftlichen Klasse* (1960) 2, pp. 211–255. The excerpts of Stobaeus IV, 23–24 H, are also useful in this regard.

[11] *Odyssey* 11. 424–434. [12] Fr. 7, Diehl, *Anthologia Lyrica* I³ 3 (1952) pp. 52–58.

[13] See especially *Theogony* 590–612.

[14] Xenophon, *Symposium* 2.9, cf. Plato *Meno* 73 AB, Aristotle *Politics* 1260 a 21. Xenophon notes that Socrates did not see fit to educate his own shrewish wife, Xanthippe.

[15] Diogenes Laertius 6.1.12.

possible, even serving in the army. The impracticability of thus making men out of women was seen by Aristotle and the dictum of Socrates challenged. Aristotle agreed that women had virtue, even as slaves and children, but maintained that the male was by nature superior to the female,[16] and therefore "neither the temperance, nor the courage, nor the justice of a man and a woman are the same, as Socrates thought, but man has a ruling courage (*archikê andreia*), woman a subordinate (*hupêretikê*), and so also for the other virtues."[17] However much Aristotle's ideas may have reflected the prevailing Greek attitude, they were not accepted in philosophical circles. Or rather, they were accepted often enough in practice, though rejected in theory. Epicurus' garden was exceptional in welcoming women as well as men: it was called a brothel.[18] Crates' wife and disciple Hipparchia shared completely in the ascetic life of the Cynic, but was subjected to every sort of indignity.[19] The Arcadian Axiothea was a remarkable exception at the Academy.[20] Zeno envisioned women sages in his ideal state,[21] but in practice had nothing to do with them.[22] Nevertheless, the Stoics taught that all mankind, including women, had the same nature and virtue[23] and that all were teachable: women, like farmers and artisans, could become sages.[24] Cleanthes wrote a book, *Concerning the Proposition that the Virtue of Man and Woman Is the Same*.[25] Later Stoics, such as Hierocles and Antipater, praised the value of marriage even for the sage.[26]

Several long fragments preserved by Stobaeus present the liberal yet practical views of Musonius Rufus, a Stoic philosopher of the time of Nero who was influenced by Roman tradition. In his *That Women*

[16] Aristotle, *Politics* 1259 b 1.   [17] Aristotle, *Politics* 1260 a 21–24.
[18] See A. J. Festugière, *Epicurus and his Gods* (Cambridge, Mass. 1956) 29–30.
[19] Diogenes Laertius 6.7.96–97.   [20] Aristotle fr. 64 Rose.
[21] Diogenes Laertius 7.1.33; see Paul Barth, *Die Stoa*[6] (Stuttgart 1946) 37.
[22] Athenaeus 13, 563 E (*Stoicorum Veterum Fragmenta*, ed. J. von Arnim, Leipzig, 1921, I, 58–59, fr. 247).
[23] Clement of Alexandria, *Stromateis* IV 8, 59 (*St. Vet. Frag.* III 59, fr. 254).
[24] Lactantius *Divinae institutiones* 3.25 (*St. Vet. Frag.* III 59, fr. 253).
[25] Diogenes Laertius 7.5.175.
[26] See the fragments of the books *On Marriage* of Hierocles and Antipater in Stobaeus IV 22, 21–25 ed. Hense.

Also Should Practice Philosophy[27] Musonius argues that woman is basically the same as man and has equal need of the various virtues; therefore even women must study philosophy, by which the virtues are developed. Musonius' practical sense, however, restrains him from arguing that women are to perform the same functions as men: rather a woman studies philosophy so that she may perform her womanly duties well. This argument is pursued further in his *Whether Daughters Should Be Educated Side by Side with Sons*.[28] Both men and women have the same virtues: even courage (*andreia*) is not proper to men alone, for women need courage lest they desert the right from fear or pain. The example of the Amazons is introduced to demonstrate that women can be courageous not only in domestic matters but in war as well. Such activity, of course, is unusual for women, and in general they are to be given lighter tasks, such as weaving, because they are weaker. Musonius does envision the occasion, however, when some men might do lighter work and some women heavier, if the condition of their bodies allowed or circumstances required.

Plutarch himself had a high opinion of women, which is expressed frequently in both the *Lives* and the *Moralia*. Among his ethical writings several works are devoted to the role of women, especially in marriage. The *Praecepta conjugalia*, addressed to two of Plutarch's former students now newly married, gives numerous small rules for the guidance of husband and wife. It is the woman's part to be subordinate to her husband, obedient, quiet, and modest, while the husband's is to respect and cherish her. Moreover, he is to educate her, to be not only "father and revered mother and brother," as Homer says, but "guide, philosopher, and teacher of that which is most lovely and divine" (145 CD). If the wife is trained in philosophy she will not believe in charms and will laugh at those pretending to pull the moon down from the sky. She will not desire costly jewels and finery, but rather the ornaments of virtue which were the glory of Theano and Cleobulina, of Gorgo and Timoclea and Claudia and

---

[27] Stobaeus II 31, 126 (= Musonius, ed. Hense, pp. 8–13).
[28] Stobaeus II 31, 123 (= Musonius, ed. Hense, pp. 13–19).

Cornelia.[29] Thus without extravagance she may live a happy and distinguished life. That a woman could and should be educated was also maintained by Plutarch in a work *That a Woman Also Should Be Educated* (VII, 125-127 ed. Bernadakis) of which only a few short excerpts are preserved. Plutarch's own wife, Timoxena, was not a stranger to letters, for she is mentioned as the author of a book, *On Love of Ornament*, which Plutarch recommends to the young bride in the *Praecepta conjugalia* (145 A).

Plutarch's finest statement of the nature and excellence of women, however, is in the *Amatorius*. There, in a dialogue which supposedly took place while he and his young wife were attending the festival of Eros at Thespiae, making a thank offering to the god, he introduces the questions of the relative merits of homosexual and heterosexual love. After a eulogy of the god Eros reminiscent of Plato's *Symposium* and *Phaedrus*, Plutarch sets forth his own opinion that this god works most effectively and honorably in the love of husband and wife. He presents the various arguments in support of marriage adduced by the Stoics,[30] based chiefly on considerations of utility and comfort. But beyond that he finds in the union in love of man and wife an unaging bond which brings out the best qualities of both and is the true beginning of that ladder of love described by Plato in the *Symposium*. He supports this argument with the histories of Camma the Galatian[31] and of Empone the wife of Sabinus,[32] both of whom through

---

[29] Theano was the wife of Pythagoras; a saying of hers is quoted by Plutarch in *Praecepta conjugalia* 142 CD. Cleobulina, or Eumetis, the wise daughter of Cleobulus, was present at a meeting of the seven sages in Corinth, according to Plutarch, *Septem sapientium convivium*, 148 C. Gorgo was the daughter of Cleomenes and wife of Leonidas (see Herodotus 5.51, 7.239). Claudia is undoubtedly the Claudia Quinta who effortlessly pulled the ship bearing the sacred stone of the Magna Mater off a bar in the Tiber (see Livy 29.14 *et al.*). Cornelia, of course, is the mother of the Gracchi.

[30] See the references given by Flacelière, *Dialogue sur l'amour*, 20-24, and by Hubert in the Teubner edition (Plutarch *Moralia* IV).

[31] 768 B-D. The story of Camma is also told in *Mul. Virt.* 20 (see below pp. 103-106) and helps date the *Mulierum Virtutes* (cf. above, p. 2).

[32] 770 D-771 C. Julius Sabinus in A.D. 69 supported the revolt in Gaul of Julius Civilis against Vespasian. The loyalty of his wife Empone (Tacitus *Epponina*, Dio *Peponilla*) is also reported by Tacitus, *Historiae* 4.67 and Dio Cassius 66.3, 16.

steadfast love displayed the highest virtue. Plutarch's exaltation of woman and of conjugal love is unique in classical Greek literature, and reveals an important part of his character. This philosophical ideal was realized in, and no doubt inspired by, Plutarch's own home life, as we learn from the moving letter of consolation which he wrote to his wife on the death of one of their children (*Consolatio ad uxorem*). Plutarch there reveals the love, respect, and understanding which united him to his wife.

The keen interest in women as human beings which these works reveal naturally expressed itself in the *Lives*, Plutarch's major work. Long before Plutarch composed the *Mulierum Virtutes* for Clea, he had presented in the *Lives* numerous portraits of extraordinary women. The description of Porcia testing with a knife whether she was a true child of Cato [33] leaps immediately to mind, or of Cleonice preferring to die rather than suffer Pausanias' drunken violence,[34] or of Thebe contriving the murder of her tyrant husband.[35] This same interest in the deeds of great persons, women as well as men, underlies the *Mulierum Virtutes*.

We know little of collections before Plutarch of the actions of famous women. Photius noted that Sopater excerpted the *Accounts of Deeds Done Courageously by Women* of one Artemon of Magnesia, not otherwise known.[36] Sopater also excerpted a book of Apollonius the Stoic, *Women Who Were Philosophers or Otherwise Accomplished Something Noteworthy, or through Whom Houses Were Joined in Good Will*.[37] We know no more of this collection or its author, although Von Arnim suggests that this Apollonius may be Apollonius of Tyre, who in the first century B.C. wrote a catalogue of philosophers and their books, beginning with Zeno.[38] Sopater used yet another collection,

---

[33] Plutarch, *Brutus* 13.2–6.
[34] Plutarch, *Cimon* 6.4–6.
[35] Plutarch, *Pelopidas* 35.3–7.
[36] Photius *Bibliotheca* cod. 161, 103 A Bekker. See *RE* s.v. Artemon 19, II, 2 (1896) 1447.
[37] Photius (above, n. 36) 104 B Bekker.
[38] *RE* s.v. Apollonios 94, II, 1 (1896) 146. He is followed by Schmid-Stählin II⁶ 1, 258.

anonymous, which listed *Women Lifted up to Great Fame and Brilliant Reputation*.[39] All three of these works have been suggested at various times as the source of an extant anonymous collection,[40] which under the title *Women Intelligent and Courageous in Warfare* gives fourteen brief histories of remarkable women, of whom ten are barbarian (Semiramis, Zarinaia, Nitocris of Egypt, Nitocris of Babylon, Theiosso [Dido], Atossa, Rhodogyne, Lyde, Tomyris, and Onomaris) and four Greek (Argeia, Pheretime, Thargelia, and Artemisia). In all except two of the stories the source of the account is recorded: Herodotus provides five stories, Ctesias two, and Timaeus, Hellanicus, Aeschines the Socratic, Xenophilus, and Menecles one each. The notices do not so much give stories about the women (as does the *Mulierum Virtutes*) as present the highlights of their careers. Following these histories is a list, "Houses which were ruined through women," with a few words noting how various mythical families were destroyed by women—for example, "that of Theseus through the love of Phaedra for Hippolytus."

A fifth collection is mentioned by Suidas. He preserves a notice of one Charon of Carthage, who wrote, besides a book on the Tyrrhenians and biographies of men in four books, biographies of women, likewise in four books.[41] Again, nothing else is known of this writer. Undoubtedly other collections of this type existed which have not survived even in title. Considering the sparseness of the remains we cannot affirm to what degree Plutarch's work belongs to this genre. It is useful to remember nevertheless that none of the women found in the *Anonymus de mulieribus* of Westermann is the subject of an anecdote in the *Mulierum Virtutes*.

Plutarch was led to assemble his collection of stories from a particularly appropriate motive. After the death of Leontis, a woman

---

[39] Photius (above, n. 36) 104 A Bekker.
[40] Anton Westermann, *Paradoxographoi, Scriptores rerum mirabilium Graeci* (Braunschweig 1839) 213–218 and pp. xli–xlii. See also V. Rose, *Anecdota Graeca et Graecolatina* I (Berlin 1864) 14.
[41] Suidas s.v. Charon (no. 137 Adler). Cf. Müller *FHG* IV 360. Schwartz, *RE* s.v. Charon 9, III, 2 (1899) 2180, dates him to the Hellenistic period, before 146 B.C.

unknown to us,[42] Plutarch had a long conversation with Clea, touching upon the consolation philosophy had to offer on such an occasion. Afterward he elaborated for Clea one topic of this conversation, the proposition that men and women have one and the same virtue. He will not accept, he writes her, Thucydides' famous statement in the funeral oration of Pericles (2.45.2), that a good woman should not be spoken of outside her own home whether for good or for evil. More fitting is that of Gorgias (*Fragmente der Vorsokratiker* 82 B 22), who stated that a woman's reputation should be known to many, but not her appearance. These opinions reflect in varying degrees the traditional Greek belief that a woman's place is inside, separate from the world of men. Plutarch, however, rather approves of the Roman practice, which allowed women as well as men to be publicly honored after their deaths.[43] This custom he takes as a precedent for this work in honor of the deceased Leontis.

The *Mulierum Virtutes* is historical and expository in form,[44] and will please not so much from the presentation as from the examples themselves, that is, women who did brave deeds. Plutarch protests that in thus relating stories about women he is not attempting to beguile his readers, but to convince them rationally, proving the proposition that the virtue of men and women is the same not by logical demonstration but by historical example. His defense of his method is important for the proper understanding not only of this work but also of the *Parallel Lives*, and is worth quoting in full:

> There is no better way to learn the similarity and difference of the virtue of men and women than to place lives beside lives and deeds beside deeds as though products of a great art, observing whether the ambition of Semiramis to accomplish great things had the same character and stamp as that of

---

[42] She is perhaps identical with or related to --]*leou thugatêr Leontis*, the dedicator of an inscription at Delphi about the time of Vespasian. See Daux, *BCH* 83 (1959) 490-493 esp. 493 n. 2 (= *SEG* XVIII 216).

[43] This practice is also referred to in *Camillus* 8.3, as a reward voted by the senate to the women, cf. Livy 5.50.7. Cicero *De oratore* 2.11 (44), however, believed that Popilia the mother of Catulus was the first to be so praised. Plutarch mentions the funeral orations given by Julius Caesar for his aunt Julia and wife Cornelia (*Caesar* 5.2-4).

[44] 243 A: *to historikon apodeiktikon echonta*.

Sesostris,[45] or the good sense of Tanaquil the same as that of King Servius,[46] or the resolution of Porcia the same as that of Brutus,[47] and that of Timoclea the same as that of Pelopidas,[48] according to their most important common element and quality. For the virtues, because of the various constitutions of individuals, take on certain differences, peculiar colors as it were, and they assimilate themselves to the underlying habits, bodily temperament,[49] nourishment, and manner of life of the individual: Achilles was brave in one way, Ajax in another, and the intelligence of Odysseus was not like that of Nestor, nor were Cato and Agesilaus just in the same way, nor did Irene[50] love her man as did Alcestis, nor was Cornelia high-minded as Olympias.[51] But not on this account do we create many different courages and intelligences and justices, provided only that the individual dissimilarities do not force one out of its proper category (243 B-D).

This passage illustrates how much the *Parallel Lives* were in Plutarch's mind when he wrote the *Mulierum Virtutes*. Half of the examples are from the *Lives*, and what is more indicative, the principle of comparison stated is the essential feature of the *Parallel Lives*. In this paragraph he defines two types of comparison, one between men and women, and the other between two persons of the same sex. The two types of comparison, he argues, are essentially the same, since the virtue of women is the same as that of men. In the *Mulierum Virtutes* he presents a catalogue of virtuous deeds of women, yet he makes no express comparisons: he presumes that his readers are already well acquainted with the deeds of men.

[45] The two are also mentioned together in *De Iside* 360 B. For Semiramis, see Diodorus 2.4-20 and the *Anonymus de mulieribus* 1 (= Ctesias, *FGrHist* 688 F 1b, 1c). For Sesostris, see Herodotus 2. 102-110.
[46] Cf. Plutarch's account of Tanaquil and Servius in *De fortuna Romanorum* 322 E-323 D.
[47] Porcia's resolution appears in two vignettes in *Brutus*, 13.2-6 and 53.4-5.
[48] Timoclea's courage is reported in *Alexander* 12 as well as in *Mul. Virt.* 24: see Chapter III below.
[49] *Krasesi sômatôn*: cf. Galen's book entitled *hoti ta tês psuchês êthê tais tou sômatos krasesin hepetai* (Kuhn IV 767ff.).
[50] Surely not the courtesan friend of a minor Ptolemy at Ephesus (Athenaeus 13, 593 AB) as often suggested, following Wyttenbach. Yet no suitable Irene is known.
[51] The character of Cornelia is touched upon in the lives of the Gracchi (e.g. *Tiberius* 1.4-5, *Gaius* 19), that of Olympias in the life of Alexander (see *Alexander* 10.4, 39.4-5).

Introduction

Plutarch's statement, moreover, reveals another affinity with the *Parallel Lives*, and with much of the *Moralia*. This is the conviction that one can arrive at a better understanding of virtue by studying the lives and deeds (*bious kai praxeis*) of men. This is his reason for writing biography, to discover through his actions the character of a man.[52] The same principle of using historical examples to discover moral truth underlies many of the essays in the *Moralia*.[53] The innumerable historical or semihistorical anecdotes in the *Lives* are another reflection of Plutarch's use of this method of discovering moral insights and presenting them to us. Nor is this method as obvious as it might appear: Musonius, for example, in arguing that women possess the same virtue as men, used only one example, the daring of the Amazons, and that from the legendary past, not from history.[54] Seneca is closer to the manner of Plutarch, when he cites Lucretia, Cloelia, Cornelia the mother of the Gracchi, and Cornelia the wife of Livius Drusus as evidence that women can show virtue.[55] Plutarch, however, presents a catalogue of twenty-seven accounts of virtue in women. This catalogue is for Plutarch a philosophical treatise in itself, as he clearly asserts in the introduction. The proposition that the virtue of men and women is the same is to be proved not by argument but by the clear testimony of history.

Finally, Plutarch professes in his introduction that he will pass over the anecdotes which are repeated by everyone (*ta agan periboêta*) and those with which a well-read person like Clea would already be familiar. He will make an exception, however, to this general rule of avoiding well-known stories if he feels that some detail worth hearing has escaped those narrating the common, widespread stories (243 D). This affirmation, in view of his recognized integrity, prohibits the

---

[52] See esp. *Alexander* 1, *Pompey* 8, *Nicias* 1, *Cimon* 2 and Friedrich Leo, *Griechisch-römische Biographie* (Leipzig 1901) 184-186.

[53] E.g. *De garrulitate* 505 A–511 E, a series of examples recalling unfortunate events in history caused by loquacity, *De fraterno amore* 488 D–489 F (examples of the love of Xerxes and Ariamenes, Seleucus II and Antiochus, Eumenes II and Attalus), and *Amatorius* 768 B–D, 770 D–771 C (the stories of Camma and Empone).

[54] Stobaeus II, 31.123 (= Musonius ed. Hense, p. 15).

[55] *Ad Marciam de consolatione* 16.

assumption that Plutarch assembled these stories by rifling some earlier anthology of women's deeds. The principles which Plutarch followed in selecting his anecdotes may be better ascertained after the stories have been examined individually. Since, however, the proposition has been advanced and repeated that Plutarch in the *Mulierum Virtutes* merely excerpts an earlier anthology, that question demands a prior investigation. The theory arose from a comparison of Plutarch's collection with Polyaenus' *Strategemata*, in which are found a majority of the stories told by Plutarch. A careful examination of the relation of the collections of Plutarch and Polyaenus will be a profitable prelude to the investigation of the individual anecdotes of the *Mulierum Virtutes*.

II

THE *MULIERUM VIRTUTES* AND POLYAENUS' *STRATEGEMATA*

Of the twenty-seven stories collected in the *Mulierum Virtutes*, nineteen are found in the seventh and eighth books of Polyaenus' *Strategemata*.[1] This work in eight books by the rhetor from Macedonia[2] was dedicated to Marcus Aurelius and Lucius Verus ca. A.D. 162. The prefaces to the various books explain the aim of the author. As the Parthian War loomed ever nearer, Polyaenus took it upon himself to collect examples of generalship, for the use of the emperors, presenting in short anecdotes illustrative stories from many authors.

The correspondence between the collections of Plutarch and Polyaenus (see page 14) had been explained until eighty years ago as a direct borrowing from Plutarch by Polyaenus. Wyttenbach, in the introduction to his notes on the *Mulierum Virtutes*, says simply, "Certe ex hoc Plutarchi libro multa descripsit capita Polyaenus Strategem. Lib. VIII." Cobet had no doubt that the *Mulierum Virtutes* was the

---

[1] The best text is that re-edited by J. Melber after E. Wölfflin, Leipzig 1887 (Teubner). References in this chapter to the introduction to this edition are made thus: Melber, Introduction, p. 1.

[2] See Suidas s.v. Polyainos (no. 1956 Adler). On Polyaenus and his work see F. Lammert, *RE* s.v. Polyainos 8, XXI 2 (1952) 1432-36 and s.v. Strategemata, IV 1 A (1931) 174-181.

14 The "Mulierum Virtutes" and Polyaenus' "Strategemata"

PLUTARCH–POLYAENUS				POLYAENUS–PLUTARCH			
1	8.25.2	14	8.31	7.45.2	5	8.38	19
2	8.65	16	8.35	.48	10	.39	20
3	8.66	17	8.36	.49	8	.40	24
4	8.33	18	8.37	.50	6	.41	25
5	7.45.2	19	8.38	8.25.2	1	.42	27
6	7.50	20	8.39	.31	14	.63	11
7	8.64	24	8.40	.33	4	.64	7
8	7.49	25	8.41	.35	16	.65	2
10	7.48	27	8.42	.36	17	.66	3
11	8.63			.37	18		

source of Polyaenus' stories.[3] Alfred von Gutschmid remarked that the last part of the eighth book "Polyaenus ex Plutarchi libro de virtute mulierum deprompsit, cum alias Plutarcho non usus est."[4] Finally, Wölfflin in the introduction to his edition of Polyaenus (Leipzig 1860) maintained his author's dependence on Plutarch.[5] In 1884, however, Otto Knott in a study "De fide et fontibus Polyaeni" argued that the similarity between the two authors was due to the use of a common source by Plutarch and Polyaenus.[6] This view was accepted without further discussion or treatment by Melber[7] in his

---

[3] *Mnemosyne* 4 (1855) 241: "Iuvenibus suaserim eleganter librum pseudo-Plutarcheum ita comparare cum Polyaeno in lib. VIII, ut quid vir viro praestet intelligere et sentire discant; videbunt enim multa apud scriptorem antiquiorem recte et venuste dicta a militari viro et scribendi imperito subinepte et perperam reficta esse." He later accepted the genuineness of the *Mulierum Virtutes* (see above, Chapter I, n. 2).

[4] *Philologus* 11 (1856) 149 = *Kleine Schriften* I (Leipzig 1889) 176.

[5] Cited by J. Melber, "Über die Quellen und den Wert der Stratagemensammlung Polyäns" *Jahrbücher für classische Philologie*, Suppl. Bd. 14 (1885) 664.

[6] *Commentationes philologae ienenses* 3 (1884) 75–80.

[7] See above, n. 5, pp. 417–688, and especially pp. 596, 654, 664, and 683. Adolf Schirmer, *Über die Quellen des Polyaen* (Altenberg, 1884) 17–18, also accepted Knott's conclusion, and treating the possibility that Polyaenus 7.45.2 is derived from Nicolaus of Damascus as a fact, supposed that Nicolaus is the common source of Polyaenus and Plutarch except for the stories Polyaenus 8.35–42 (= *Mul. Virt.* 16–20, 24, 25, 27) which, he says, no historian would have recounted in such an arbitrary order, and so must be from an anthology.

extensive study of the sources of Polyaenus, and remains the accepted opinion today.[8]

A thorough examination of Plutarch and Polyaenus, however, completely vindicates the earlier opinion. Knott's arguments, though at first sight persuasive, are found to be without foundation, except in the case of one story, that of the Persian women (Poly. 7.45.2, *Mul. Virt.* 5).

First consider the difference in disposition of the two sets of stories, which Knott believes an indication of Polyaenus' independence from Plutarch.[9] The arrangement of the last two books of the *Strategemata* in relation to the stories found also in Plutarch is shown in the following table:

Stories concerning:	Chapters	Stories found in *Mulierum Virtutes*
Individual barbarian men	7. 1–41	—
Groups of barbarian men	.42–46	7.45.2
Groups of barbarian women	.47–50	7.48–50
Individual Roman men	8. 1–24	—
Groups of Romans	.25	8.25.2
Individual Barbarian women	.26–29	—
Individual Roman women	.30–32	8.31
Individual Greek women	.33–63	8.33, 35–42, 63
Groups of Greek women	.64–71	8.64–66

The table reveals that Polyaenus divided his collection of *strategemata* into categories, and that the difference between the disposition of the stories in Plutarch and Polyaenus was necessary if the latter was to incorporate Plutarch's anecdotes into his own scheme. Three stories of

---

[8] See Schmid-Stählin II[6] 2, 754, n. 10; W. Nachstädt in Plutarchus *Moralia* II, 225; Ziegler, *RE* 859, and F. Lammert, *RE* s.v. Strategemata 180 (he does not mention this problem in his article in *RE* s.v. Polyainos). Various students of individual stories have nevertheless questioned the opinion of Knott and Melber; see e.g. Jacoby, *Comm.* to *FGrHist* 310 F 6 note 80 (p. 26), on the story of the Argive women (Poly. 8.33 = *Mul. Virt.* 4).

[9] It is perhaps to state the obvious to remark that the postulation of a common source in no way explains the difference in the disposition of the two collections. One of the authors must still have changed the order from that which he found in his source.

barbarian women acting in common found in the *Mulierum Virtutes* (10, 8, 6) were collected in one spot by Polyaenus (7.48–50). The one story of Roman women acting together (*Mul. Virt.* 1) is found among Polyaenus' anecdotes of Romans (8.25.2), and the story of Cloelia (*Mul. Virt.* 14) is joined by Polyaenus (8.31) with those of the other Roman heroines. The whole last half of the *Mulierum Virtutes* (16–27), which contained anecdotes concerning individual women, is found in exactly the same order, though with some stories omitted,[10] in Polyaenus 8.35–42, in the section devoted to this category of stories. Stories by Plutarch concerning groups of women (*Mul. Virt.* 7, 2, 3) are found collected together in Polyaenus in the same fashion (8.64–66). However, the two accounts (*Mul. Virt.* 4 and 11) which had been considered by Plutarch as stories of group bravery in Polyaenus (8.33 and 63) are regarded as concerning individuals, and are placed in that section (8.33–63). Indicatively, these stories which are not in the category assigned them by Plutarch also are not grouped with other stories found in Plutarch, but have found positions at the beginning and end of their new category. Of the stories which are found both in Polyaenus and in Plutarch, only the account of the Persian women (7.45.2) is found to be in an unexpected position, that is, among the stories of barbarian men (7.42–46) rather than among those of barbarian women (7.47–50).

The different disposition of the anecdotes in the *Mulierum Virtutes* and the *Strategemata*, therefore, is the result of the different principles of organization in the two works. Plutarch divided his collection into two parts, stories of women acting together (*Mul. Virt.* 1–15) and individually (16–27).[11] Polyaenus, on the other hand, divided the stories also according to the nationality of the women, as is shown by the table above. This different arrangement of the stories in itself indicates nothing concerning their source. The exact repetition of the sequence of stories in the various categories, however, and especially of the eight stories of individual bravery (*Mul. Virt.* 16–20, 24–25, 27 = Poly. 8.35–42), is striking evidence for the later author's use of Plutarch.

---

[10] *Mul. Virt.* 21–23, 26. See below, p. 28.
[11] See above, p. 1.

The "Mulierum Virtutes" and Polyaenus' "Strategemata"

There remains to be considered the relation between the individual pairs of stories. That which Knott found most convincing for his argument was *Mul. Virt.* 4 and Polyaenus 8.33, the story of Telesilla and the Argive women. The full Polyaenus passage with the parallel sections of Plutarch may be quoted here:

Mulierum Virtutes 4	Polyaenus 8.33
... ἐπεὶ δὲ Κλεομένης ὁ βασιλεὺς τῶν Σπαρτιατῶν πολλοὺς ἀποκτείνας (οὐ μήν, ὥς ἔνιοι μυθολογοῦσιν, ἑπτὰ καὶ ἑβδομήκοντα καὶ ἑπτακοσίους πρὸς ἑπτακισχιλίοις) ἐβάδιζε πρὸς τὴν πόλιν, ὁρμὴ καὶ τόλμα δαιμόνιος παρέστη ταῖς ἀκμαζούσαις τῶν γυναικῶν ἀμύνεσθαι τοὺς πολεμίους ὑπὲρ τῆς πατρίδος.	Κλεομένης Σπαρτιατῶν βασιλεὺς κτείνας ἐν παρατάξει Ἀργείων ἄνδρας ἑπτακισχιλίους ἑπτακοσίους ἑβδομήκοντα ἑπτὰ ἐβάδιζεν ἐπὶ τὸ Ἄργος ὡς κατὰ κράτος αἱρήσων τὴν πόλιν· Τελέσιλλα ἡ μουσικὴ τὰς Ἀργείας ὁπλίσασα προήγαγεν εἰς μάχην.
ἡγουμένης δὲ τῆς Τελεσίλλης ὅπλα λαμβάνουσαι καὶ παρ' ἔπαλξιν ἱστάμεναι κύκλῳ τὰ τείχη περιέστεψαν, ὥστε θαυμάζειν τοὺς πολεμίους.	αἱ δὲ ἔνοπλοι παρὰ ἔπαλξιν ἱστάμεναι, κύκλῳ τὰ τείχη φραξάμεναι
τὸν μὲν οὖν Κλεομένη πολλῶν πεσόντων ἀπεκρούσαντο· τὸν δ' ἕτερον βασιλέα Δημάρατον, ὡς Σωκράτης φησίν, ἐντὸς γενόμενον καὶ κατασχόντα τὸ Παμφυλιακὸν ἐξέωσαν.	Κλεομένη μὲν ἀπεκρούσαντο, Δημάρατον δὲ τὸν ἕτερον βασιλέα ἐξώσαντο καὶ τὴν πόλιν ἁλῶναι κινδυνεύουσαν ἀνέσωσαν.
οὕτω δὲ τῆς πόλεως περιγενομένης, τὰς μὲν πεσούσας ἐν τῇ μάχῃ τῶν γυναικῶν ἐπὶ τῆς ὁδοῦ τῆς Ἀργείας ἔθαψαν, ταῖς δὲ σωθείσαις	

ὑπόμνημα τῆς ἀριστείας
ἔδοσαν ἱδρύσασθαι τὸν
Ἐνυάλιον. τὴν δὲ μάχην οἱ
μὲν ἑβδόμῃ λέγουσιν ἱσταμένου
μηνός, οἱ δὲ <u>νουμηνίᾳ</u>
γενέσθαι τοῦ νῦν μὲν τετάρτου,
πάλαι δ' <u>Ἑρμαίου παρ'</u>   τοῦτο τὸ στρατήγημα τῶν
Ἀργείοις, καθ' ἣν <u>μέχρι νῦν</u>   γυναικῶν <u>μέχρι νῦν</u> Ἀργεῖοι
τὰ Ὑβριστικὰ τελοῦσι,   τιμῶσι, <u>νουμηνίᾳ</u> μηνὸς
γυναῖκας μὲν ἀνδρείοις   <u>Ἑρμαίου τὰς</u> μὲν γυναῖκας
<u>χιτῶσι καὶ χλαμύσιν</u>, ἄνδρας   ἀνδρείοις <u>χιτῶσι καὶ χλαμύσι</u>,
δὲ <u>πέπλοις</u> γυναικῶν καὶ   τοὺς δὲ ἄνδρας <u>πέπλοις</u>
καλύπτραις <u>ἀμφιεννύντες</u>...   γυναικείοις <u>ἀμφιεννύντες</u>.

The comparison shows an extraordinarily close agreement between words and phrases, far closer than is ever found when Plutarch himself tells the same story twice.[12] Nothing is said in Polyaenus which is not said in Plutarch, and although four short phrases are original with Polyaenus, they are trivial differences and do not affect the sense. On the other hand a number of items found in Plutarch are not found in Polyaenus. Thus the two instances in which Plutarch gives two alternatives in his story—on the date of the battle of Sepeia and on the number killed there—Polyaenus in each case preserves only one alternative. Knott objected that Polyaenus accepts the variant number of men killed, 7,777, which Plutarch expressly rejects. Polyaenus, however, was not accustomed to give variants (we note this also in 8.31, Cloelia, as compared with Plutarch's version, *Mul. Virt.* 14); nor was he a diligent searcher after historical truth. The exact number was chosen simply because Polyaenus found it more vivid than Plutarch's preferred *pollous*. To confirm the conclusion that Polyaenus used Plutarch, we find that Polyaenus here reproduces (anonymously) the citation from Socrates of Argos, which Plutarch without doubt introduced from his own reading.[13] Polyaenus must have taken this

[12] See below pp. 24–26.
[13] See the discussion of *Mul. Virt.* 4, below, p. 52.

story directly from Plutarch's *Mulierum Virtutes*, not from any common source.

This comparison, which Knott considered an excellent demonstration of Polyaenus' independence from Plutarch, proves in fact just the opposite. Knott fails to notice the difference in purpose (not to say talent) between the work of Plutarch and Polyaenus, which readily explains the usually slight changes made by the latter when borrowing stories from the *Mulierum Virtutes*. Polyaenus wished to present in as brief a form as possible anecdotes of successful stratagems. To this desire for brevity he sacrificed small details, sentences, or whole paragraphs of his source, and preserved only the kernel of the original account. He wrote hurriedly[14] and therefore followed wherever possible the words of his source, but for the same reason he also made a number of small mistakes.

The striking similarity of words and phrases between the corresponding anecdotes of the *Mulierum Virtutes* and the *Strategemata* is most obvious in the shorter stories, which Polyaenus could use with negligible abridgement. An example is the story of the Celtic women:

Mulierum Virtutes 6	Polyaenus 7.50
Κελτοῖς, πρὶν ὑπερβαλεῖν Ἄλπεις καὶ κατοικῆσαι τῆς Ἰταλίας ἣν νῦν νέμονται χώραν, στάσις ἐμπεσοῦσα δεινὴ καὶ δυσκατάπαυστος εἰς πόλεμον ἐμφύλιον προῆλθεν. αἱ δὲ γυναῖκες ἐν μέσῳ τῶν ὅπλων γενόμεναι καὶ παραλαβοῦσαι τὰ νείκη διῄτησαν οὕτως ἀμέμπτως καὶ διέκριναν, ὥστε φιλίαν πᾶσι θαυμαστὴν καὶ κατὰ πόλεις	Κελτοῖς στάσις ἦν ἐμφύλιος. ἤδη δὲ καὶ ἐς πόλεμον ὡπλισμένων, αἱ γυναῖκες αὐτῶν [ἐν μέσῳ] στᾶσαι τῆς παρατάξεως τὰ ἐγκλήματα διῄτησαν καὶ διέκριναν, ὥστε τοὺς ἄνδρας φίλους γενομένους διαλλαγὰς ποιήσασθαι

[14] See Melber, Introduction, p. VI, "Polyaenus igitur omnes libros intra paucos annos deinceps emisit." He was also engaged in the courts at the time: see book II, preface.

καὶ κατ᾽ οἴκους γενέσθαι πρὸς   καὶ κατὰ οἴκους καὶ κατὰ πόλεις.
πάντας. ἐκ τούτου διετέλουν   αὖθις, εἴποτε Κελτοὶ
περί τε πολέμου καὶ εἰρήνης   βουλεύοιντο πολέμου πέρι καὶ
βουλευόμενοι μετὰ τῶν γυναικῶν   εἰρήνης ἢ τῶν ἄλλων ὅσα
καὶ τὰ πρὸς τοὺς συμμάχους   κοινὰ πρὸς ἀλλήλους ἢ τοὺς
ἀμφίβολα δι᾽ ἐκείνων   συμμάχους, ἕκαστα γνώμῃ τῶν
βραβεύοντες. ἐν γοῦν ταῖς   γυναικῶν ἐβραβεύετο. ἐν γοῦν
πρὸς Ἀννίβαν συνθήκαις   ταῖς πρὸς Ἀννίβαν συνθήκαις
ἐγράψαντο, Κελτῶν μὲν   γέγραπται, Κελτῶν μὲν ἐγκαλούντων
ἐγκαλούντων Καρχηδονίοις   Καρχηδονίοις τοὺς Καρχηδονίων
τοὺς ἐν Ἰβηρίᾳ Καρχηδονίων   ἐπάρχους καὶ στρατηγοὺς εἶναι
ἐπάρχους καὶ στρατηγοὺς   δικαστάς, ἢν δὲ Καρχηδόνιοι
εἶναι δικαστάς· ἂν δὲ   Κελτοῖς ἐγκαλῶσι, τὰς
Καρχηδόνιοι Κελτοῖς ἐγκαλῶσι,   Κελτῶν γυναῖκας δικάζειν.
τὰς Κελτῶν γυναῖκας.

The reader will note at a glance that the account of Polyaenus reproduces almost exactly the words of Plutarch and records nothing that is not in his account, while at the same time omitting some details. Exactly similar to this pair are *Mul. Virt.* 16 (Pieria) and Polyaenus 8.35 and *Mul. Virt.* 11 (Milesian women) and Polyaenus 8.63.[15] Only slightly different are those cases in which Polyaenus reports only one episode from several collected in a single chapter by Plutarch: thus *Mul. Virt.* 3 part 2 (Chian women) and Polyaenus 8.66, *Mul. Virt.* 17 part 2 (Polycrite) and Polyaenus 8.36, and *Mul. Virt.* 27 part 1 (Pythes' wife) and Polyaenus 8.42. There is one difficulty in this last pair, because Polyaenus in his account calls Pythes' wife Pythopolis, although she is not named by Plutarch. However, to postulate a common source is no solution: if Plutarch had found the name of the woman in his source, he would have given it. Rather, Polyaenus, unhappy with his heroine's anonymity, seems to have christened her with a

---

[15] The fact that Polyaenus 8.63 says that the decree of the Milesians was moved by a woman, whereas Plutarch clearly ascribes it to a man, is surely a trivial mistake or alteration by Polyaenus, and not evidence for a common source giving two variants.

The "Mulierum Virtutes" and Polyaenus' "Strategemata" 21

name inspired by the river Pythopolites mentioned by Plutarch in this chapter.[16]

In all of these stories Polyaenus' dependence on Plutarch is evident from the often exact repetition of words and phrases and from the absence of any facts not in Plutarch. Even in those cases, such as *Mul. Virt.* 4 (Argive women) quoted above, in which Plutarch's account was so long that Polyaenus felt it necessary to abridge extensively to fit the story to his format, the same features are still present. In this category are *Mul. Virt.* 2 (Phocian women) and Polyaenus 8.65, *Mul. Virt.* 7 (Melian women) and Polyaenus 8.64, *Mul. Virt.* 8 (Tyrrhenian women) and Polyaenus 7.49, *Mul. Virt.* 14 (Valeria and Cloelia) and Polyaenus 8.31, *Mul. Virt.* 24 (Timoclea) and Polyaenus 8.40 and *Mul. Virt.* 25 (Eryxo) and Polyaenus 8.41.

The treatment of the Eryxo story demonstrates how Polyaenus tailored these stories by Plutarch to fit his own collection. First, he began abruptly with the tyranny of Learchus, passing over the reign of Arcesilaus II and shifting the description of Learchus' activity from the reign of Arcesilaus to Learchus' tyranny. This change condensed Plutarch's account but does not significantly alter the story. Then he rewrote the murder scene completely, at the same time preserving Plutarch's phrasing, as a comparison shows:

Mulierum Virtutes 25	Polyaenus 8.41
ταῦτα δ' ἔπραττεν ἡ Ἐρυξὼ μετὰ Πολυάρχου τοῦ πρεσβυτάτου τῶν ἀδελφῶν. ὁρισθέντος δὲ καιροῦ πρὸς τὴν σύνοδον, ὁ Πολύαρχος εἰς τὸ δωμάτιον τῆς ἀδελφῆς παρεισήχθη κρύφα, νεανίσκους ἔχων δύο	... καὶ δὴ νύκτωρ ἄνευ τῶν δορυφόρων ἧκε πρὸς τὴν Ἐρυξὼ καὶ εἴς τι δωμάτιον εἰσελθὼν περιπίπτει Πολυάρχῳ τῷ πρεσβυτάτῳ

---

[16] He may also have been influenced by the name Cratesipolis in 8.58. Pythopolis as a personal name is otherwise unknown, although Friedrich Bechtel, *Die historischen Personennamen des Griechischen* (Halle 1917) lists the analogous forms Athenopolis and Hephaestopolis. According to Stephanus of Byzantium s.v., Pythopolis was the name of Pythes' city.

σὺν αὐτῷ ξιφήρεις, φόνῳ   τῶν Ἐρυξοῦς ἀδελφῶν ἔνδον
πατρὸς ἐπεξιόντας, ὃν ὁ Λάαρχος   λοχῶντι καὶ δύο νεανίσκους
ἐτύγχανεν ἀπεκτονὼς νεωστί.   ξιφήρεις ἔχοντι, ὑφ' ὧν
μεταπεμψαμένης δὲ τῆς   κατακεντηθεὶς ἀπέθανε.
Ἐρυξοῦς αὐτὸν ἄνευ δορυφόρων
εἰσῆλθε, καὶ τῶν
νεανίσκων αὐτῷ προσπεσόντων
τυπτόμενος τοῖς ξίφεσιν ἀπέθανε.

The confrontation of these passages readily shows the manner in which Polyaenus considerably shortened Plutarch's account by omitting whole phrases, while preserving his words wherever possible. This is accomplished even though he introduced Polyarchus after mentioning the arrival of Learchus, not before as Plutarch had. Polyaenus' aim was to give the essential story as succinctly as possible, without departing from his source more than necessary. Finally, he completed his abridgement of this story by omitting the paragraph describing the mission of Eryxo and Polyarchus to Egypt.

In two instances Polyaenus followed the greater part of Plutarch's account closely, but abridged and rewrote the ending. Thus his version of the fall of Salmantica (7.48) reports the two treaties and the trick of the women in words almost identical with those of *Mul. Virt.* 10, and omits the notices on the Masaesylians and Banon. A difference occurs in the last sentence:

Mulierum Virtutes 10   Polyaenus 7.48

... τοὺς μὲν καταβαλόντες,   ... τοὺς μὲν κατέβαλον, τοὺς
τοὺς δὲ τρεψάμενοι διεξέπεσον   δὲ ἐτρέψαντο καὶ ἀθρόοι
ἀθρόοι μετὰ τῶν γυναικῶν.   διεξεπαίσαντο (Korais, but
πυθόμενος δ' ὁ Ἀννίβας καὶ   διεξεπέσαντο F). Ἀννίβας
διώξας τοὺς μὲν καταληφ-   τὴν ἀνδρείαν τῶν γυναικῶν
θέντας ἀνεῖλεν· οἱ δὲ τῶν   θαυμάσας ἀπέδωκε δι'
ὁρῶν ἐπιλαβόμενοι παραχρῆμα   αὐτὰς τοῖς ἀνδράσιν αὐτῶν

The "Mulierum Virtutes" and Polyaenus' "Strategemata" 23

μὲν διέφυγον, ὕστερον δὲ
πέμψαντες ἱκετηρίαν εἰς
τὴν πόλιν ὑπ' αὐτοῦ
κατήχθησαν, ἀδείας καὶ
φιλανθρωπίας τυχόντες.

τήν τε πατρίδα καὶ τὰ
χρήματα.

Polyaenus' concluding statement is only half the length of Plutarch's. This was accomplished by ignoring the latter's report of the flight to the mountains and describing the Salmantican repatriation as a direct result of Hannibal's admiration for the bravery of the women. The women's bravery was the subject of this account of Plutarch, as of his whole work. The modification by Polyaenus is completely in accord with Plutarch's tone; nor does it add a statement of fact independent of Plutarch's account. This story must also have been taken by Polyaenus from Plutarch.[17] In similar fashion Polyaenus in 8.39 shortened the conclusion of the Camma story (*Mul. Virt.* 20) from six lines to two, replacing Plutarch's description of the frantic efforts of Sinorix to overcome the poison with a shorter yet still melodramatic ending. There is no need to postulate a common source which cited two variants.

Three of Plutarch's long stories Polyaenus wished to condense so much that he found it necessary to rewrite them in his own words. As in the other stories, however, he reports nothing not found in Plutarch. The story of the Trojan women (*Mul. Virt.* 1 and Poly. 8.25.2) is reduced from 22 Teubner lines in Plutarch to 10 in Polyaenus, yet the account is the same in both. The one difference, Polyaenus' quotation of the exhortation of Rhome in direct discourse, is not a variant, but his own stylistic device, used also in other accounts.[18]

The differences between *Mul. Virt.* 18 (Lampsace) and Polyaenus 8.37, were sufficient to persuade Jacoby that the two versions were

---

[17] V. Benjarano, *Zephyrus* 6 (1955) 107 also believes Polyaenus used Plutarch in this case.
[18] See Melber, Introduction, p. IX.

independent, and he printed both texts in parallel columns as a fragment of Charon of Lampsacus (*FGrHist* 262 F 7).[19] These differences, however, are not sufficient to establish Polyaenus' independence. Polyaenus condensed Plutarch's account to less than half its original length, and therefore rewrote much of it. But the thought divisions are the same, as are many of the shorter phrases. The only difference in fact is the name *Phoxos* in Polyaenus for *Phobos* in Plutarch. This must be considered either the result of Polyaenus' haste or the error of a copyist. In all other respects Polyaenus, using his own words and passing over many details, preserves the account of the *Mulierum Virtutes*.[20]

Plutarch's narrative of Aretaphila (*Mul. Virt.* 19) is longer than most others in his collection, and therefore Polyaenus in 8.38 abridged it drastically: his version is only one-sixth as long as Plutarch's. Yet in his new version of the story, the chief points of the old are preserved, and none new added, so that there is no doubt of his use of Plutarch. A small mistake, however, reminds us once more of Polyaenus' haste, even carelessness. According to Plutarch, the tyrant Nicocrates had killed the priest Melanippus and taken his priesthood, then killed Phaedimus and married his wife Aretaphila. Polyaenus by an oversight says that the tyrant killed the priest Melanippus and married his wife Aretaphila.

This demonstration of Polyaenus' dependence upon the *Mulierum Virtutes*, which is based upon the striking similarity of words and phrases in the two authors, and the fact that Polyaenus adds nothing not in Plutarch, though omitting much, is confirmed by a comparison with other versions of these stories which are preserved in Plutarch.

---

[19] In his Comm. to *FGrHist* 262 F 7–8 (p. 12) he refers to "die gemeinsame quelle... von Plutarch and Polyaen, die wir nicht benennen können." See also Melber, "Über die Quellen" p. 596. Jacoby's opinion on the relation of Plutarch and Polyaenus varied: in his Comm. to *FGrHist* 139 F 2 he said that Poly. 8.40 was from *Mul. Virt.* 24 (Timoclea) or *Alexander* 12, and to *FGrHist* 310 F 6 (p. 45) that Poly. 8.33 was drawn from *Mul. Virt.* 4 (Argive women), but to *FGrHist* 500 F 1, n. 3 (p. 248) he states that Poly. 8.36 was "aus gleicher quelle" as *Mul. Virt.* 17 (Polycrite).

[20] It is interesting that Knott did not attempt to use these differences to support his argument. *Phobos* is the reading of all the manuscripts of Plutarch. It is changed to *Phoxos* by Nachstädt.

The "Mulierum Virtutes" and Polyaenus' "Strategemata"

The hypothesis of a common source for Polyaenus and Plutarch presumes that the coincidence of words and phrases may be explained by supposing that each author followed the common source very closely. However, in those cases in which Plutarch tells the same account twice, both times obviously from the same source, the two versions differ from each other both in language and method of presentation, but Polyaenus always agrees with the version of the *Mulierum Virtutes*. Consider these passages from *Mul. Virt.* 14 (Valeria and Cloelia), *Publicola* 19, and Polyaenus 8.31:

Publicola 19

ὡς δ' οὔτε τινὰ φυλακὴν
ἑώρων οὔτε παριόντας
ἄλλως ἢ διαπλέοντας,
ὁρμὴν ἔσχον ἀπονή̲ξ̲α̲σ̲θ̲α̲ι̲
πρὸς ῥεῦμα πολὺ καὶ
δ̲ί̲ν̲α̲ς̲ β̲α̲θ̲ε̲ί̲α̲ς̲ . . .

ἀκούσας δὲ τὸ ὄνομα
τῆς Κλοιλίας, προσέβλεψεν
αὐτὴν ἵλεῳ καὶ φαιδρῷ
τῷ προσώπῳ, καὶ
κελεύσας ἵππον ἀχθῆναι
τῶν βασιλικῶν
κεκοσμημένον
εὐπρεπῶς ἐδωρήσατο.

Mulierum Virtutes 14	Polyaenus 8.31
μιᾶς δ' αὐτῶν ὄνομα Κλοιλίας προτρεψαμένης ἀναδησάμεναι περὶ τὰς κεφαλὰς τοὺς χιτωνίσκους παρεβάλοντο πρὸς ῥεῦμα πολὺ καὶ δ̲ί̲ν̲α̲ς̲ β̲α̲θ̲ε̲ί̲α̲ς̲ νέουσαι	μία δὲ ἐξ αὐτῶν Κλοιλία προὔτρεψεν ἁπάσας ἀναδήσασθαι τοὺς χιτωνίσκους περὶ τὰς κεφαλὰς καὶ διανήξασθαι τὸ ῥεῦμα τοῦ ποταμοῦ δ̲ί̲ν̲α̲ι̲ς̲ β̲α̲θ̲ε̲ί̲α̲ι̲ς̲ δύσπορον.

αὐτῆς δὲ τῆς Κλοιλίας   Κλοιλία προλαβοῦσα
εἰπούσης ἑαυτήν,   τὰς ἄλλας ὡμολόγησε.
ἀγασθεὶς ὁ Πορσίνας   Πορσίνας ὑπεραγασθεὶς
ἐκέλευσεν ἵππον   τὸ ἀνδρεῖον τῆς κόρης
ἀχθῆναι κεκοσμημένον   ἵππον αὐτῇ λαμπρῶς
εὐπρεπῶς, καὶ τῇ   κεκοσμημένον ἐδωρήσατο
Κλοιλίᾳ δωρησάμενος   καὶ τὰς παρθένους
ἀπέπεμψεν εὐμενῶς   πάσας ἐπαινέσας
καὶ φιλανθρώπως   Ῥωμαίοις ἀπέπεμψεν.
πάσας.

The account of *Mul. Virt.* 14 is directly dependent upon that of *Publicola* 18-19, as is shown in the commentary (below pp. 81-82), and yet there is a far greater divergence between these two versions than between *Mul. Virt.* 14 and Polyaenus. Plutarch apparently did not like to repeat exactly an earlier account, whether his own or that of his source, but chose each time to tell the story anew. The same phenomenon may be observed in the other cases where Plutarch told a story twice: *Mul. Virt.* 1 (Trojan women), *Romulus* 1, and *Quaestiones Romanae* 265 BC; *Mul. Virt.* 8 (Tyrrhenian women) and *Quaestiones Graecae* 296 B-D; *Mul. Virt.* 11 (Milesian women) and *De anima* (preserved in Gellius 15.10); *Mul. Virt.* 20 (Camma) and *Amatorius* 768 B-D; and *Mul. Virt.* 24 (Timoclea) and *Alexander* 12. In each case the account of Polyaenus repeats the words and phrasing of the version of the *Mulierum Virtutes*, omitting details preserved only in Plutarch's other version and including those found only in the version of the *Mulierum Virtutes*.

Only one story does not fit this pattern: that of the Persian women, Polyaenus 7.45.2. In the first part of *Mul. Virt.* 5 Plutarch described how the Persian women shamed their fleeing men into standing their ground and eventually defeating the Medes under Astyages. Polyaenus tells the same story, but in quite different words, a fact surprising in so short a story, which could have been copied almost directly from Plutarch. Most important, however, Polyaenus names the satrap, Oibares, who led the flight of the Persians. He is not mentioned in Plutarch. The conclusion follows that Polyaenus in this case did not use Plutarch.[21] This in no way refutes the argument for the general dependence of Polyaenus on the *Mulierum Virtutes*. Polyaenus' account of the Persian women, as was noted above (p. 16), does not belong to his section containing stories on the barbarian women (7.47-50), as do the stories taken from the *Mulierum Virtutes*, but is part of his section on barbarian men (7.42-46), where it is coupled with a story about Persian men (7.45.1). This position suggests that it was not found in a collection of deeds of women, such as the *Mulierum Virtutes*, but in some other context. It seems to be a coincidence that Plutarch also found the story interesting enough to include among his examples of bravery in women.

This comparison between the collections of Polyaenus and Plutarch not only reveals the dependence of Polyaenus upon the *Mulierum Virtutes* but defines more precisely Polyaenus' method in composing his anthology. When a story in which he is interested is short enough, he copies it almost verbatim into his own collection (7.50, 8.35, 8.63). If the account in his source has several parts, he often chooses one and passes over the others (8.36, 8.42, 8.66). Longer stories he abridges, leaving out descriptive phrases and parenthetical remarks, but still preserving the words and phrasing of his original (7.49, 8.31, 8.33, 8.40, 8.41, 8.64, 8.65). Sometimes in this process of abridgement he substitutes a brief summarizing sentence for a descriptive paragraph (7.48, 8.39). Finally, if the story in his source is considerably longer than his own format allows, he will paraphrase the account, trying to preserve the important facts in the briefest possible compass (8.25.2, 8.37, 8.38). In all these instances he shows an absolute dependence upon the account furnished him by Plutarch. He will convert a hortatory address or decree from reported to direct speech,[22] but he will not depart from his source as Plutarch did in composing, for

---

[21] The sources of Plutarch and Polyaenus for this anecdote are considered in the discussion of *Mul. Virt.* 5 in Chapter III.

[22] E.g., 8.25.2 and 8.65. Cf. Melber, Introduction, p. IX.

example, the two different prayers of Camma in *Mul. Virt.* 20 and *Amatorius* 768 B–D.

His carelessness is evident in the small mistakes which have been remarked, such as writing *Phoxos* for *Phobos* (8.37), or the confusion of Melanippus and Phaedimus (8.38). His repetition of slightly different versions of the same story is another indication of haste. Thus his story of the Spartan women in 8.71, unfortunately only partially preserved, repeats the stratagem found in 7.49, describing how the Spartan women saved the lives of their foreign husbands, who had been imprisoned by the Spartans. In 7.49 he had followed Plutarch (*Mul. Virt.* 8, Tyrrhenian women); in 8.71 he follows Herodotus (4.145–146) and, faithful to his new source, makes the men Minyans, descendants of the Argonauts, instead of Tyrrhenians. Polyaenus seems to have made no connection between the two stories, which are in fact different versions of the same account.[23]

The *Mulierum Virtutes* was excellently suited for the needs of one trying to assemble a vast collection of stratagems in the shortest possible time. In this book Plutarch had gathered twenty-seven brief anecdotes of virtue in women, most of which described courage in the face of an enemy and were suitable for inclusion in Polyaenus' collection. Polyaenus did not use eight stories which he must have felt did not suit the aims or format of his work. Thus he omitted those accounts which contained no stratagem or trick of war: the Ceian women (*Mul. Virt.* 12), Phocian women (13), Micca and Megisto (15), Stratonice (21), the Pergamene woman (23), and Xenocrite (26). The story of Micca and Megisto, moreover, is exceptionally long, and would have been very difficult to adapt to Polyaenus' condensed format. Plutarch's story of the Lycian women who turned back Bellerophon (*Mul. Virt.* 9) was unsuitable both because it concerned mythical times (from which Polyaenus drew only a few stratagems found in book I) and because three of the four accounts given by Plutarch limit the role of the women to persuasion only. The anecdote of Chiomara (*Mul. Virt.* 22) might have found a place in Polyaenus' collection,

[23] Plutarch's account is a rationalized version of Herodotus. See below pp. 64–65.

although it does not strictly report a stratagem, but Polyaenus may have believed that the story of the just murder of a brutish Roman centurion should not be included in a book written for the use of the Roman emperor.

The establishment of Polyaenus' use of Plutarch's *Mulierum Virtutes* destroys the hypothesis that Plutarch and Polyaenus derived their collections from a common anthological source. This hypothesis was the cornerstone of the argument that considered Plutarch's *Mulierum Virtutes* simply an excerpt from an earlier and larger collection of women's deeds, and minimized Plutarch's influence in these accounts. Having proved Plutarch's independence from Polyaenus, it is now necessary to examine the individual stories of his collection with respect to their possible sources, their historical value, and the contribution of Plutarch to each.

III
COMMENTARY

Mulierum Virtutes I: THE TROJAN WOMEN [1]

In this first story in his catalogue of women's deeds, Plutarch draws from that wealth of legend which surrounded the foundation of Rome. The majority of the fugitives from ravaged Troy, he tells us, were driven by a storm and wandered to Italy, where they anchored at the Tiber. The men roamed about seeking information, but the women, tired of wandering on the sea, decided that it was best to settle down where they were, since they could never return to Troy. Therefore, spurred on, as they say (*hôs phasi*) by one Rhome, they burned the ships. When the men ran up, the women greeted them with embraces and kisses, to soothe their anger. (This is why, Plutarch adds, Roman matrons even now kiss their relatives in greeting.) The Trojans then made the best of necessity, and settled there with the Latins.

Similar accounts of the same story are narrated by Plutarch in *Romulus* 1 and *Quaestiones Romanae* 6, 265 BC. In the latter Plutarch remarks that the story had been set in many different places, but that he follows the version of Aristotle, who located it in Italy.[2]

Fortunately from other sources we are able to reconstruct fully and certainly the account of Aristotle, and compare it with the versions of Plutarch. Dionysius of Halicarnassus reports that Aristotle said that the Achaeans returning from Troy were blown off course

---

[1] This is one of the stories from the *Mulierum Virtutes* used by Polyaenus in his *Strategemata* (8.25.2). See Chapter II and especially p. 23.

[2] This version of the story, together with Dionysius of Halicarnassus, *Roman Antiquities* 1.72.3-4, and Festus s.v. Romam (p. 269 Müller, p. 329 Lindsay), is given as Aristotle fr. 609 Rose and *FGrHist* 840 F 13. Other stories of Trojan women burning their ships are collected by F. Cauer, *De Fabulis Graecis ad Romam conditam pertinentibus* (Berlin, 1884) 14-17. Cf. Ulrich Höfer, *Konon* (Griefswald 1890) 62-63. The central position of Rhome in the earliest foundation legends is discussed by A. Alföldi, *Die trojanischen Urahnen der Römer*, Prog. Basel (Basel 1957).

and wandered into Latium. There, their ships were burned by the captive women brought from Troy, who were afraid of being carried into slavery.[3] Thus they were forced to settle in Latium. According to Festus,[4] Heraclides Lembos reported that some of the Achaeans returning from Troy were driven by a storm to Italy, where sailing up the Tiber they arrived at the site of Rome. There the captive women, tired of the voyage and urged on by the maiden Rhome, burned the ships. The Achaeans therefore named after this girl the city which they were forced to establish. Festus is probably quoting here from the *Histories* of Heraclides. The complete agreement of the accounts quoted by Dionysius and Festus shows that Heraclides' version is taken from Aristotle. This conclusion is confirmed by the fact that Heraclides Lembos is known to have written an epitome of Aristotle's *Politeiai* and *Nomima Barbarika*.[5]

This account of Aristotle which is ascertained from the versions of Dionysius and Festus was used by Plutarch, but not followed faithfully. In the *Quaestiones Romanae* Plutarch cites Aristotle for his information on the origin of the Roman women's custom of saluting their relatives with a kiss.[6] As part of this he includes some details of Aristotle's account of the burning of the ships. Plutarch's connection of Aristotle with an account of this custom confirms the hypothesis that this story is taken from Aristotle's *Nomima Barbarika*.[7] In this version Plutarch does not identify exactly the men whose ships the Trojan women burned,[8] but in the later version of the *Romulus*[9] the

---

[3] *Roman Antiquities* 1.72.3-4.

[4] P. 269 Müller, p. 329 Lindsay. Servius Danielis to Vergil *Aeneid* 1.273 and Solinus *Collectanea* 1.2 report less fully than Festus the version of Heraclides.

[5] See H. Bloch, "Herakleides Lembos and his Epitome of Aristotle's *Politeiai*," *TAPA* 71 (1940) 27-39, esp. p. 37.

[6] For this custom see Athenaeus 10, 440 EF = Polybius VI, 11ᵃ, 4 Büttner-Wobst and *RE* s.v. Ius osculi, X 2 (1919) 1284-85.

[7] Heraclides summarized the *Nomima Barbarika* as well as the *Politeiai*: Arist. fr. 611, 44 Rose on the Tyrrhenians, 611, 58 on the Thracians.

[8] They are called simply *hoi andres*, which does not define their relationship to the women, who would be wives if the men were Trojans or concubines if they were Achaeans.

[9] The *Romulus* was written after the *Quaestiones Romanae* for the latter are cited *Rom.* 15.7. See Ziegler *RE* 860.

men are described as fugitives from Troy—that is, Trojans. This is an unmistakable departure from the account of Aristotle, who has called them Achaeans. Yet in other matters Plutarch continues to follow the philosopher. In the *Romulus* he retells the story of the Trojan women for a purpose different from that behind the *Quaestiones Romanae*, to explain the origin of the city of Rome. Therefore he returns to the account of Aristotle himself, from which he introduces Rhome, the noble Trojan who encouraged the women to burn the ships. At the same time he again mentions Aristotle's explanation of the custom of kissing, although in this context it is not strictly relevant. Finally, Plutarch's version in the *Mulierum Virtutes*, which is probably later than the *Romulus*,[10] is again modified to suit its context, although the differences between the two later versions are slight. In *Mul. Virt.* 1 Plutarch finds it unnecessary to state that Rhome is the eponym of Rome, but once more explains the origin of the women's kiss of greeting. Since he wishes in this version to present the burning of the ships as a noble act, he discusses fully the motivation of the women, their weariness with wandering and the hopelessness of returning to Troy. Moreover, he clearly states that the men are Trojans.

What is the meaning of Plutarch's deviation from the account of Aristotle? It is certain that Plutarch knew Aristotle's account and did

[10] The chronology of the *Lives* is uncertain. The massive work of C. Stoltz, *Lunds Universitets Årsskrift* N.F. Avd. 1, XXV (1929), no. 3 (see esp. pp. 58–95), accepted by Ziegler *RE* 899–903 and C. Theander, *Eranos* 56 (1958) 12 does not succeed in refuting Mewaldt, *Hermes* 42 (1907) 564–578, who maintained that cross-citations by Plutarch from the *Romulus* to the *Lycurgus*, from the *Numa* to the *Camillus*, and from the *Camillus* to the *Romulus* meant that the pairs *Theseus-Romulus*, *Lycurgus-Numa*, and *Themistocles-Camillus* were composed at the same time. Since the latter two pairs because of their self-citations are admittedly earlier than *Pericles-Fabius*, the tenth (see *Per.* 2.5) in the series of *Lives*, *Theseus-Romulus* also must be among the first ten pairs of lives. (See Mewaldt's review of Stoltz, *Gnomon* 6 [1930] 431–434 and Flacelière's review of Ziegler, *REG* 63 [1950] 302–303.) Nor is it correct to interpret Plutarch's statement in *Theseus* 1 to mean that *Theseus-Romulus* is one of the last pairs of lives, as do Stoltz and Ziegler: see Flacelière *REG* 61 (1948) 67–68 and W. Bühler, *Maia* 14 (1962) 281. Since the *Romulus* belongs to the first half of the *Parallel Lives*, it is almost certain to have been written before the *Mulierum Virtutes*, which belongs to Plutarch's last years (see p. 2 above).

not simply repeat the mistake of an earlier compiler.[11] He had read Aristotle's *Politeiai*[12] and cites Aristotle on Roman history (*Camillus* 22.4 = Arist. fr. 610 Rose). In the *Quaestiones Romanae* he cites Aristotle not for the frequently repeated foundation legend, but for the peculiar manner of salutation, a detail not connected with Aristotle by Dionysius and Festus.[13] Plutarch therefore read Aristotle, but in writing these three versions, especially those of the *Romulus* and the *Mulierum Virtutes*, he was most likely writing from memory. Thus an absolutely precise repetition of Aristotle's account is not to be expected. The principal difference in his new version of Aristotle's story, however, must have been his acceptance of the legend of the Trojan origin of Rome widespread in his time. Vergil and Livy unequivocally supported the Trojan origin of Rome, but are only the most conspicuous of the writers who accepted this legend. If confirmation from earlier writers were necessary, Hellanicus (*FGrHist* 4 F 84) had told the same story as Aristotle of the burning of the ships, yet had specified that the Trojan women had come with Aeneas and Odysseus and therefore could not have been captives, as we learn from Dionysius of Halicarnassus (*Rom. Ant.* 1.72.2). In the presence of such contemporary opinion and ancient testimony, Plutarch without apology modified the story of Aristotle.

In his commentary to Lycophron 921, Tzetzes refers to this story of Plutarch, but reports that Rhome was a Trojan captive of the Greeks, the exact opposite of Plutarch's statement.[14] This is undoubtedly a mistake of Tzetzes, who also would have added this note

---

[11] R. Flacelière, Plutarque *Vies* I (Paris, 1957), 53, rightly criticizes the reference of Rosenberg, *RE* s.v. Romulus, I, 1 A (1914), 1077, to the "Zusammenstellungen des unbekannten Gelehrten, den Plutarch im Leben des R. benutzt," remarking that "cette hypothèse est à la fois gratuite, inutile et invraisemblable."

[12] See his reference to the pleasure of reading Aristotle's *Politeiai*, *Non posse suaviter vivi*, 1093 C (quoted below p. 131).

[13] The *Politeiai* were also an important source for the customs discussed in the *Quaestiones Graecae*: see Giesen *Philologus* 60 (1901) 446–471.

[14] Tzetzes states, "But Plutarch says that Rhome was the Trojan captive who advised the rest of the women to burn the Greek ships."

to his commentary from memory, and surely was influenced by the story of the Trojan captive Aethilla which he reported in the same note.

Mulierum Virtutes 2: THE PHOCIAN WOMEN (1) [15]

Plutarch prefixes his account of the heroic act of the Phocian women with the statement that this act had never been celebrated by a famous writer (*endoxou men ou tetuchēke suggrapheôs*), reminding us of his determination voiced in the preface to the *Mulierum Virtutes* to avoid stories which were well known. Although the "desperation of the Phocians" is reported by Pausanias, and was proverbial to Polybius, the resolution of the women, their acceptance of death on a pyre before capture and enslavement, is in fact recorded only by Plutarch.

The background of Phocian-Thessalian warfare was first presented in a brief flashback by Herodotus (8.27–28). After the victory of Xerxes, he relates, the Thessalians sent heralds to Phocis, "since they had always had a grudge against them, and especially after their most recent defeat." Herodotus then relates the two battles which made up the "most recent defeat," that is, the slaughter of the Thessalian infantry by a night sortie of picked Phocians who had been colored white according to the stratagem of the Elean seer Tellias, and the equally ingenious destruction of the Thessalian cavalry through pots hidden in the earth.

Pausanias, in his outline of the most important events of Phocian history, presents a more complete account of the same war (10.1.3–11). He, like Herodotus, dates the conflict shortly before the Persian invasion ("before the Persians marched against the Greeks"; cf. Her. 8.27.2: "not many years before this expedition of the king"). Pausanias records the two engagements mentioned by Herodotus, but he reverses their order and adds two other episodes not found in the earlier writer, the massacre of the night reconnaisance mission of three hundred Phocians led by Gelon, and a battle in which the

[15] This is one of the stories from the *Mulierum Virtutes* used by Polyaenus in his *Strategemata* (8.65). See Chapter II and especially p. 21.

Phocians were led by the generals Rhoeus of Ambrossus and Daiphantus (MSS. Daiphantes) of Hyampolis and by the *mantis* Tellias of Elis, in whom the Phocians rested their hopes.[16]

Before the battle the Phocians made a desperate decision: they gathered all their women, children, and property together in one place, built a funeral pyre, and left men behind who, if their compatriots were defeated, were to kill the women and children, burn their bodies and the Phocians' worldly goods on that great pyre, and then seek death themselves. With this dreadful alternative before them, the Phocians were filled with courage and overcame the Thessalians. On this resolution of the Phocians, Pausanias comments that "from this, all unfeeling resolutions are called by the Greeks 'Phocian desperation' (*aponoia Phôkikê*)."[17]

In *Mul. Virt.* 2 Plutarch relates one incident of the larger story which he had told in detail in the life of Daiphantus, now lost.[18] But

---

[16] The position of the Elean seer among the Phocian leaders is noteworthy. Pausanias called him, "the one who had the most important position among the magistrates (*archontes*)" (10.1.8), but it is uncertain whether he was actually a general: see Busolt-Swoboda, II 1451 note 4. J. A. O. Larsen, *CP* 55 (1960) 234 notes that the presence of Tellias is consistent with the dating of the battle shortly before the Persian War.

[17] The desperate decision of the Phocians is not unique, although they were fortunate that in their case the resolution was never put into action. Not so with others. Polybius recalls "Phocian desperation" in his account of the siege of Abydus (16.29–35), during which the besieged resolved that when the wall fell they would execute the women and children and throw their gold and silver into the sea with curses (16.31). In the same place he mentions the less extreme measure of the Acarnanians, which he himself had recorded earlier (9.40.4–6, cf. Livy 26.25.11–14). The Xanthians particularly favored such an escape from slavery. Herodotus tells us (1.176) that before going out to defend themselves against Harpagus, the general of Cyrus the Great, they burnt their women and children in a great pyre. Again, when Brutus after Pharsalus marched against Xanthus, Appian writes (*Bellum civile* 4.76–80) that the men slaughtered their wives and children, put them in a heap, and burned them, slaying themselves on the flaming pyre. Appian refers to the account of Herodotus, and adds that the same thing was done when the city was attacked by Alexander. (Arrian, *Anabasis* 1.24.4 mentions the surrender of Xanthus, but no more.) Livy narrates the dramatic sacrifice of the citizens of Astapa during the second Punic War (28.22.23). All these peoples perished with the fall of their city.

[18] 244 B: "The detailed account of the matter (*to kath' hekaston tês praxeôs*) has been written in the life of Daiphantus, but the deed of the women is as follows." The life of Daiphantus is also listed in the Lamprias catalogue (38) and was excerpted by Sopater (Photius *Bibliotheca* cod. 161, p. 104 B Bekker).

first he gives an account of the origin of the conflict mentioned by neither Herodotus nor Pausanias. There was a truceless war, he tells us, caused by the murder of all the Thessalian magistrates and tyrants in the Phocian cities, followed by the Thessalians' retaliatory killing of two hundred fifty Phocian hostages. Then the Thessalians invaded Phocis through Locris, having passed a resolution to kill the Phocians and enslave their women and children. Daiphantus, one of the three Phocian archons, moved the resolution described by Pausanias. But then, according to Plutarch, it was suggested that the women be consulted, to gain their consent for such a drastic plan. The women assembled, and not only approved Daiphantus' proposal, but voted him a crown, "because he advised the best for Phocis." Even the children, they say, voted approval on their own account. Following this unanimous action, the Phocians marched forth and defeated the Thessalians at Cleonae near Hyampolis. This resolution, Plutarch adds, was called by the Greeks Phocian desperation (*Phôkeôn aponoia*); the victory the Phocians still celebrate with a festival, the Elaphebolia, at Hyampolis.

The story of Plutarch is completely independent of the Herodotean account, although it does not contradict it. There are certain similarities with the account of Pausanias, but the fact that *Mul. Virt.* 2 reports an incident consciously excerpted from the more complete and detailed account of the Thessalian war in the life of Daiphantus must be kept constantly in mind.[19] Pausanias' source (rather than Pausanias himself) conflated the Herodotean account with material found also in Plutarch. The reference to "Phocian desperation" in both accounts, and the fact that Pausanias' notice of the three leaders, Rhoesus, Daiphantus, and Tellias complements Plutarch's

---

[19] The fullest discussion of the relation of these three accounts is by M. Sordi: "La guerra tessalo-focese del V secolo," *RivFC* N.S. 31 (1953) 235–258. Her conclusions are examined by Larsen, *CP* 55 (1960) 232–234 (in a review article on Sordi's book, *La lega tessala fino ad Alessandro Magno* [Rome 1958]). For earlier treatments see Macan and Stein to Herodotus 8.27–28, L. Weniger, *Archiv für Religionswissenschaft* 9 (1906) 223–230, H. Hitzig, *Jahrbücher für classische Philologie* 109 (1874) 123–127, Busolt, *Gr. Gesch.* I² 700, Beloch, *Gr. Gesch.*² I 2, 205–206.

"Daiphantus... himself the third archon," demonstrates that Plutarch and Pausanias used a common source. Pausanias' omission of the chief element in Plutarch's version, the decree of the women, assures us that he did not use this passage in Plutarch. Nor did he use Plutarch's life of Daiphantus,[20] although he elsewhere used the lives of Philopoemen[21] and Epaminondas,[22] as is clear from the negligible role of Daiphantus in his account and his silence on the cause of the war given by Plutarch. Furthermore, the common source of Plutarch and Pausanias must not have mentioned the central fact of Plutarch's story, the vote of the women.

This common source calls the decree of the Phocians "Phocian desperation." Therefore this part of the story must be earlier than Polybius, who refers (16.32.2) to the already proverbial Phocian desperation (*tên legomenên Phôkikên aponoian*) in recounting a like decision of the besieged citizens of Abydus.[23] The source of Plutarch, however, must belong to at least the fourth century, for it was known already to Aeschines. The orator recalls to the Athenians "the enmity toward the Phocians, which the Thessalians had had from ancient times when the Phocians took their hostages (*homêrous*) and flogged (*katêloêsan*) them to death" (2.140), which is echoed by Plutarch's *homêrous katêloêsan*. *Katêloêsan* is a very rare word (found in Aeschines and Plutarch only in these passages) and its use to describe the treatment of the hostages in the Thessalian-Phocian conflict must derive from a single source.[24] Hiller von Gaertringen suggested that the source of Plutarch might be Ephorus,[25] and this is not unreasonable in view of his propensity to enlarge upon Herodotean notices. In this

---

[20] As suggested by G. Daux, *Pausanias à Delphe* (Paris 1936) 138 n. 1.
[21] See H. Nissen, *Kritische Untersuchungen über die Quellen... des Livius* (Berlin 1863) 287–290.
[22] See Peper, *De Plutarchi "Epaminonda"* (Diss. Jena 1912) 15–25.
[23] See above, n. 17. The expression was also known to Stephanus of Byzantium, who says s.v. Phocis, "... there is also a proverb, Phocian desperation, for those resolving upon unfeeling acts." Cf. "unfeeling resolutions" in Pausanias.
[24] For the meaning see Photius *Lexicon* s.v. *katêloiôsen* "not simply *he killed*, but *beating with sticks*."
[25] *RE* s.v. Daiphantos 1, IV 2 (1901) 2012–2013.

case the additional material would have come from a Phocian source, presumably a Phocian local history, despite Jacoby's doubt that there ever was such a work on Phocis.[26] Aeschines, who would not be acquainted with a Phocian local history, would have read a popular historian like Ephorus.

The story of Plutarch in *Mul. Virt.* 2 has a particular focus which is not shared by that of Pausanias. Neither Pausanias nor his source was especially interested in "Phocian desperation," and his account, as M. Sordi notes, cannot be called a romanticized story based on that proverb.[27] Pausanias is equally interested in all four engagements. The concentration on the decree of the Phocians in *Mul. Virt.* 2, and the addition of the romantic element with the decree of the women, is the contribution of Plutarch himself, and was prompted by his desire in this work to celebrate the bravery of women. Plutarch also made use of additional sources in this account, which he identifies in the first sentence: "The deed of the Phocian women ... is attested both by the important rites which the Phocians even now perform at Hyampolis and by ancient decrees ..." Of the decrees which are testimony to his story, that of the men was known to Pausanias, that of the women is found only in Plutarch. The feast to which he refers he names at the end of his story: "The feast which is most important of all, the Elaphebolia, they celebrate in Hyampolis up to this day to Artemis for that victory." Elsewhere Plutarch tells us that he visited a friend at Hyampolis and attended this feast.[28] At one of the discussions which are so attractively depicted in the *Symposiaca* he could have heard of these decrees from his Phocian friends, one of whom even claimed to be a descendent of Daiphantus.[29] Perhaps he even

---

[26] *FGrHist* III b p. 423.   [27] *RivFC* N.S. 31 (1953) 249–250.
[28] *Symposiaca* 4.1.1 (660 D). He also associates the feast with Daiphantus, *Non posse suaviter vivi* 1099 F: "By Zeus, even we celebrate the victory of Daiphantus at Hyampolis, as you know, and Phocis is filled with sacrifices and honors." An inscription from Hyampolis (*IG* IX, 90), dated to the first half of the first century B.C., mentions "the great Elaphebolia." For the relation of this festival to the Attic Elaphebolia, see Martin Nilsson, *Griechische Feste von religiöser Bedeutung* (Leipzig 1906) 221–225. Cf. also Pausanias' note (10.35.7): "(at Hyampolis) they especially reverence Artemis."
[29] *De sera numinis vindicta* 558 A. Cf. Theander, *BLund*, 1950–51, p. 31.

saw them inscribed on a stele commemorating the battle and the women's courage.[30] Some acquaintance with a purported decree or a paraphrase of it is suggested by the details in his account: the name of the mover (Daiphantus) with patronymic, the rider proposing to consult the women, and the additional clause in the decree of the women proposing to crown Daiphantus. Plutarch's use of *phasin* (they say) in referring to the children's decree suggests that he felt less confidence in his authority for this element. Thus Plutarch could rightly state that the story of the women had not been told before by a famous writer, even though his source for the background of the war had been known to Aeschines.

Plutarch used these same sources, the feasts and the decrees, when he gave his full account of these events in the life of Daiphantus. In the life the emphasis would be not on the women but on Daiphantus himself. The origin of the *aspondos polemos* would undoubtedly have been treated more fully. It is clear from comparison with *Mul. Virt.* 14, in which the first paragraphs quickly summarize several chapters in the life of Publicola, that the passage in *Mul. Virt.* 2 on the origin of the war which sets the scene for the act of the women, is a much condensed summary of the account of the life. The battles described by Pausanias without doubt were also treated in the *Daiphantus*, although they were omitted by Plutarch from the summary in *Mul. Virt.* 2. Thus Plutarch's notice that the Thessalians attacked Phocis after gathering forces from all their cities is equivalent to Pausanias' report of the invasion *panstratiai*, but Plutarch skips over the massacre of Gelon's mission which in Pausanias is the immediate cause of the desperate resolution of the Phocians. Pausanias records the two Phocian stratagems reported by Herodotus, the buried pots and the "ghost army" of whitened soldiers. These do not appear in the summary

[30] The erection long after the fact of such inscriptions commemorating great events in a city's history has been recently attested by the discovery of the Themistocles inscription at Troezen (*Hesperia* 29 [1960] 198-223; bibliography of discussions to date by S. Dow, *CW* 55 [1962] 105-108); cf. also the inscriptions of the oath of Plataea (Tod, *GHI* II, no. 204) and the oath of the founders at Cyrene (*SEG* IX, 3 most recently discussed by A. J. Graham *JHS* 80 [1960] 94-111).

account of *Mul. Virt.* 2, but Plutarch was certainly familiar with them and probably included them in the *Daiphantus*.³¹ The life of Daiphantus was one of those written on local heroes outside of the framework of the *Parallel Lives*, together with those of Aristomenes and Aratus, and would have been particularly valuable because of Plutarch's close association with Phocis and his ability to add material from local tradition and personal observation. The story in *Mul. Virt.* 2 is based on the material treated in this life, with a special emphasis on the decree of the women.

The references of Herodotus and Pausanias establish the date of this story in the period shortly before the invasion of Xerxes. According to the rather awkward summary of *Mul. Virt.* 2 the Thessalian attack on Phocis opposed by Daiphantus was intended to punish a Phocian uprising against the tyrants and magistrates whom the Thessalians had established or at least supported in the Phocian cities.³² The relative chronology of the engagements is not certain, but the order followed by Pausanias, who depends ultimately upon a Phocian source, need not be challenged. All three writers support the assumption that all the engagements belong to one war.³³ J. A. O. Larsen argues that the fighting was prolonged over a rather long period of time. He correctly notes, however, that the pass of Hyampolis was the natural route for

---

[31] Polyaenus misunderstood a detail of Plutarch's condensed account: he reports that the women resolved to "ourselves go up on the pyre with our children, kindle the wood, and burn to death" (8.65), although Pausanias explicitly states, and Plutarch undoubtedly meant, that the women should be killed by the soldiers before their bodies were burnt on the pyre.

[32] This is the interpretation of Busolt, *Gr. Gesch.* I² (1893) 699 and Beloch, *Gr. Gesch.*² I 1 339, followed by F. Schober, *RE* s.v. Phokis, XX 1 (1941) 482–483, and with important modifications re-establishing the date in the period testified by Herodotus, M. Sordi, *RivFC* N.S. 31 (1953) 235–258. Eduard Meyer, *Geschichte des Altertums*² (Stuttgart 1937) III, 266 and 708, maintains, however, that although the Thessalians more than once attacked Phocis, "freilich ist die Unterwerfung der Landschaft nie gelungen" (p. 708). Perhaps rightly. The summary in Plutarch is awkwardly written, and may have distorted important facts. It is noteworthy that Aeschines (2.140, quoted above p. 37) who is dependent upon the same source, states that the Phocians killed the Thessalian hostages, and not vice versa. The Attic orators, however, are notoriously inaccurate even for Athenian history.

[33] See M. Sordi, *RivFC* N. S. 31 (1953) 252–253.

any Thessalian drive southward, and that therefore we need not doubt the report of frequent battles there.[34]

Mulierum Virtutes 3: THE CHIAN WOMEN [35]

Plutarch's account of the Chian women is tripartite, the first part narrating the causes of the foundation of Leuconia, the second the war between the Chian settlers of that city and the Erythraeans, and the third the bravery shown much later by the Chian women when their city was besieged by Philip V. The two parts concerning Leuconia should be considered first.

Once, when a noble was being married at Chios, the then king Hippoclus for a joke leaped upon the bride's carriage, whereupon he was killed by the groom's friends. The city was polluted, and the god ordered that all those involved in the murder leave the city. So a large number of the citizens left Chios, expelled the Corones from Leuconia and settled there, holding it with the Erythraeans.[36] Later, Plutarch continues, there arose a war with the Erythraeans, who were then the most powerful of the Ionians, and not being able to hold out against them, the Chians agreed to leave the city under a safe-conduct, with nothing other than a tunic and a cloak each.[37] But their women mocked them for this weakness, and persuaded them to take shield and spear, saying to the Erythraeans that to a man of courage his spear is his tunic, and his shield his cloak. Thus they marched out armed, and the Erythraeans, taken aback, yielded to them. Plutarch concludes,

---

[34] *CP* 55 (1960) 233–234.
[35] The second part of this chapter is one of the stories from the *Mulierum Virtutes* used by Polyaenus in his *Strategemata* (8.66). See Chapter II and especially p. 20.
[36] Wilamowitz would read *Kolôneis* for *Korôneis*, citing Strabo (13, 589), but M. B. Sakellariou, *La Migration grecque in Ionie* (Athens 1958) 200 calls attention to a modern place-name Koroneia on Chios, which might reflect this old name. Leuconia, according to *RE* s.v. Leukonia, XII 2 (1925) 2283, is mentioned only in this passage, Polyaenus 8.66, Thucydides 8.24.3, and Frontinus, *Strategemata* 2.5.15. Frontinus, moreover, does not specifically name Leuconia, and may refer to another occasion.
[37] Note the similarity between the terms of this treaty and that made by the Salmanticans, *Mul. Virt.* 10. These terms were not unusual: cf. the historical fragment published by C. Bonner, *TAPA* 72 (1941) 27–28 lines 5–7 and his commentary, pp. 29–30.

"The Chians thus saved themselves, having been taught by their women to be brave."

The historical setting of this war is difficult to ascertain. A war between the Erythraeans and the Chians is also the background of two different anecdotes by Frontinus (*Strategemata* 2.5.15) and Anticlides (*FGrHist* 140 F 5 = Athenaeus 9, 384 DE). Herodotus 1.18.3 mentions a war in which Miletus aided the Chians against Erythrae. In *Mul. Virt.* 17 Plutarch reports a joint expedition of Miletus, Erythrae and other Ionians against Naxos. Miletus and Erythrae are also said by Strabo 13, 588, to have founded Parium together with Paros. Finally, Hippias of Erythrae (*FGrHist* 421 F 1 = Athenaeus 6, 258 F– 259 F) tells us that the Erythraean aristocrats were aided by the Chian tyrants Amphiclus and Polytecnus in their efforts to overthrow king Cnopus. It seems that alliances were formed and broken between the three cities, each city being at various times ally and opponent of the others. A coherent picture does not appear to emerge. Plutarch remarks that Erythrae, when it was the most powerful city of the Ionians, fought the Chian colony of Leuconia. The decisive role of the Erythraean general in the siege of Naxos (*Mul. Virt.* 17) suggests that this enterprise was roughly at the same time. Yet Herodotus notes that at Lade the Erythraeans supplied only eight ships, against 100 from Chios and 80 from Miletus. Although the Erythraeans may have been reluctant to aid in the defense of Miletus, it is clear that they were no longer a great power.[38] These wars must be placed considerably earlier than Lade, before Miletus and Chios had reached their full strength.

W. G. Forrest has attempted, not without reservations, to see in the notice of Hippias on the expulsion of Cnopus with Chian help the key to the changing alliances.[39] During the Lelantine war, he suggests, Erythrae under Cnopus was allied with Chalcis against Miletus, and therefore was opposed by Miletus in its battle with Chios. Then the aristocrats, gaining aid from their enemy Chios, expelled Cnopus

---

[38] Note also Herodotus' slighting notice of Erythrae in his list of Ionian cities, 1.142.4.
[39] *Historia* 6 (1957) 168 n. 9.

(who fled to Delphi, which was friendly to Chalcis) and instituted a period of friendship with Miletus, signaled by aid in the Naxian war and the joint settlement of Parium. The date in the period of the Lelantine war is confirmed by Eusebius, who places the founding of Parium in 708. Finally, Erythrae showed itself again friendly to Chalcis on the Acanthus dispute. This hypothesis is a tempting resolution of the problem, but leaves certain difficulties. Plutarch places the founding of Leuconia soon after the death of king Hippoclus. It seems unlikely that there were still kings in Chios at the end of the eighth century. However, Plutarch's description of the war with Erythrae as simply "later" than the settlement of Leuconia perhaps allows a rather long period to intervene. Cnopus is called by Strabo (14, 633) a son of Codrus and the founder of Erythrae, although Hippias is clearly describing a revolt of a much later date. Finally, there is no reason to refer the various notices of Chian-Erythraean conflict to a single war. The two cities were very close, and there must have been a number of occasions for dispute. Compare the long history of Samian-Milesian rivalry over Priene and the Mycale peninsula. Nor is it to be forgotten that Plutarch reports that the Erythraeans fought the Chian colonists of Leuconia, something different from fighting the Chians in Chios. The evidence provides us with a certain picture only of the numerous wars among the Ionian states and the fluidity of their various alliances in the archaic period.[40]

There is no hint as to Plutarch's source for the story. It seems ultimately to derive from a Chian source (the pro-Chian bias precludes Erythraean origin), but we have little trace of Chian local history besides the works on the *Foundation of Chios* by Ion of Chios

[40] Jacoby (Comm. to *FGrHist* 500 F 1) refuses to commit himself on the date of the war, but calls attention to Rubensohn, *RE* s.v. Paros, XVIII 2, pt. 3 (1949) 1808 and Hiller, *IG* XII 5, xii, no. 1219, who date the war in the mid-seventh century. See also R. Herbst, *RE* s.v. Naxos, XVI 2 (1935) 2088. A. G. Dunham, *History of Miletus* (London, 1915) 64–65, treats it separately from the Lelantine war, calling it simply "an early war," and considers it the product of a struggle by Miletus for the trans-Aegean trade.

and Hellanicus. There is no reference to a Chian constitution by Aristotle. Jacoby's statement that there is no account of the sources for the war remains true.[41]

The third part of this chapter Plutarch introduces as an almost parenthetical addition. The Chian women showed no less courage, he says, many years later against Philip the son of Demetrius (Philip V), who, when he was besieging the city, proclaimed that the slaves should revolt and join him, and that he would reward them with freedom and marriage to the wives of their present masters. But the women with wondrous spirit mounted the walls with the slaves who themselves were indignant and with rocks and missiles drove off Philip, nor did a single slave desert to him.

This siege of Chios by Philip V may be dated to 202–201, at the time of his battle with the Samians off Chios. The siege is reported in a fragment of Polybius (16.21–2): "Philip was at a loss, since the business of the siege was going against him, and the enemy was coming down on him with many heavily armed ships . . . Inasmuch as the present state of affairs did not permit capture (of the city), he withdrew, contrary to the expectation of his enemies. For Attalus' men had been hoping to overpower him while he was still preparing the mines."[42] Although Chios is not mentioned, the connection with the Plutarch passage need not be doubted.[43] No source is mentioned by Plutarch, but it is quite possible that Plutarch drew upon Polybius himself for his account. He used Polybius for an event of the year 189 in Galatia (see the discussion of *Mul. Virt.* 22). The story seems to be included here because of its similarity to the account of the defense of Argos by the Argive women which immediately follows.

[41] Comm. to *FGrHist* 421 F 1 n. 11 (p. 160).
[42] Appian *Bellum Macedonicum* 4.1 reports incorrectly that Philip actually took Chios as well as Samos.
[43] See David Magie, *Roman Rule in Asia Minor* (Princeton 1950) p. 942, n. 42 and references there cited. I. I. Rospatt, *Philologus* 27 (1868) 680 n. 28 seems the first to have made a strong case for the besieged city in Polybius being Chios.

Mulierum Virtutes 4: THE ARGIVE WOMEN [44]

Plutarch, Pausanias, and Herodotus give accounts of Cleomenes' invasion of Argos, but the element central to the stories of Plutarch and Pausanias, the defense of the city by Telesilla and the Argive women, is not found in Herodotus. This defense is the particular interest of a rich Argive tradition, the development of which can be traced in the variants preserved by Plutarch and Pausanias. The analysis of these variants, therefore, and their relation to Herodotus, will make clear the nature of the Argive tradition, its use by Plutarch, and its authority for the history of Cleomenes' invasion.[45]

Plutarch's narrative is the most complex of the three. Telesilla, a woman of good family, had taken up poetry on the advice of an oracle, and achieved some reputation among the women. When Cleomenes of Sparta, after the battle of Sepeia and the near extermination of the Argive hoplite force, led his troops against Argos, Telesilla roused the young women to take up arms, mount the walls, and drive off the enemy. Cleomenes was repulsed, but according to the Argive historian Socrates, the other king, Demaratus, fought his way into the city and held the Pamphyliakon[46] before he was expelled and the city saved. The battle was either on the seventh of the month, or at the new moon, when the Hybristika, a festival involving an exchange of clothing between men and women, was celebrated. Finally, Herodotus is wrong in describing the aftermath of the battle at Argos: the Argive women, to remedy the shortage of men, took as husbands not *douloi* but *perioikoi*.

The version of Pausanias (2.20.8–10) has much in common with

---

[44] This is one of the stories from the *Mulierum Virtutes* used by Polyaenus in his *Strategemata* (8.33). See Chapter II and especially pp. 17–19.

[45] F. Jacoby has studied this tradition with his usual care and thoroughness in his commentary to Socrates of Argos (*FGrHist* 310 F 6); his work is the foundation of the following discussion.

[46] The Pamphyliakon is probably a quarter of the city (thus Jacoby, Comm. to *FGrHist* 310 n. 105 [p. 30], following Wilamowitz, *Die Textgeschichte der griechischen Lyriker*, Abhandlungen Göttingen, Phil.-hist. Kl., N.F. 4 n. 3 [Berlin 1900] 78 and Vollgraff, *BCH* 33 [1909] 186–187). There is no entry s.v. in *RE*.

that of Plutarch. Pausanias saw in Argos a relief of Telesilla, with books thrown down at her feet, holding a helmet and about to put it on. This representation of the poetess he explains by a short history: when Cleomenes had defeated the Argives, and had burnt the fugitives in the sacred grove, he marched against Argos. But Telesilla, having sent the slaves (*oiketas*) and those too young or old to bear arms to guard the wall, armed the women and led them against the Spartans. When the Spartans discovered that the women were not terrified, but received their onslaught, they withdrew, deciding that to be defeated by women or to defeat them was equally inglorious. This battle, adds Pausanias, was predicted by the oracle to the Argives reported in Herodotus, of which he quotes the first three lines.[47] Numerous differences show that there is no direct relation between Pausanias and Plutarch. Yet the treatment of Telesilla and of the women's defense of Argos proves that the two accounts represent two slightly divergent branches of a common Argive tradition.

The narrative of Herodotus (6.75.3–84.1) is complementary to these two; it overlaps their accounts, but concentrates on different events. Herodotus recounts Cleomenes' campaign in Argos as the Argive explanation for Cleomenes' madness and suicide. Cleomenes, he relates, invaded the Argolid after receiving an oracle that he would take Argos. The Argives met him at Sepeia near Tiryns, but had been made so timorous by an ambiguous oracle which they had received in conjunction with the Milesians that they were easily outwitted and defeated. When they fled to the holy grove of the demigod Argos, Cleomenes disregarded their right of sanctuary and burned the grove. Too late he realized that this was the fulfillment of the oracle that he would take Argos. Discouraged, he returned home without attempting

---

[47] Suidas s.v. Telesilla gives a similar yet briefer account. This is derived from Pausanias, for it refers to the stele seen by him and otherwise faithfully reproduces details of his account. Whether it entered the encyclopedia directly from Pausanias, or via the Constantinian excerpts (as did much material from Pausanias, see Adler, *RE* s.v. Suidas, IV 1 A [1931] 705), a collection of oracles (thus Adler, note to Suidas s.v. Telesilla [IV p. 518 no. 260]), or from a collection of women's deeds (thus Jacoby, Comm. to *FGrHist* 310, n. 81 [p. 26]) is not relevant here: Suidas' article sheds no light on the earlier tradition of the Telesilla story.

"*Mulierum Virtutes*" 4: The Argive Women

more. The Argives were so reduced in number that the slaves took control of the city until the young sons of the fallen could reestablish their rights. Cleomenes' sacrilegious burning of the grove of Argos, said the Argives, provoked the divine vengeance to punish him with his horrible end.

Two facets of Herodotus' narrative are noteworthy: the oracle which had been given to the Argives, and the omission of the story of Telesilla. Nothing in Herodotus suggests that he knew of the defense of Argos described in Plutarch and Pausanias. Since Herodotus used both Argive and Spartan sources for his account,[48] it is incredible that an attack upon Argos, which included even the penetration of the city by King Demaratus, would not have left some trace upon his narrative. There is none.

The oracle reported by Herodotus[49] is clearly related to the story of Telesilla; both describe the triumph of the female in Argos over the male. Either one is dependent on the other, or both the oracle and the story were composed after the battle of Sepeia, and reflect the same Argive view of the events. In fact, the oracle demonstrably was written before Sepeia. It is obscure and ambiguous, characteristics which mark a prophecy delivered before the fact, when the outcome is still in doubt. An oracle *ex eventu* is by nature clear and precise, because it is written to prove a particular point with regard to an event already known.[50] The oracle itself, therefore, proves the truth of Herodotus' assertion (6.19) that it was given, along with its twin on

---

[48] Thus Jacoby, Comm. to *FGrHist* 310 n. 78 (p. 26).

[49] Herodotus 6.77.2 (in Rawlinson's translation):

> Time shall be when the female shall conquer the male, and shall chase him
> Far away, gaining so great praise and honor in Argos;
> Then full many an Argive woman her cheeks shall mangle;
> Hence, in the times to come 'twill be said by the men who are unborn,
> "Tamed by the spear expired the coiled terrible serpent."

[50] H. W. Parke and D. E. W. Wormell, *The Delphic Oracle* I (Oxford 1956) 158–159, remark the vanity of modern attempts to find a "correct" interpretation of this oracle. See How and Wells to Herodotus 6.77. Roland Crahay, *La littérature oraculaire chez Hérodote* (Paris 1956) 172–175, discusses some of the contradictory interpretations proposed by scholars; he himself believes the oracle an invention of Cleomenes.

the fall of Miletus, when the Argives sent to Delphi "concerning the safety of their city" before the defeat at Sepeia.[51] This oracle, therefore, cannot be considered as evidence for the events which followed Sepeia. This is confirmed by Herodotus, who can give only a contrived and unconvincing explanation of the oracle's relevance to the battle. If he could give no better, it was because there was no better available, either at Sparta where he gathered most of his information on Cleomenes, or at Argos, which he visited.[52] It follows that the Telesilla story, which gives a report of the events following Sepeia closely related to the oracle but completely unknown to Herodotus, must have originated after Herodotus' investigations, and drawn inspiration from the oracle reported by him, and not from the events themselves.[53]

An analysis of the story of Telesilla, once it is seen to be invention and not true history, reveals that successive Argive historians elaborated various aspects of the story. Two broad stages may be noted: the first, a reaction to the account of Herodotus, and the second, a controversy between writers of *Argolika* and *Lakonika*.[54]

As for so many other cities, Herodotus' narrative seems to have been the incentive for the Argives to present their own version of local history.[55] The original attempt of the *Argolika* to offset the uncomplimentary account by Herodotus of Cleomenes' invasion would have been the story which is the basis of Plutarch's narrative in *Mul. Virt.* 4: Telesilla persuading the women to mount the walls and

[51] The gratuitous forecast of the fate of Miletus would only have been volunteered sometime after the battle of Lade, but probably before the city had fallen, thus establishing the date of the oracle, and the battle of Sepeia, ca. 494 B.C. This date has been disputed: 494 is favored by recent writers (see those cited n. 66 below and Bengston *Gr. Gesch.*² 156) although it is challenged without argumentation by Jacoby, Comm. to *FGrHist* 310 n. 90 (p. 28). T. Lenschau, *Klio* 31 (1938) 416–420 and others before him dated the battle to 519 B.C.

[52] See Jacoby *RE* suppl. II (1913) 273, lines 57–64.

[53] Pausanias (2.20.10) quotes the oracle from Herodotus, but remarks: "Herodotus explained the oracle, perhaps understanding it, and perhaps not."

[54] See Jacoby, Comm. to *FGrHist* 310 n. 84 (p. 27).

[55] Jacoby, Comm. to *FGrHist* 310 n. 92 (p. 28), argues that in the case of Argos this development took place only after Hellanicus.

defend them against Cleomenes. The anecdote in *Apophthegmata Laconica* 223 BC 4, 5 belongs to the same stage of the tradition.[56] Herodotus is the point of departure for the story of the women defending the city; it is even possible that the oracle was known only through Herodotus.[57] Telesilla, a famous poetess of the period, was a natural choice for the leader of the women.[58] This part of the tradition accepted Herodotus' account of the battle of Sepeia, as is seen from Plutarch's narrative in *Mul. Virt.* 4. Another version more opposed to Herodotus existed, which attributed Cleomenes' victory to his rupture of a seven-day truce.[59] This may be from the same account as two other notices involving the number seven:[60] Plutarch rejects as a fable (*ou mên hôs enioi muthologousin*) an account which set the number killed by Cleomenes at 7,777,[61] and reports a variant which dated the battle of Sepeia on the seventh day of the month.[62] The correction of 7,777 to simply many (*pollous*) was perhaps made by Plutarch himself, and not taken from his source.[63] In *Coriolanus* 38 he criticizes with the same word (*muthologousin*) the reference by his source Dionysius of Halicarnassus (*Roman Antiquities* 8.56) to a talking statue, and substitutes his own more credible interpretation. Even if this correction is not the work of Plutarch, but expresses a variant in the Argive tradition, it is probable that it was introduced into this

---

[56] Note 223 B 4: "(Cleomenes) failed because the women took down the weapons from the temples and with them held him off."

[57] See Jacoby, Comm. to *FGrHist* 310 n. 78 (p. 26).

[58] Too little is known of Telesilla to conclude that her poems had a martial air which suggested the association. The reference of Maximus of Tyre, *Dissertationes* 37.5 (p. 439 Davis, London 1740), "the poems of Tyrtaeus stirred up the Spartans, and the songs of Telesilla the Argives," is probably based upon the Argive tradition rather than Telesilla's poetry. Her fragments and important testimonia are collected by Diehl, *Anthologica Lyrica* II (1925) 61 and J. M. Edmonds, *Lyra Graeca* II (1924) 236–245. See also Paul Maas, *RE* s.v. Telesilla, V 1 A (1934) 384–385; Schmid-Stählin I 1, 449–450; Bergk, *Poetae Lyrici Graeci* III (1882) 380–381.

[59] *Ap. Lac.* 223 AB 2, 3.

[60] Jacoby, Comm. to *FGrHist* 310 n. 81 (p. 26).

[61] This variant was accepted by Polyaenus (8.33).

[62] See also Aristotle *Politics* 5.2.8 (1303 a 6).

[63] As implied by Jacoby, Comm. to *FGrHist* 310 n. 86 (p. 27), who thinks rather of a Hellenistic compiler of the anonymous variants cited in Plutarch's account.

account by Plutarch himself. We know that other variants playing on the number seven were known to him from their appearance in the *Apophthegmata Laconica*, which, although not published by Plutarch, were among his papers.[64]

A more explicit Argive correction, already known and accepted by Aristotle,[65] expressly rejected Herodotus' use of the term *douloi* and substituted *perioikoi* in the description of the conditions in Argos effected by the tremendous loss of citizens at this time. The value of the notices of Herodotus and the Argive writers concerning the role of the *douloi* and *perioikoi* in establishing fifth-century Argive history has been the subject of several recent studies, and need not be discussed here.[66] The reason for the correction is evident: Herodotus' statement that Argos was in the hands of *douloi* must have been painful indeed to a pride already rendered sensitive by the steady decline of Argive power in the sixth and fifth centuries. The result is that the account of the *Argolika* on this point openly contradicts Herodotus: in the story of the defense of Argos by Telesilla it does not challenge Herodotus so obviously, but is incompatible with Herodotus rather than contradictory. The misinterpretation of Herodotus (who does not say that the slaves married Argive women) may perhaps be the result of a preconceived notion that Herodotus could be refuted by a reference to the strange custom dictating that married women had to wear beards when they slept with their husbands.[67]

---

[64] See Ziegler, *RE* 865–867. [65] Aristotle, *Politics* 5.2.8 (1303 a 6).

[66] See Fritz Gschnitzer, *Abhängige Orte im griechischen Altertum* (Zetemata 17, Munich 1958) 74–77; R. F. Willetts, *Hermes* 87 (1959) 495–506 (who argues that the *douloi* were serfs, as were Aristotle's *perioikoi*: according to Newman, Comm. to the *Politics ad loc.*, serf is the common meaning of *perioikos* in Aristotle); W. G. Forrest, *CQ* N.S. 10 (1960) 221–241 (who explains *douloi* as a political tag); F. Kiechle, *Philologus* 104 (1960) 181–200. See also the earlier studies of P. A. Seymour, *JHS* 42 (1922) 24–30 and S. Luria, *Klio* 26 (1933) 211–228 (whose comparison with the *Lêmnia kaka* is unfounded, see Jacoby, Comm. to *FGrHist* 310 n. 91 [p. 28].)

[67] This practice and the festival of the Hybristika are discussed and parallels cited by Nilsson, *Griechische Feste* 371; Frazer, *Pausanias* vol. III, p. 197; How and Wells to Herodotus, 6.77; and W. R. Halliday, *Annual of the British School at Athens* 16 (1909–10) 212–219.

"Mulierum Virtutes" 4: The Argive Women

This Argive revision of Herodotus was no doubt a factor which influenced Plutarch to include this story in his collection, for elsewhere also he demonstrates an obvious pleasure in correcting a Herodotean account from a local historian. In particular, the case of the Argive *perioikoi* would be an example of Herodotus' use of a word with a bad connotation when a better was available, a practice condemned by Plutarch in the *De Herodoti malignitate*.[68]

Pausanias presents a new stage in the development of the Argive tradition. Like Plutarch, he remarks Telesilla's activity as a poetess and preserves the Herodotean account of the victory of Cleomenes at Sepeia. Although the latter incident is reported in rather more detail than in Plutarch, here also the oracle to Cleomenes, a Spartan element, is omitted. But in his account of Cleomenes' attack on Argos the walls are defended by men—aged, youths and slaves—while the women play the part of true soldiers, actually coming to grips with the Spartans and sustaining their assault unafraid. This version preserves traces of a Laconian justification of Cleomenes' retreat, which accepted the Argive story of the female defense of Argos, but argued that the Spartans withdrew only because they were ashamed to fight women. The Argive response to the Laconian justification, also given by Pausanias, was that the Spartans had actually engaged with Argive women before they decided to retreat, thus rendering impossible any Spartan claim to gallantry.

In the basic narrative of Plutarch the women keep to the protection of the walls. Pausanias, to rebut a Spartan version of the story, makes the women join battle before the city. Socrates of Argos, in the passage cited by Plutarch, gives a stronger response to the Laconian defense. According to him, not only did the Spartans engage with the women, but led by King Demaratus they forced their way into the city, and captured the Pamphyliakon, only to be expelled ignominiously from the city. This imaginative account seems to have been

---

[68] 855 B. Another defense of the Argives against Herodotus, made with the help of common knowledge rather than local historians, is found in the same work, 863 BC.

inspired by a historical incident from the recent past.[69] In 271 B.C. Argos was almost captured by Pyrrhus of Epirus, but he was killed in the street-fighting after having gained control of much of the city. He seems to have been hit by a stone or tile thrown by a woman from above.[70] This fact was novelistically elaborated by the patriotic Argive writers: Pausanias reports, for instance, citing the Argive Lyceas, that it was no ordinary woman who threw the tile, but Demeter herself.[71] According to Polyaenus (8.68), the Argive women gained great renown by killing Pyrrhus. After such a glorious victory, the Argives were willing to hear of similar deeds in earlier centuries; Socrates' version of Telesilla's victory would add glory both to the ancient battle and the recent. It was probably also at this time that the stele with the relief of Telesilla seen by Pausanias was set up, as well as the statue mentioned by Tatian (*Oratio ad Graecos* 33). The sculptor of the statue, Niceratus, was active in Pergamum between 276 and 263 B.C.[72]

Jacoby rightly ascribes to Socrates only the single sentences directly attributed to him by Plutarch: "According to Socrates (*hôs Sôkrates phêsin*), they drove out the other king, Demaratus, after he had gotten in and gained control of the Pamphliakon." The citation is an addition to the basic narrative, which finished the description of the women's defense of the city with "after many casualties they were expelled." Between this phrase and the mention of the honors given after the battle to the Argive women, Plutarch added the variant from Socrates.[73] Plutarch's addition of the variant from Socrates is a

---

[69] Remarked by Jacoby, Comm. to *FGrHist* 310 n. 90 (p. 27), cf. n. 100 (p. 29).

[70] Thus Pausanias 1.13.7–9 (= Hieronymus of Cardia, *FGrHist* 154 F 15). Similar but more detailed and dramatic is the version of Plutarch, *Pyrrhus* 34 (from Phylarchus? See Jacoby, Comm. to *FGrHist* 154 F 15, II BD p. 547, and Kroymann, *RE* suppl. 8 [1956] 484–485, s.v. Phylarchos.)

[71] Pausanias 1.13.8 (= Lyceas, *FGrHist* 312 F 1). It is doubtful whether Zonaras 8.6 (who says that a woman in her excitement fell on Pyrrhus from a roof and killed him) represents genuine Argive tradition.

[72] Lippold, *RE* s.v. Nikeratos 4, XVII 1 (1936) 314–316. See Jacoby, Comm. to *FGrHist* 310 n. 100 (p. 29).

[73] Jacoby, Comm. to *FGrHist* 310 F 6 (p. 46) and n. 88 (p. 27). This view is opposed by F. Kiechle, *Philologus* 104 (1960) 180–181, who argues that the whole Telesilla story

product of his own wide reading, and not drawn from an intermediary.[74]

The story of the Argive women in this chapter is a literary invention of Argive writers, based upon the account of Herodotus. Plutarch reports in his basic narrative one version of the developed Argive tradition, and introduces the variants of Socrates and perhaps that giving the date of the battle of Sepeia and the number of dead from his own reading in Socrates and other writers.

Mulierum Virtutes 5: THE PERSIAN WOMEN

Plutarch, Nicolaus of Damascus (*FGrHist* 90 F 66, 43-44), Justin (1.6.13-15) and Polyaenus (7.45.2) narrate in roughly similar fashion the victory of Cyrus over Astyages and the Medes. The Persians had been routed, and all seemed lost, when the Persian women ran up to meet their fleeing men, and lifting up their skirts, cried out, "Where are you heading, cowards? Do you think to flee back here, whence you were born?" The Persians were shamed, and turning to face the Medes, defeated them.

The accounts of Justin, Nicolaus, and Plutarch are very similar, and must be presumed to depend on a common source. Moreover, this source must be Ctesias, for it is known that this fragment of Nicolaus is an excerpt from Ctesias,[75] and Justin seems also to depend on him

---

in Plutarch is taken from Socrates; Plutarch, however, usually names his sources only for variants, not for a simple narrative. If the whole story were from Socrates, there would be no reason to introduce his name here. The action of Telesilla is equally reasonable as an *aition* for the scorn the women later showed their mates without the addition from Socrates, and therefore it is not necessary to connect this part of the account with Socrates, as Kiechle believes.

[74] See Jacoby, Comm. to *FGrHist* 310 F 6 (p. 46). Plutarch cites Socrates twice in *Quaestiones Romanae* 26 and 52 (*FGrHist* 310 F 3, 4), once in *Quaestiones Graecae* 25 (F 5) and once in *De Iside* 364 F (F 2). All these citations are from the *Peri hosiôn* (named in F 2), and considering the association of the Telesilla story with the Hybristika, this notice may also be from that work, rather than from the *Periêgêsis* (see Jacoby, Comm. to *FGrHist* 310, n. 15 [p. 22]).

[75] Jacoby, Comm. to *FGrHist* 90 F 66 (p. 251): "scheint reines exzerpt ohne jede zutat N.s oder aus anderen quellen." Cf. Jacoby, *RE* s.v. Ktesias, XI 2 (1922) 2056-58. This view is challenged unconvincingly by R. Laqueur *RE* s.v. Nikolaos 20, XVII 1 (1936) 375-384.

3+P.H.M.

in this part of the work.[76] Plutarch used Ctesias extensively in his life of Artaxerxes; we may therefore presume that he drew upon him directly in this passage.[77] He mistakenly has the women flee to the city Pasargadae rather than the mountain of the same name, as is stated in Nicolaus and therefore in Ctesias. The mistake was facilitated by Ctesias' mention of the city in the same passage.[78] The mistake is the more excusable if, as is reasonable, Plutarch was narrating the incident from memory.

The account of Polyaenus differs from those of Plutarch, Nicolaus, and Justin in ascribing the rout of the Persians to the cowardice of the satrap Oibares. Therefore Polyaenus does not follow Plutarch, as so often,[79] nor Nicolaus, for neither mentions the role of Oibares in the rout. In the account of this campaign, however, Nicolaus often mentions Oibares, and it is possible that Ctesias mentioned him on this occasion also, although this reference was omitted in the excerpts of Nicolaus, Justin, and Plutarch. Such an identical omission by three different excerptors is unlikely, but there is nothing in Polyaenus contradicting this Ctesian tradition, and his account may also be ultimately derived from Ctesias.[80]

Justin and Polyaenus narrate the story only as far as the defeat of

---

[76] See Jacoby *RE* s.v. Ktesias col. 2056, lines 17-22.

[77] He did not take the story from Nicolaus. He only cites Nicolaus once (*Brutus* 53 = *FGrHist* 90 F 99), and that not from his historical compilation but from the life of Caesar.

[78] See the account of Nicolaus. According to Stephanus of Byzantium s.v. Passargadae [sic] = Anaximenes of Lampsacus (*FGrHist* 72 F 19), Cyrus founded the city after the battle. Cf. Strabo 15, 730 C. Pasargadae was also the name of the leading tribe of the Persians, to which the Achaemenids belonged (Her. 1.125.3).

[79] See above pp. 26-27.

[80] J. Melber, *Über die Quellen*..., pp. 453-456, compares this passage with Polyaenus 7.6.1 and 7.6.9 and concludes that each comes from a different source. He attributes 7.6.9 to Ctesias, thus denying that he can be the source of 7.45.2. But 7.6.9 does not necessarily refer to the same incident as 7.45.2; Nicolaus records several battles between Astyages and Cyrus; for the flight to Pasargadae mentioned in Polyaenus 7.6.9 compare especially Nicolaus, *FGrHist* 90 F 66, 36. Both accounts may therefore be from Ctesias. Melber's argument is further weakened when we note the close resemblance between 7.6.1 and 7.45.2. These share ultimately a common source, although the original (Ctesian?) account has been watered down, perhaps from prudishness, in 7.6.1 by the intermediate source from which Polyaenus drew 7.6.1-5.

the Medes, but Plutarch and Nicolaus go on to mention the gold given by Cyrus and later kings to the Persian women[81] whenever the king entered Pasargadae.[82] Plutarch's story is further enlarged, however, by the notice, absent from the other authors, that Ochus, to avoid making this distribution, would not enter the city, whereas Alexander entered the city twice, and gave double to the women with child. This addition is very similar to a notice in *Alexander* 69.1. In fact, the passages in the life of Alexander and in the *Mulierum Virtutes* are different versions of one account, which Plutarch wrote with a different emphasis in each book, fitting each version to its context. For this reason the city (Pasargadae) and the pregnant women are mentioned in *Mul. Virt.* 5, where the origin of the story is of interest, but not in the life, which is concerned only with the royal custom continued by Alexander. The anecdote about Ochus could not have been told by Ctesias, the source of Nicolaus and of the first part of the Plutarch story. This anecdote is connected in both Plutarchian versions with Alexander, to magnify by contrast the generosity of the latter. We must conclude, therefore (and this is suggested also by the absence of Cyrus from the version in the *Alexander*), that the source of the Ochus and Alexander section of *Mul. Virt.* 5 is different from the source which gives the battle and the establishment of the custom by Cyrus. This second source would have come to Plutarch's notice while he was preparing to write the life of Alexander.[83]

The account of the Persian women, short though it is, thus has two sources, which were combined by Plutarch, probably from memory: one, Ctesias, who was also source for Nicolaus and Justin, who

[81] Xenophon, *Cyropaedia* 8.5.21, exaggerates Cyrus' generosity, saying that he gave money to men as well as women.
[82] Not Persepolis as suggested by Wyttenbach and repeated by Nachstädt. Nicolaus explicitly states Pasargadae, and is confirmed by Plutarch, who in *Alexander* 69 immediately after referring to the gift of gold speaks of Alexander's respect for the tomb of Cyrus, which according to Strabo (15, 730 A) was at Pasargadae. The archaeological and literary evidence for Pasargadae has been assembled most recently by H. Treidler, *RE* s.v. Pasargadai, Suppl. Bd. 9 (1962) 777-799.
[83] Plutarch (*De Iside* 363 C, cf. 355 C) ascribes another unfavorable story about Ochus to Dinon (*FGrHist* 690 F 21). The connection with Alexander in this case, however, precludes the use of Dinon by Plutarch here.

narrated the battle and the foundation of the gold distribution by Cyrus the Great; the other, drawn from a writer on Alexander, relating the observances of the custom by Alexander and contrasting it with the miserliness of Ochus.

The similar story of the Laconian woman who reproached her sons as they fled from battle in the *Apophthegmata Lacaenarum* (*Mor.* 241 B, 4) is at best only distantly related to the story of the Persian women. It had already been used by the philosopher Teles,[84] to whom it is ascribed by Stobaeus along with other Spartan apophthegms found in this collection.[85] It is possible that the Spartan version is a translation of the Persian story into the Greek philosophical tradition, and therefore may derive ultimately from Ctesias. Other instances of such self-exposure are discussed in connection with *Mul. Virt.* 9, the Lycian Women.

Mulierum Virtutes 6: THE CELTIC WOMEN [86]

The fairness and good sense of the Celtic women, Plutarch tells us, was such that they arbitrated all the men's disputes, to the extent that when the Celts made a treaty with Hannibal, it was prescribed that if the Celts felt wronged, the judges of the matter should be the Carthaginian governors and generals in Spain, but if the Carthaginians, the judges should be the Celtic women.

This treaty is undoubtedly that made by Hannibal with the Celts between the Pyrenees and the Rhone while marching toward Italy.[87] The terms of the treaty are not given elsewhere. Plutarch's source is

---

[84] *Teletis Reliquiae*² ed. Hense (Tübingen 1909) p. 58 lines 8–12 = Stobaeus 4.44.83 (p. 989 Hense).

[85] According to Nachstädt, the *Apophthegmata Laconica*, including the *Apophthegmata Lacaenarum*, is a collection "ex vetere illo apophthegmatum Laconicorum corpore, quo iam Plato et Aristoteles usi erant." (*Plutarchi Moralia* II, 167, cf. pp. 110–111.) This view is rejected by Jacoby, Comm. to *FGrHist* 591 (Aristocrates) n. 5 (p. 365).

[86] This is one of the stories from the *Mulierum Virtutes* used by Polyaenus in his *Strategemata* (7.50). See Chapter II and especially pp. 19–20.

[87] Mentioned by Livy 21.24. See Polybius 34.10 and Camille Jullian, *Histoire de la Gaule* I (Paris 1909) 462 n. 3 and G. De Sanctis, *Storia dei Romani* III, 2 (Turin 1917) 16, n. 25.

not known, although it is more than likely the same as that which described Hannibal's capture of Salmantica, *Mul. Virt.* 10.[88]

A similar report of the political sagacity of Celtic women is found in the Paradoxographus Vaticanus Rohdii: "These (*scil.* the Gauls) when they deliberate about war take counsel with the women, and whatever the women decide prevails. But if when they make war they are defeated, they cut off the heads of the women who had advised that the war be undertaken, and throw them out of the country."[89] Both notices report a custom quite foreign to Greek ways. In the account of Plutarch, however, the custom seems to enter only as *aition*, genuine or invented, for the historical fact of the unusual terms of the peace treaty.

Mulierum Virtutes 7: THE MELIAN WOMEN[90]

In this story Plutarch relates the sending out from Melos of a colony under Nymphaeus. The Melians landed in Caria, and were given land by the Carians who inhabited Cryassa. When these later had a change of heart and decided to kill the Melians at a feast, a Carian girl named Caphene, much in love with Nymphaeus, revealed their plot to him. The invitation came, and Nymphaeus told the Carians that it was the Greek custom to go to a feast with their wives. The Carians agreeing, he ordered the women each to carry a sword under her clothes, but the men to go unarmed. During the feast, the Carians set upon the Melians, but they, taking their swords from their wives, defended themselves and killed their attackers. The Melians then took possession of the territory and settled a new city, Nea Cryassa, while Caphene married Nymphaeus and was honored by all. Lest we miss the moral Plutarch adds: "Well may we wonder at the courage and the silence of the women, and the fact that not one among so many

---

[88] Jullian (above, n. 87) suggests "ce mystérieux Silénus," Hannibal's companion and historian (*FGrHist* 175). See the discussion of *Mul. Virt.* 10, below.
[89] In *Rerum Naturalium Scriptores Graeci Minores* I (Leipzig 1877) ed. Otto Keller, p. 112 no. 46.
[90] This is one of the stories from the *Mulierum Virtutes* used by Polyaenus in his *Strategemata* (8.64). See Chapter II and especially p. 21.

even unwillingly through fright was a coward." In this account Plutarch is interested not in the virtue of the barbarian girl (as in the case of Lampsace, *Mul. Virt.* 18) but with that of the Greek women who aided their husbands.

We have no other information of this colony of Melos. Cryassa is identified by Stephanus of Byzantium s.v. as a city in Caria, named from the Carian Cryassos, but Nea Cryassa is not mentioned. Oldfather suggests[91] that the source of this story is the *Karika* of Apollonius of Letopolis (Apollonius of Aphrodisias, *FGrHist* 740) although he is cited only by Stephanus of Byzantium (and once by the *Etymologicon Magnum*), and so late an author (Jacoby writes "Kaiserzeit?") is unlikely to have been used by Plutarch. The only other author of *Karika* of which we have any fragments is Philip of Theangela (*FGrHist* 741), of perhaps the third century B.C. In the complete absence of any historian of Melos,[92] or any reference to an Aristotelian constitution, not even a guess as to Plutarch's source may be made. It has a definite Melian, or Greek, bias. The motif of the barbarian girl aiding Greek colonists may be compared with the story of Lampsace, *Mul. Virt.* 18.[93] Contrary to Dümmler,[94] the Melian colonists were surely Dorian.

Mulierum Virtutes 8: THE TYRRHENIAN WOMEN[95]

In this episode Plutarch narrates the fate of the Tyrrhenians driven from Lemnos and Imbros by the Athenians. His story falls into two parts; first, the settlement of the Tyrrhenians in Laconia, their subsequent arrest, and their escape by changing clothes with their wives, and second, their colonization, under Spartan auspices and the Spartan leaders Delphus and Pollis, of Melos and of Lyttus in Crete. The whole

---

[91] *RE* s.v. Kaphene, X 2 (1919) 1893.
[92] Cf. Jacoby, Comm. to *FGrHist* III B (p. 400).
[93] F. Dümmler, *RhMus* N.F. 42 (1887) 185, remarks that this type of novelistic touch is "vor dem Epos in der ionischen Volkssage vorhanden."
[94] *Athenische Mitteilungen* 13 (1888) 301: see the discussion of *Mul. Virt.* 8 and the colonization of Melos from Sparta soon after the Dorian invasion referred to in n. 99 below.
[95] This is one of the stories from the *Mulierum Virtutes* used by Polyaenus in his *Strategemata* (7.49). See Chapter II and especially p. 21.

chapter has been considered to be drawn from Ephorus, because of certain correspondences between Conon, Nicolaus of Damascus, Ephorus as reported by Strabo, and Plutarch.[96] The account of the escape of the men from prison by their wives' stratagem is very similar to the escape of the Minyans recorded by Herodotus (4.146). Plutarch's reference to Tyrrhenians on Lemnos is similar to that made by Philochorus (*FGrHist* 328 F 100).

The two parts of this chapter must be considered separately, discussing first the second part, which is in fact derived from Ephorus. According to Conon (*FGrHist* 26 F 1, 36), Philonomus, a non-Dorian, betrayed Laconia to the Dorians, and received in return Amyclae, which he settled with people from Lemnos and Imbros. In the third generation they clashed with the Dorians and left Amyclae. Some Spartans joined them, and they sailed for Crete, with the Spartans Pollis and Delphus as leaders. On the way they settled Melos; in Crete they took Gortyn without resistance and lived there with the surrounding natives. The account of Conon is attributed to Ephorus by Höfer[97] (and all others after him), who compared it with Strabo 8.5.4 (*FGrHist* 70 F 117): "Ephorus says that the Heraclidae . . . gave Amyclae to the man who betrayed Laconia to them." The same writer is the source of Nicolaus of Damascus (*FGrHist* 90 F 28),[98] who likewise relates how the Heraclidae awarded Amyclae to the traitor Philonomus, who after an absence returned with some Lemnians, distributed land in Amyclae to the new settlers, and ruled there as king. A certain consistency connects the stories of Conon, Strabo, and Nicolaus of Damascus, and the narrative of Ephorus seems to show clearly through: Philonomus betrays Laconia to the Heraclidae, and receives Amyclae as a reward. After an absence he returns with men from Lemnos and Imbros, settling in Amyclae. After three generations the descendants of these new settlers quarrel with

---

[96] This is the opinion of Höfer, *Konon* 71–73, and Luigi Pareti, *Storia di Sparta arcaica* I (Florence 1917) 124–130. The paragraphs immediately following repeat their arguments with only minor changes.
[97] Höfer, *Konon*, 72.
[98] See Jacoby, Comm. to *FGrHist* 90 F 28–33.

their Dorian neighbors and leave for Crete under Pollis and Delphus. On the way they settle Melos;[99] in Crete, Gortyn.

Another story of Conon (*FGrHist* 26 F 1, 47) mentions the expedition of Pollis and Delphus in connection with Althaemenes of Argos. The inference that the account of Althaemenes' colonizing activity in Crete and Rhodes is also derived from Ephorus is confirmed by Strabo (10.4.18, *FGrHist* 70 F 149), who on the authority of Ephorus says that Crete was colonized by the Dorians under Althaemenes in the time of Eurysthenes and Procles.[100] Since Eurysthenes and Procles were the first generation after the Heraclidae, while Althaemenes was the second, the synchronism between the two accounts ascribed to Ephorus is not perfect, but the difference is easily explained by an overlapping of the two generations.

The account of Ephorus thus defined is clearly discernible in the second part of Plutarch's narrative in *Mul. Virt.* 8. As related by Plutarch, the Pelasgians from Lemnos and Imbros in Laconia, after political differences with the Spartans, force the Spartans to give them money and ships to allow them to leave. The Spartans also provide three leaders, Pollis, Delphus,[101] and Crataedas and promise that the emigrants will be considered colonists and kin of the Lacedaemonians. Some settled at Melos, but those with Pollis sailed on to Crete and, upon the fulfillment of a strange oracle connected with the cult-statue of Artemis carried from Brauron,[102] settled at Lyttus. Conon 36 gives Gortyn as the Spartan colony, whereas Plutarch

---

[99] Melos is also called a Spartan colony by Thucydides 5.84.2. Cf. Herodotus 8.48: "In race, the Melians are from Sparta."

[100] Höfer, *Konon*, 73-74.

[101] Thus the majority of the editors restore the names from Conon, after Wyttenbach, not without hesitation: the MSS. have *adelphon kai krataida*. Nachstädt suggests in his apparatus *adelphon ⟨autou⟩ Krataidan* with Xylander.

[102] W. R. Halliday, *Greek Questions of Plutarch* (Oxford, 1928) 111, suggests the connection of the Artemis carried by the Lemnians from Brauron with the cult of Britomartis Chersonesus: see Strabo 10.4.14 (479): "the seaport of Lyttus is the so-called Chersonese, where there is the temple of Britomartis." Preller-Robert, *Griechische Mythologie*[4] I, 313, n. 7, explain the resemblance of the cult at Brauron to that of the great goddess on Lemnos by the abduction from Brauron of the maidens worshipping Artemis.

names Lyttus, but there need be no difficulty. Plutarch connects only Pollis with the founding of Lyttus (although in *Quaestiones Graecae* 21 Pollis and Delphus are said to have fought together in the first wars against the Cretans, see below); the others may have settled at Gortyn. Moreover, in *FGrHist* 70 F 149 Ephorus himself remarks that Lyttus was a Dorian colony. The unusual detail with which Plutarch described the founding of this colony is also notable in another passage of Plutarch, *Quaestiones Graecae* 21 (296 B-D). This passage is associated with *Mul. Virt.* 8 and with Ephorus by its reference to the Lemnians in Sparta and the colonization of Crete under Pollis and Delphus. To explain the term *hoi katakautai*, Plutarch here relates that the colonists under Pollis and Delphus, while fighting with the native Cretans,[103] left many men unburied. Later, when time had rendered the duty objectionable, Pollis attempted to make the obligation more attractive by establishing honors to be given to those who buried the dead, and gave them this name, which means "burners." Then Pollis and Delphus divided into two separate groups, but promised to preserve an *adeian adikêmatôn*. For the other Cretans were accustomed to rob each other, but these two cities neither did wrong nor stole nor killed.

That Ephorus treated the colonization of Crete in some detail is evident from the accounts of Althaemenes and Pollis and Delphus noted above. According to Strabo, Ephorus recorded the most important facts about the Cretan constitutions (10.4.16, *FGrHist* 70 F 149). In his account he would have been concerned with the issue, important in his day, of the relation between the Cretan and Spartan constitutions,[104] and he must have treated the customs and religious practices of the Cretans as well.[105] The description, therefore, of the

[103] The fighting mentioned in connection with the colony in both Plutarch passages confirms that both refer to Lyttus; according to Conon 36 the Dorians took Gortyn without opposition.

[104] See Jacoby, Comm. to *FGrHist* 70 F 149 (p. 79), quoting Schwartz *RE* s.v. Ephoros, VI 1 (1907) 13.

[105] See Jacoby, Comm. to *FGrHist* III B, p. 307 (Kreta): "Ephoros—der über Kreta ausführlich gehandelt hat, und bereits den unterschied zwischen der vordorischen idealverfassung, den dorischen sitten, und den realen zuständen seiner zeit machte." Customs were for the Greeks part of *politeia*.

customs of the Dorian colonists found in *Quaestiones Graecae* 21, as well as the account of the landing in *Mul. Virt.* 8, would readily find a place in Ephorus' descriptive narrative of Crete.

Yet another correspondence between Ephorus and Plutarch may be noted. The paraphrase of Ephorus by Strabo, arguing that the Laconian laws are older than the Cretan, "for (the Lyttians), since they are colonists (*apoikoi*), preserve the customs of the mother city" (10.4.17, *FGrHist* 70 F 149), is cognate to Plutarch *Mul. Virt.* 8 (247 E): "Therefore they consider themselves both to be related in race to the Athenians through their mothers and to be colonists (*apoikoi*) of the Spartans."[106]

Thus the second part of Plutarch's narrative in *Mul. Virt.* 8 can be traced to Ephorus. To judge from the episodes preserved by Plutarch, Ephorus treated the Cretan Dorian colonies in some detail—rather more than is suggested by the notices in Strabo and the condensed narratives of Nicolaus and Conon.

It has been generally accepted that the first part of Plutarch's narrative is also taken from Ephorus.[107] Certain similarities between accounts encourage this conclusion. The settlers from Lemnos and Imbros in Sparta are also mentioned by Ephorus (in Conon, *FGrHist* 26 F 1, 36) as noted above (p. 59). According to Plutarch, the Tyrrhenians were useful to the Spartans in the Helot War; this war is also placed by Ephorus (*FGrHist* 70 F 117) in the earliest period of the Dorian occupation.[108] The Tyrrhenians wished to share in the

---

[106] Cf. the promise of the Lacedaemonians to the colonists, that they would be considered "colonists (*apoikoi*) and kin (*suggeneis*) of the Lacedaemonians" (247 E). Jacoby suggests (Comm. to *FGrHist* 70 F 149, p. 80) that it is possible that Aristotle in *Politics* 2.7.1, 1271 b 28, "the Lyttians are colonists of the Laconians," used Ephorus. Polybius 4.54 parallels Plutarch closely: "Lyttus, being a colony (*apoikos*) of and related (*suggenês*) to the Lacedaemonians..." For Spartan connections with Lyttus, see also Pausanias 4.19.4, from which we learn that archers from Lyttus and other Cretan cities aided the Spartans against Aristomenes. The sources for the history of Lyttus are gathered by M. Guarducci, *Inscriptiones Creticae* I, 180-182. Another people which recalled a distant relation with Athens were the Bottiaeans; see Plutarch *Qu. Gr.* 35 (299 A) and Aristotle fr. 485 Rose.

[107] See the authors cited above, n. 96.

[108] Pausanias puts it some generations later, under Alcamenes (3.2.7).

government, an issue which Ephorus in the same passage remarked as a source of friction between Spartans and *perioikoi*. The unrest of the Tyrrhenians in Plutarch finally resulted in their emigration, as in Ephorus (Conon 36) the Lemnians left Amyclae because of stasis with the Dorians. The conclusion suggests itself that Ephorus rewrote Herodotus' story of the Minyan emigrants from Lemnos who settled first at Sparta and then colonized Thera (4.145-148) to fit his own story of the establishment of the Heraclidae in Sparta and their colonization of Crete, and that this version of Ephorus is given by Plutarch in abridged but essentially unaltered form.[109]

A close examination of the differences between the accounts of Ephorus and Plutarch, however, does not support this argument. A first indication is that Plutarch, following Ephorus, uses the name Pelasgians in the second part of this chapter for the people he called Tyrrhenians in the first. Ephorus, however, never calls the immigrants to Laconia Tyrrhenians but Lemnians, or as here, Pelasgians (that is, non-Dorians).[110] Plutarch in writing this chapter overlooked this difference, thus preserving an indication that the two halves are from different sources. Moreover, Plutarch does not name or even imply a connection with Philonomus or Amyclae, nor does he mention the two generations between the arrival of the Tyrrhenians in Laconia and the colonization of Melos and Crete. He remarks the acceptance of the Tyrrhenians into the Laconian community, but by their aid in the Helot War, a war which according to Ephorus (*FGrHist* 70 F 117) is in the time of Agis, of the third generation of Heraclidae. Moreover, Ephorus states that the war began because Agis deprived the *perioikoi* of rights that they had had before, a statement which is inconsistent with Plutarch's narrative. Finally, Ephorus' description of the Dorian conquest of Laconia and the establishment of the Spartan state is in the first three books (thus *FGrHist* 70 F 117, which is in question here)

---

[109] Thus Pareti (above, n. 96) p. 128.
[110] Thus Ephorus explains Pelasgians in *FGrHist* 70 F 113; note also that the followers of Althaemenes in Conon 47 are called Pelasgians to distinguish them from their Dorian fellow-colonists.

whereas his account of the colonization of Crete (including *FGrHist* 70 F 149) must be placed in the fourth or fifth books. It is unlikely that Plutarch or his source would have combined the two stories from separate parts of Ephorus' narrative. The account in the first part of *Mul. Virt.* 8, therefore, may not be ascribed to Ephorus.

If the relation of the first part of Plutarch's story to Ephorus is questionable, that to Herodotus is not. The names and certain details have been changed but the story remains the same. According to Herodotus (4.145-148), the Minyans, descendants of the Argonauts, were driven off Lemnos by the Pelasgians who had raided Brauron. They came to Laconia and thanks to their relation to the Argonauts, the companions of Castor and Pollux, were welcomed, given citizenship (by being distributed among the tribes) and allowed to marry Spartan wives. But when they demanded a share in the kingship, they were imprisoned. They were freed by their wives, who entered the prison on the pretext of visiting their husbands, then exchanged clothes with the men, and remained behind while the men left the prison dressed as women. First the men fled to Taygetus, and then all were allowed to leave, some joining with Theras in the colonization of Melos and Thera, others going to other regions. In Plutarch, Herodotus' story has been revised and rewritten to place the central anecdote of the men's escape in a new and more historical setting.[111] Therefore, the legendary Minyans become Tyrrhenians, long recognized as inhabitants of Lemnos. Upon arrival in Sparta the Tyrrhenians do not claim connection with mythical heroes, but show themselves useful allies in the Helot War. The new attempt at historicity is noticeable in the different words with which the two authors describe the offense of the newcomers. Herodotus says that the Minyans *exubrisan*, asking for a share in the kingship, *kai alla poieuntes*

---

[111] The same stratagem described by Herodotus and Plutarch is transferred to a completely different occasion (though still connected with Sparta) in the story of Chilonis, the wife of Theopompus, Polyaenus 8.34. The story of Herodotus is given without alteration by Valerius Maximus 4.6 ext. 3 and Polyaenus 8.71 (the latter unfortunately fragmentary). Boccaccio retells the story with some original variations in *De mulieribus claris* 29.

ouk hosia. In Plutarch they are suspected of "coming together for a revolution (*epi neôterismôi*) and planning to change the established order (*ta kathestôta*)." Both authors mean the same thing, but Herodotus' statement is in the old religious-ethical terminology, whereas Plutarch's account, in the style of later historiography, uses purely political terms. In like manner Herodotus' explanation for the delay in the execution of the conspirators—that the Lacedaemonians kill people only at night—is replaced by the legalistic statement that the accusers were looking for better evidence. Finally, the place of the colony to Thera is taken by the expedition to Crete as described by Ephorus. In Plutarch we find a "historicized" version of Herodotus.[112]

It has been demonstrated above that Ephorus cannot be the source of Plutarch's revised version of the Herodotean story. Unfortunately, our knowledge of other historians, especially Spartan and Cretan local historians, is so slight that we cannot suggest who Plutarch's source was.

Plutarch, when he presented together in *Mul. Virt.* 8 these two stories, that modified from Herodotus by an unknown writer, and that on the colonization of Crete by Ephorus, preserved the name Pelasgian in one and Tyrrhenian in the other, applying them both to the wanderers from Lemnos and Imbros. The question of the Pelasgians and Tyrrhenians on Lemnos has been much discussed;[113]

---

[112] Contrast J. Bérard, *REA* 51 (1949) 234, who admits that the account of Plutarch has been contaminated by Herodotean elements, but argues "il ne paraît pas que les deux aventures, par ailleurs différentes, doivent être confondues."

[113] The tradition of the Pelasgians and Tyrrhenians on Lemnos, and their relation with the Pelasgians in Attica and the raiders of Brauron has been treated at length by Jacoby, Comm. to *FGrHist* 328 (Philochorus) F 99-101, pp. 405-419, esp. 409-413 and notes. See also his Comm. to *FGrHist* 4 (Hellanicus) F 4. Important earlier studies are by E. Meyer, *Forschungen zur alten Geschichte* I (Halle 1892) 6-28, L. Pareti, *RivFC* 46 (1918) 162-190, F. Schachermeyr, *Etruskische Frühgeschichte* (Berlin 1929) 267-273 and *RE* s.v. Pelasgoi, XIX 1 (1937) 252-256. More recently, there is J. Bérard, *REA* 51 (1949) 224-245 and F. Lochner-Hüttenbach, *Die Pelasger* (Arbeiten aus dem Institut für vergleichende Sprachwissenschaft, 6, Wien 1960) 108-111 (who founds his discussion on a collection of all references to the Pelasgians in ancient literature). W. Brandenstein, *RE* s.v. Tyrrhener, VII 2 A (1948) 1909-1920 (the Tyrrhenians before they came to Etruria) is of little help for this problem.

here it is necessary only to consider what is contributed by Plutarch's account.

Plutarch's short notices concerning the Tyrrhenians on Lemnos and Imbros is quite similar to that of the early-third-century atthidographer Philochorus (*FGrHist* 328 F 100): "The Tyrrhenians who inhabited Lemnos and Imbros put out in their ships, seized Brauron in Attica, and after carrying off the virgins... lived with them." The same writer adds (*FGrHist* 328 F 99, 101) that the Tyrrhenians are also called Pelasgians. These statements of Philochorus, according to Jacoby,[114] represent the scholar's attempt to reconcile the contradictory reports of Herodotus and Hecataeus. Plutarch's source may not have used Philochorus, although he gives an account similar to his: if Jacoby's hypothesis is true, Hecataeus had already called the marauders at Brauron Tyrrhenians.[115] Certainly the joining of the two accounts into the narrative found in Plutarch would be easiest after the clear identification by Philochorus of the Tyrrhenian ravishers from Lemnos with the Pelasgians, but they may have been joined before: the names had been connected already in the fifth century by Hellanicus, who called the Pelasgians in Italy Tyrrhenians (*FGrHist* 4 F 4), by Sophocles (Frag. 270 ed. Pearson) and Thucydides (4.109.4).[116] Other atthidographers may have suggested the solution preserved by Plutarch before Philochorus. Whether derived from Philochorus or not, the notice of the Tyrrhenians of Lemnos in Plutarch is a product of the attempt to subject history to certain critical techniques which arose after Herodotus.[117]

More striking evidence of the attitude of Plutarch's source to Herodotus is his reference to the children of the Athenian women and the Lemnian raiders. Herodotus had said (6.138) that these children,

[114] Comm. to *FGrHist* 328 F 99–101, p. 411.
[115] Comm. to *FGrHist* 328 F 99–101, p. 411.
[116] The last two influenced by Hellanicus? See Jacoby, Comm. to *FGrHist* 328 F 99–101, p. 412. The relation of Myrsilus of Lesbos (*FGrHist* 477 F 8–9) to Hellanicus is discussed by Jacoby in n. 35 (pp. 314–315).
[117] The explanation of F. Lochner-Hüttenbach, *Die Pelasger*, 110: "Ohne Zweifel is für Plutarch die Quelle Herodot..., daneben auch noch Philochoros oder einer von dessen Quellen," is too simple.

thanks to their Attic blood, so outshone the pure-bred Pelasgian children, and showed such ambition against their fathers, that it was finally necessary for the Pelasgians to kill their own sons before they were overthrown by them. This is clearly a pro-Athenian account, providing an excuse for Miltiades' subjection of Lemnos and Imbros. In Plutarch, however, the children of the Athenian women are *mixobarbaroi* and as such expelled from the island by the Athenians. (It is not clear whether according to this version the Tyrrhenians themselves were allowed to remain on Lemnos until Miltiades conquered the island.) The expulsion of the children of the Athenian women reflects a new kind of nationalism and pride in race, the same as that found in Pericles' famous limitation of Athenian citizenship to children of two Athenian parents. Its most eloquent expression, however, is in the *Menexenus* of Plato (245 D), written sometime after 387 B.C., in which Socrates, supposedly quoting Aspasia, praises Athens thus:

> For neither the Pelopses nor the Cadmuses nor the Aegyptuses nor Danauses nor the many others, who by nature are barbarians, though by custom Greeks, live with us, but we dwell here ourselves Greeks, not *mixobarbaroi*, so that the hate of the alien nature which has been engendered is pure.

It is with this same feeling that Xenophon (*Hellenica* 2.1.15) can report Lysander's capture of a city allied to Athens and his enslavement of its people, and then, with a sort of verbal shrug, add "the inhabitants were *mixobarbaroi*." Plutarch's source for this part of his account, therefore, not only rewrote Herodotus in order to make him conform better with what seemed good history, but also was influenced by an attitude toward the barbarians and *mixobarbaroi* which was strong in Athens in the first half of the fourth century.

To conclude, the account of the Laconian colonization of Crete depends on Ephorus, and its historicity must be considered on that basis. Plutarch's version adds some details to what is preserved of Ephorus' account in Strabo, Nicolaus, and Conon, but is chiefly useful for the better conception it allows of the extensive and detailed treatment of the Cretan Dorians provided by Ephorus. The first part of Plutarch's account, on the Lemnian migration to Laconia, is a rewriting of Herodotus on a more "historical" basis. The author did not accept Herodotus' hypothesis concerning the Pelasgians on Lemnos, and provides us instead with another and later (first half of the fourth century) viewpoint of the story.[118] In general, the handling of Herodotus' account by Plutarch's source reveals once more both the indebtedness of the fourth-century writers to Herodotus and their dissatisfaction with his methods.

Mulierum Virtutes 9: THE LYCIAN WOMEN

The myth, or saga, of Bellerophon and the Chimaera was first mentioned by Homer (*Iliad* 6.156-195) and retold by Hesiod, Pindar, Sophocles, Euripides, and most of the poets which followed them.[119] According to Homer, Bellerophon was at the court of Proteus when the wife of Proteus conceived a passion for him. He rebuffed her, whereupon she accused him to her husband of attempted seduction, and Proteus sent him to the king of Lycia to have him killed. The Lycian king ordered him to slay the Chimaera, hoping that he would be killed by it. But Bellerophon not only slew the Chimaera but subsequently defeated the Solymi and Amazons. When the king set up an ambush of his soldiers, Bellerophon killed them all. Thereupon the king recognized his divine parentage and gave Bellerophon his daughter and half his kingdom. Hesiod and others add that Bellerophon slew the Chimaera with the aid of the winged horse, Pegasus.

The four versions of the story given by Plutarch in this chapter do

---

[118] It is not known how much truth there is in the tradition of a Lemnian raid on Brauron. However, the attempt to date this raid (as does J. Bérard, *REA* 51 [1949] 235) before the founding of Melos, by reference to Plutarch's account places too much faith in the chronological exactitude of such tradition.

[119] The numerous stories of Bellerophon are collected and discussed by Rapp in W. H. Roscher, *Lexicon der griechischen und römischen Mythologie* I (1884-1890) 757-774, Bethe, *RE* s.v. Bellerophon, III 1 (1894) 241-251, and Karl Robert, *Griechische Heldensage* I (Berlin 1920) 179-185. Ludolf Malten, "Bellerophontes," *Jahrbuch des deutschen archaeologischen Instituts* 40 (1925) 121-160 considers the Asiatic origins of the saga.

not follow this poetic tradition. They are examples of the rationalization of the myths introduced by the Ionians, the chief exponents of which were Hecataeus, Herodorus and Euhemerus.[120] These writers attempted to reduce the myths to stories which might take place even in their own day. This is also the object of the stories related by Plutarch in this chapter.[121]

Plutarch begins with an admission that his story sounds like a myth, but maintains that it has some support,[122] and proceeds to relate four versions. According to the first, Amisodarus,[123] as they say, (*hôs phasin*), whom the Lycians call Isaras,[124] came from the Lycian colony at Zeleia[125] with some pirates under the command of one Chimarrhus, who had a ship with a lion for a figurehead and a serpent at the stern. This man gave much trouble to the Lycians until he was killed by Bellerophon, who pursued him on Pegasus. Bellerophon likewise repulsed the Amazons, but was not rewarded justly by Iobates, the Lycian king. Therefore Bellerophon in anger waded into the sea and begged his father Poseidon to make the land sterile and fruitless. As he walked back from the shore a great wave followed him and covered the plain.[126] The Lycian men pleaded with Bellerophon to no avail,

---

[120] See F. Wipprecht, *Zur Entwicklung der rationalistischen Mythendeutung bei den Griechen* I (Tübingen 1902). I have not seen vol. II (1908).

[121] The Bellerophon saga was also explained allegorically: see Olympiodorus *in Plat. Gorg.* XLIV, 4.

[122] "What is said to have happened in Lycia sounds fabulous (*muthôdes*), but has nevertheless a certain report for confirmation" (247 F).

[123] Cf. *Iliad* 16.328–329: "... Amisodarus, who raised the irresistible Chimaera."

[124] Isaras as a personal name is found only here.

[125] In Homer, the Trojans' ally Pandarus, ruler of Zeleia, was from Lycia. See *Iliad* 2.824–827, quoted by Strabo 13.585. Leaf, *Strabo on the Troad* (Cambridge 1923) 63–64, notes that Homer does not call the Zeleians "Lycians," as Strabo thought. The coin showing a Chimaera attributed to Zeleia (Head, *Numismatic Chronicle*, n.s. 15 [1875] 285–288) is now identified only as Ionian of uncertain mint (thus B. V. Head, *Historia Nummorum*[2] [Oxford 1911] 565, and *Guide to The Principal Coins of the Greeks* Pl. I no. 18). I am indebted to G. K. Jenkins of the British Museum for calling my attention to this change of opinion.

[126] This element of the myth had a basis in fact. The Lycian coast was several times inundated. O. Benndorf and G. Niemann, *Das Heroon von Gjölbaschi-Trysa* (Wien 1889) 50 n. 1 cite Dio Cassius 63.26.5 (a flood in A.D. 68) and the Oracula Sibyllina 3.439–441, 4.112–113, 5.126–129.

but when the women came to meet him with upraised skirts, he turned back in shame, and the wave with him.

This account is only partly rationalistic. The Chimaera of the poet has become the pirate Chimarrhus. It was a common euhemeristic device to see wicked men behind the monstrous Chimaera, although no known version speaks of Chimarrhus: more commonly there is a woman Chimaera with two sons, Leon and Dracon.[127] The monster's tripartite form has been explained by the ornaments of the pirate's ship. We may compare Philochorus' account of Triptolemus sailing in a ship with a winged snake for a figure-head rather than going in a chariot drawn by dragons (*FGrHist* 328 F 104), or Palaephatus' substitution of a ship named Pegasus for Bellerophon's winged horse.[128] From the phrasing of Plutarch's version ("pursued him with Pegasus") Pegasus might even be a normal horse. Nevertheless, Poseidon is Bellerophon's father, and the hero's prayer causes the sea to break its natural boundaries and cover the land.

Plutarch's second version represents a conscious effort to remove the principal mythical element preserved in the first story, the wave sent by Poseidon ("but some, explaining away the mythical element of the story, deny that he led up the sea with curses, but say that..."). According to this version, the land was actually below sea-level, but protected by a natural dike, through which Bellerophon cut a channel, thus flooding the plain.[129] This version also made more normal the action of the women, who only flocked about Bellerophon (*athroas perichutheisas*), filling him with shame and placating his anger.

Others, however, rationalized the myth in a completely different manner: they said that the Chimaera was a mountain facing the sun which reflected such rays in the summer as to dry up the crops.

---

[127] See Heraclitus *De incredibilibus* 15 (*Mythographi Graeci* III, 2, pp. 78–79), Olympiodorus (above, n. 121), Scholiast Lycophron 17, Scholiast *Iliad* 6.181. Another version in Schol. Lycophron explains the Chimaera as the three peoples against whom Bellerophon fought: the Solymi, the Amazons, and the Lycians.

[128] Palaephatus, *De incredibilibus* 29 (*Mythographi Graeci* III, 2, pp. 37–39).

[129] Heracles also was credited with cutting such channels: cf. his flooding of a plain in Thrace (Strabo VII fr. 44 M.) and his flood-control scheme for the Phenian plain (Pausanias 8.14.1–3).

Bellerophon cut off the smoothest part of the mountain and remedied the evil.[130] He found no gratitude and planned to avenge himself, but was won over by the women. Ctesias (*FGrHist* 688 F 45, c. 20; F 45e) refers to a mountain in Lycia named Chimaera, and Palaephatus and various scholiasts[131] explain the Bellerophon myth by referring to the hero's ridding the mountain of lions and snakes. The association of the Chimaera with this mountain in Lycia was the more reasonable because it was volcanically active, as reported by writers from Ctesias to modern travelers.[132] No other account, however, tells us that the mountain was dangerous because of the rays which it reflected.

Finally, Plutarch refers to Nymphis in the fourth book of his *On Heraclea* (*FGrHist* 432 F 7) for the least fabulous account. The local historian wrote that Bellerophon had killed a wild boar which was ravaging the countryside, but was not rewarded. Therefore, he called down upon the Lycians the wrath of Poseidon, who made the soil saline and therefore sterile.[133] Yet Bellerophon was placated by the women who entreated his mercy, and prayed to Poseidon to abandon his anger. For this reason the Xanthians used to take their names not from their fathers but from their mothers.[134] Nymphis' account is "least mythical" because it makes Bellerophon a purely human figure. It does not require a hero to kill a boar, nor to be heard by Poseidon. For Nymphis, Bellerophon was an extraordinary man, but no more. In the previous stories the fabulous Chimaera and Pegasus had been eliminated, but Bellerophon was still considered more than human, whether praying to his father Poseidon, cutting without

---

[130] This passage is quoted with the notice "Plutarch speaks thus about the Chimaera in his *monobiblos* concerning the virtue of women," by the Anonymous *De incredibilibus* 8 (in *Mythographi Graeci* III, 2, p. 91).

[131] Palaephatus (above, n. 128). Cf. Scholiast *Iliad* 6.181 and Servius to *Aeneid* 6.288.

[132] See Malten (above, n. 119) 157 and *RE* s.v. Chimaira 2 and 3, III 2 (1899) 2281–82.

[133] Poseidon was also said to have ruined the land near Troezen with brine, until he had been properly appeased (Pausanias 2.32.8).

[134] Cf. Her. 1.173, Nicolaus of Damascus *FGrHist* 90 F 103k, Heraclides Lembos *Politeiai* 15 (Arist. fr. 611, 43 Rose, from Aristotle's *Constitution of the Lycians*).

assistance a channel for the sea, or carving a piece from the mountain. Nymphis' account, as those before, is unique. There is no other report that Bellerophon killed a boar, in Lycia or elsewhere. Other heroes, however, were famous for overpowering boars, and the stories of the Calydonian boar hunt and of the Erymanthian boar caught by Heracles may have led Nymphis to see a boar in the Chimaera of the poets.

It is not clear why Nymphis treated the Bellerophon story at all in a book *On Heraclea*. Jacoby's hypothesis that it belonged to an excursus prompted by the subjection of Lycia by Harpagus ca. 546 (Herodotus 1.176) is no more than a suggestion. Especially in the time of Nymphis, it is unlikely that a local historian would range so far afield. Nymphis was perhaps prompted to relate the story by something similar at Heraclea, such as a boar hunt or a remarkable salt deposit, of which no notice has come down to us.[135] Nymphis may possibly have established a connection between Lycia and Lycus, the king of the Mariandyni who welcomed Heracles and allowed him to found Heraclea in his territory.[136]

Nymphis related that Bellerophon was turned from his anger by the Lycian women, and connected this with the well-known Lycian use of metronymics.[137] He does not mention the self-exposure of the women, and probably rejected that element of the story.[138] In fact, only the first version in *Mul. Virt.* 9 speaks of this self-exposure: the latter three, which attempt to be less fabulous, describe the women only as entreating, persuading, or thronging about Bellerophon. The

---

[135] The passage from Ctesias cited above (*FGrHist* 688 F 45, c. 20), in which he mentions the mountain Chimaera, is an extreme example of this type of writing. While describing the unusual climate of India, to persuade his readers that he says nothing unbelievable, he reminds them of Mt. Etna, the fish-bearing springs of Zacynthus, and the flaming mountain in Lycia.

[136] Lycus is mentioned by Nymphis in book 1 (*FGrHist* 432 F 4–5), whereas Plutarch's reference is to book 4. But the change from fourth (Δ') to first (A') is not difficult paleographically.

[137] E. Kornemann *RE* s.v. Mutterrecht, Suppl. 6 (1935) 566–567 discusses the relation of the institution of matriarchy to the women's self-exposure.

[138] But Jacoby, Comm. to *FGrHist* 432 F 7, is not sure that Nymphis did not accept this detail.

first version, on the other hand, does not suggest pleading: the women oppose Bellerophon with up-lifted garments, and he retreats.

In the *Mulierum Virtutes* Plutarch twice tells of men turned back by women who exposed themselves, here and in *Mul. Virt.* 5, the Persian women.[139] The exposure of the women originally may have had a magical or religious connotation.[140] The Irish hero Cuchulinn when warm with battle was stopped in the same way as Bellerophon.[141] An interesting story of the capture of Candia given by Leo Diaconus also connects with magic such exposure, accompanied by scurrilous words, and directed against the enemy.[142] Self-exposure of women was also a part of established religion in the cult of Apis in Egypt[143] and of the mysteries at Eleusis.[144]

It is most unlikely that Plutarch found the four versions of the Bellerophon story in four separate books; equally unlikely that he found them in Nymphis himself. The listing of four different interpretations of the same unusual story, first three anonymous versions, then one that is named and accepted, suggests that they are from some scholion,[145] or from a mythological handbook. Plutarch's interest was aroused by the role of the women in placating Bellerophon. The four variants are not necessary to describe the women's *arete*, but Plutarch decided to repeat them as he found them. As frequently in the *Lives*, he first tells the more fabulous yet more interesting version, then that which is more credible.[146]

---

[139] See the discussion of *Mul. Virt.* 5, above, p. 56.

[140] See O. Gruppe, *Griechische Mythologie* II (Munich 1906) 896 n. 1; and esp. J. Moreau, *Annuaire de l'Inst. de Philol. et Hist. Orient. de l'Univ. Libre de Bruxelles*, 11 (1951) 283-300.

[141] See M.-L. Sjoestedt, *Dieux et héros des Celtes* (Paris 1940) 90-91, E. Kornemann, *Klio* 19 (1924) 356-357, R. Thurneysen *Irische Helden- und Königsage* (Halle 1921) 139.

[142] Leo Diaconus, *Histories*, in *Corpus Scriptorum Historiae Byzantinae* XI (Bonn 1828), II.6 (14 D).

[143] Diodorus 1.85.3.

[144] Clement of Alexandria, *Protrepticus* 2.27, from an orphic poem.

[145] Nymphis is frequently quoted, for example, in the scholia to Apollonius of Rhodes.

[146] Cf., e.g., *Romulus* 2.4-3.1: "Others relate what is altogether fabulous about Romulus' origin ... But the story which has the widest credence and the greatest number of vouchers is that ..."

Mulierum Virtutes 10: THE WOMEN OF SALMANTICA[147]

The fall of Salmantica in 220 B.C. is mentioned briefly by Polybius in his account of Hannibal's campaign in Spain: "The following summer he moved once more against the Vaccaei, made an attack on Helmantica (Salmantica) and took it" (3.14.1). Livy, following the same tradition, records: "vere primo in Vaccaeos promotum bellum. Hermandica et Arbocala eorum urbes vi captae" (21.5.5). Plutarch's extensive account, therefore, makes a welcome addition to our knowledge of Hannibal's activity in Spain. According to Plutarch, Hannibal had to besiege Salmantica a second time, because the citizens had broken the first treaty. Once more forcing them to surrender, he required them to leave the city wearing only a *himation*, and without weapons. Nevertheless, the women carried out swords beneath their clothes, so that when their Masaesylian guards seemed more prone to join the looting than watch the Salmanticans, the men took the swords and forced an escape, together with the women, one of whom even struck the interpreter Banon herself. Hannibal pursued them, but many escaped, and were later allowed by him to return to their city.

That Plutarch used a different tradition, and not simply a fuller version of that followed by Polybius and Livy, is seen from the difference in the names: *Helmantikê* Polybius, *Hermandica* Livy, but *Salmatikê* Plutarch. Polybius and Livy are normally considered to have used Silenus of Caleacte (*FGrHist* 175), a Sicilian Greek who accompanied Hannibal, although this remains little more than an educated guess.[148] In the face of this uncertainty no attempt may be made to assign a name to Plutarch's source, although Meyer's suggestion of Sosylus of Sparta (*FGrHist* 176), another Greek in Hannibal's following, has gained wide acceptance. He is supported by a papyrus

---

[147] This is one of the stories from the *Mulierum Virtutes* used by Polyaenus in his *Strategemata* (7.48). See Chapter II and especially pp. 22–23.
[148] See Eduard Meyer, *Kleine Schriften* II (Halle 1924) 405, A. Schulten, *Fontes Hispaniae Antiquae* III (Barcelona 1935) 26, Jacoby, Comm. to *FGrHist* 175 (II D, p. 600). Livy used Silenus through Coelius Antipater.

fragment (*FGrHist* 176 F 1), which shows that Sosylus treated the Spanish campaign very fully, as Plutarch's authority must have done. Moreover a passage in Polybius describes him in terms not unsuitable to Plutarch's source: "Concerning the stories of the writers, such as those of Chaereas and Sosylus, there is no need to speak further; for to me they seem to have the status and value not of history but of common barbershop gossip" (3.20.5 = *FGrHist* 176 T 3). However, the Chaereas (*FGrHist* 177) mentioned in this passage as well as other writers on Hannibal are possible sources for Plutarch, though known to us only by name. *Mul. Virt.* 6 (Celtic Women), which likewise concerns Hannibal and the Carthaginians, may well be from the same source.

Although the account preserved by Plutarch is not exactly "common barbershop gossip," it is exaggerated to think, with Fernandez-Chicarro, that the logical and unaffected flow of the story in both Plutarch and Polyaenus guarantees its veracity.[149] It is not surprising that Plutarch can tell a clear and logical narrative, but such a narrative is no evidence for the story's veracity. One notes that the terms of surrender given the Salmanticans that "the free men should come out in a *himation*," are quite close to those reported of the Chians, that "they should come out ... wearing one tunic and *himation* each, and nothing else" (*Mul. Virt.* 3, 245 A. See above, p. 41, n. 37). Compare also the women who concealed swords under their clothes in this story to the Melian women who did the same thing (*Mul. Virt.* 7, 246 F). On the other hand, the particulars concerning the Masaesylians and Banon the interpreter seem to be traces of on-the-scene reporting. The Masaesylians were a tribe of the northwest coast of Africa and were used by Hannibal in his Spanish campaign.[150] Both Livy and Polybius refer also to the fugitives mentioned by Plutarch in his final sentence, although according to these histories the fugitives

---

[149] *Helmantica* 5 (1954) 261. Concerning the account of Plutarch see also V. Bejarano *Zephyrus* 6 (1955) 98–108.
[150] See Schwabe, *RE* s.v. Masaesyli, XIV 2 (1930) 2057 and Polybius 3.33.15. Livy refers to a treaty the Masaesylians had with Carthage before they allied themselves in 206 B.C. with Rome (28.17).

were defeated together with members of other tribes at the river Tagus.[151] Plutarch in this case adds his own information but does not contradict that of Polybius and Livy.

Mulierum Virtutes 11: THE MILESIAN WOMEN[152]

This story, and that following on the Ceian women, are concerned with the virtue of women in the modern sense, with modesty and continence rather than bravery. Neither account is related to a historical event, and no attempt at dating is possible, or indeed necessary.

In this chapter Plutarch tells of the extraordinary malady which affected the women of Miletus, causing them to hang themselves for no apparent reason. Nothing could deter them; the pleas and the restraints of relatives and friends were equally unavailing. Finally, a wise man moved a law that the bodies of all women who hanged themselves should be borne out to their graves through the agora naked. The law was passed, and at once the women stopped their suicides, furnishing wonderful evidence, as Plutarch remarks, of their nobility and virtue, showing themselves unafraid of death, but unable to bear shame.

The same story was told by Plutarch in the first book of his *De anima* (*Moralia* VII, p. 20, ed. Bernadakis) and is preserved in a Latin translation by Aulus Gellius (15.10). This version is quite similar to that of *Mul. Virt.* 11, but shorter, and has some details not found in that work.[153] Gellius, however, does not report the notice on the cause of the disease, which certainly would have been mentioned in the *De anima*. In *Mul. Virt.* 11 Plutarch tells us, "the women fell under a strange and wondrous malady, coming from some unknown cause.

---

[151] Livy 21.5, Polybius 3.14.3.
[152] This is one of the stories from the *Mulierum Virtutes* used by Polyaenus in his *Strategemata* (8.63). See Chapter II and especially p. 20.
[153] It is unnecessary to presume with Bernadakis that the phrase "cum eodem laqueo, quo essent praevinctae" found in Gellius must have had its counterpart in the original text of *Mul. Virt.* 11. Plutarch was not such a slavish copyist of his own words.

But it was especially conjectured that the air, having taken some distracting and drug-like mixture (*krasin ekstatikên kai pharmakôdê*), had effected a swerving and derangement of their minds." This statement of a possible physical cause for the disease suggests that Plutarch may have first used the story in the *De anima*, and later repeated it in the *Mulierum Virtutes*, but this sequence is not certain. The interest in the disease may mean a medical, not a historical context.[154] However, all the other stories in the *Mulierum Virtutes* are from historical sources, and such descriptions of noteworthy diseases or other phenomena were common in Greek historians.

Mittelhaus's argument that this story is derived from Theophrastus' *Politika pros tous kairous*[155] is unconvincing, although his remark that the final sentence pointing the moral was added specially in this version seems correct.[156] His comparison with another story of Theophrastus on Milesian women (Aelian *Varia Historia* 2.38) is not apposite, for that story is probably from his *Nomoi*, not the *Politika pros tous kairous*.[157] Jacoby reasonably suggests that this story may derive from a Milesian local history.[158]

Mulierum Virtutes 12: THE CEIAN WOMEN

This chapter is not a story, as all the others in the *Virtues of Women*, but a simple notice of the virtuous habits of the Ceian women. The girls would go together to the temple areas and spend the day there, while their suitors watched them playing and dancing. In the evening at home they would wait upon each other's parents and brothers, even washing their feet. When a girl had been betrothed to a particular

---

[154] Cf. Plutarch's discussion of the causes of new diseases in the *Symposiaca* 8.9 (731 D) for a similar physical explanation of disease as caused by bad air and water.

[155] Karl Mittelhaus, *De Plutarchi Praeceptis Gerendae Reipublicae* (diss. Berlin 1911) 35–36. Cf. Dümmler's hypothesis with reference to *Mul. Virt.* 17, below, p. 95.

[156] In *De anima* Gellius reports only that the women no longer committed suicide "pudore solo deterritas tam inhonesti funeris."

[157] See O. Regenbogen s.v. Theophrastos, *RE* suppl. VII (1940) 1518.

[158] Comm. to *FGrHist* 495 note 6 (p. 245). It is not to be connected with the *Milesiaka* of Aristides.

man, all others at once gave over their suit. The result, Plutarch concludes, of this continence (*eutaxia*) of the women, was that no case of adultery or illegal seduction could be recalled for the past seven hundred years.

The concluding sentence remarking the seven hundred years of virtue among the women, is typically Plutarchian. Similar is his interest in the fact that Carvilius was the first Roman to divorce his wife,[159] or that L. Hostius, who lived after the second Punic War, was the first parricide at Rome in nearly six hundred years (*Romulus* 22.5). The story itself gives no clue as to its origin. Such notices of customs were a regular part of Greek history from Herodotus onward. Aristotle's *Constitution of the Ceians* is a possible source.[160] Plutarch himself discusses the advantages of a good constitution in encouraging sexual continence in youth in *Lycurgus* 15, certainly drawing upon fourth-century constitutional studies.

There is some question as to the nationality of the women: most manuscripts read *Kiai*, but one has *Skiai*, and Cobet suggested *Keiai*, as from the island of Ceos. This emendation was accepted by Bernadakis and Babbitt, but Nachstädt preserved the reading of the manuscripts, presumably referring it to the small town of Cios on the Bosphorus. Cobet's emendation seems preferable. I have not found a parallel for the form *Kiai* as feminine ethnic for Cios. The ethnic of Cios is *Kianos*, as is shown by many writers,[161] an inscription from Miletus regarding the Cians, their colonists,[162] and coins. Apollonius of Rhodes uses once the feminine adjective *Kianis*.[163] *Keia*, however, is the normal feminine ethnic from Ceos, and the confusion in manuscripts between "ei" and "i" is well known.[164] Furthermore, the

---

[159] Mentioned (along with other firsts) in *Quaestiones Romanae* 278 E, 267 C, *Romulus* 35.6, *Numa* 25.11. Cf. Gellius 4.3.2, 17.21.44.

[160] See Sopater's mention of Aristotle's *Politeia Kiôn*, Photius *Bibl*. cod. 161, 105 A Bekker; Arist. fr. 511 Rose. For the spelling, see below. Heraclides Lembos excerpts this constitution, cf. Arist. fr. 611, 27 Rose.

[161] See Arist. fr. 514 Rose (= Schol. Apoll. Rhod. 1.1177), Polybius 15.21-23, 18.3, Diodorus 18.72.2.

[162] *Milet* I 3 (1914) no. 41.   [163] *Argonautica* 1.1177.

[164] Cf. Suidas s.v. Kioi (1690 Adler) where the *island* Cios, i.e. Ceos, is discussed.

virtue of Ceians was proverbial: Aristophanes contrasts Chians with Ceians as types of vice and virtue.[165] Heraclides Lembos in his excerpt of Aristotle's *Constitution of the Ceians* tells us that one Aristides at Ceos, *epimeleitai gunaikôn eukosmias*, and that neither boys nor unmarried women drank wine.[166] Athenaeus quotes Phylarchus to the effect that there were no flute-girls or courtesans in the cities of Ceos.[167] In the face of this evidence it seems that Cobet's emendation is correct and that Plutarch is repeating here one of the many examples of Ceian virtue which were spread abroad.[168]

Mulierum Virtutes 13: THE PHOCIAN WOMEN (II)

This charming story of the Dionysian votaries, the Thyiades, who after a day dancing on the slopes of Parnassus fell asleep in the agora of Amphissa and were protected by the women of the town from the Phocian soldiers, may come from a historical source,[169] but may be part of the great fund of Delphic lore accumulated by Plutarch during his years as a priest at the sanctuary. Plutarch refers several times in his writings to the Thyiades at Delphi, explaining their rites and remarking their divine madness.[170] Clea, to whom this book is dedicated, was herself a leader of Thyiades.[171] Pausanias also mentions Thyiades from Delphi and Athens who met each year to celebrate

---

[165] *Frogs* 970 and scholia.
[166] Arist. fr. 611, 28 Rose.
[167] Athenaeus 13, 610 D; Phylarchus *FGrHist* 81 F 42.
[168] Another passage in Athenaeus (13, 566 E) perhaps also should be connected with Ceos. Athenaeus remarks how pleasant it is to go to the gymnasia and tracks of the island of Chios and watch the boys wrestling with the girls. Although Plutarch and Athenaeus do not describe the same practice (Plutarch clearly says that the girls played by themselves), self-control is the principal element in each story, and Wilamowitz's emendation of "Chios" to "Ceos" is possible.
[169] E.g., Demophilus' book on the sacred war, a continuation of Ephorus' history (see *FGrHist* 70 T 9, 70 F 93–96).
[170] See *Quaestiones Graecae* 293 C–F and *De primo frigido* 953 CD. The latter passage describes how the Thyiades had gone up on Parnassus in the middle of winter and were later found by a rescue party with their cloaks frozen stiff from the cold. Note also Plutarch's mention of the Sixteen at Elis, a Dionysiac group, *Mul. Virt.* 15.
[171] Plutarch, *De Iside*, 364 E.

the rite of Dionysus on Parnassus (10.4.3).[172] There seems to be no reason to doubt that the incident narrated by Plutarch actually occurred.[173] Although the story would have been of particular interest to Clea, Plutarch's method of referring to this group ("the women of Dionysus, whom they call Thyiades") demonstrates that the *Mulierum Virtutes* was written for publication and not only for Clea, who would have had no need of such an explanation.

The Sacred War here referred to is that waged by the Phocians in the mid-fourth century under the tyrants Philomelus, Onomarchus, *et al.*, against Boeotia and the other members of the Amphictyony.[174] Amphissa was captured by the Phocians in 354 or early 353 B.C. (Diodorus 16.33.3). The soldiers stationed there would have been the more dangerous because they were probably mercenaries, as were most of the Phocian troops in this war, and might therefore have mistreated even Phocian women.

Mulierum Virtutes 14: VALERIA AND CLOELIA[175]

The virgin Cloelia belongs together with Horatius Cocles and Mucius Scaevola to the heroic trio which was the incarnation in the Roman mind of the young republic's unyielding resistance to Porsenna and the Tarquins. As such, she has her place in every history of that period, is sung by the Latin poets from Vergil to Claudian,[176] and becomes a model of feminine courage.[177] It is not surprising, therefore, that

---

[172] On the Thyiades at Delphi cf. Ludwig Weniger, "Über das Collegium der Thyiaden von Delphi," *Jahresbericht über das Karl-Friedrichschen Gymnasium zu Eisenach*, Eisenach 1876, Nilsson, *Griechische Feste*, 284–5, Preisendanz, *RE* s.v. Thyiaden, VI 1 A (1936) 684–691.

[173] See E. R. Dodds, ed., Euripides' *Bacchae*², xiii–xiv.

[174] See A. W. Pickard-Cambridge, *Cambridge Ancient History* VI, 213–220, 225–227, 234–241, and H. Bengston, *Gr. Gesch.*² 302–304. For the date, see especially N. G. L. Hammond, "Diodorus' Narrative of the Sacred War," *JHS* 57 (1937), p. 64 and n. 80.

[175] This is one of the stories from the *Mulierum Virtutes* used by Polyaenus in his *Strategemata* (8.31). See Chapter II and especially pp. 21 and 25–26.

[176] See Vergil, *Aeneid* 8.651, Manilius 1.780, Silius Italicus 10.488–502, 13.828–830, Juvenal 8.265, Claudian 18.447, 29.16–17.

[177] Seneca, *Ad Marciam de consolatione* 16.2, Emporius Orator (*Rhetores Latini Minores*, ed. Halm) p. 570.

Plutarch twice narrates her story, in *Mulierum Virtutes* as an instance of virtue in women, and in *Publicola* 19 as part of his account of the Roman war with Porsenna. Other extensive and distinct accounts of this war and Cloelia's heroism are preserved by Dionysius of Halicarnassus (*Roman Antiquities* 5.21-35) and Livy (2.9-14).[178] All these accounts praise the heroism of the maiden Cloelia, who was given with other noble Roman youths as hostage to Porsenna, after the bravery of Cocles and Scaevola had convinced him that peace with the Romans was preferable to war. The girls in the group were induced by Cloelia to swim the river and return to Rome (though some say Cloelia escaped alone). Not wishing to break their faith, the Romans returned the girls to Porsenna, but the king, struck by Cloelia's daring, rewarded her with a war-horse,[179] and freed the hostages. In her honor the Romans erected a statue of her on horseback, which stood at the head of the Sacred Way.

Otto Bocksch, after an examination of the two versions of Plutarch, demonstrated that that of *Mul. Virt.* 14 was written after, and based upon, that of *Publicola* 18-19.[180] He noted that the various versions of the story which have been combined to make Plutarch's account have been more thoroughly integrated and the story of Cloelia more forcefully and simply presented in *Mul. Virt.* 14. At the same time, various refinements were added in the latter version: before swimming the river, the girls remember to tie their clothes around their heads;

---

[178] The specific account of Cloelia's heroism is found in Dionysius 5.33, Livy 2.13.6-11. Cf. also Florus 1.10.7-8, Valerius Maximus 3.2.2, Paulus Orosius 2.5.3, Cassius Dio 45.31.1 and fr. 14.4 ed. Melber (= Bekker *Anecdota* p. 133, 8), [Aurelius Victor] *De viris illustribus* 13, Servius to *Aeneid* 8.646, and the scholiast to Juvenal 8.264. The relation of these versions to each other is not clear, for various traditions have been confused. Boccaccio *De mulieribus claris* 50 is a free combination of Livy and Valerius Maximus. (On the sources of this interesting work which was not influenced by Plutarch, see L. Torretta, "Il liber de claris mulieribus," *Giornale storico della letteratura italiana* 39 [1902] 274-292).

[179] Compare the Romans' award of a fully outfitted war-horse to Coriolanus, Plut. *Coriolanus* 10 and Dion. Hal. 6.94.1.

[180] "Zum Publicola des Plutarch," *Griechische Studien Hermann Lipsius* (Leipzig 1894) 171-172. This is the reverse of H. Peter's conclusion, *Die Quellen Plutarchs in den Biographien der Römer* (Halle 1865) 49.

when interrogated by Porsenna, they are anxious not to betray Cloelia. The introductory paragraph in *Mul. Virt.* 14 provides further support for Bocksch's argument. In this paragraph Plutarch summarizes the expulsion of Tarquin from Rome and the war with Porsenna, following the account in *Publicola* 16–18, but omitting the stories of Cocles and Scaevola. Thus he mentions Tarquin's appeal to Porsenna (*Publ.* 16.1), the famine in the city (17.1), the Romans' appeal to Porsenna to judge their case (18.1) and Tarquin's insolent refusal to submit to arbitration (18.2). Another confirmation of the dependence of the Cloelia story in *Mul. Virt.* 14 upon that of the *Publicola* is that it reports no details not found in the life which could not easily have been invented by Plutarch.[181]

In both versions of this story Plutarch records two variant accounts in addition to his basic narrative. According to the first,[182] Cloelia had crossed the river on a horse, leading and encouraging the other girls as they swam, and the horse given by Porsenna to Cloelia was a confirmation of the story. (Plutarch's basic account maintained that the statue simply honored Cloelia's manly daring.) Valerius Maximus (3.2.2), Florus (1.10.8) and the author of *De viris illustribus* (13) all say that Cloelia fled on a horse, but do not say that she led the others with her. The variant preserved by Plutarch is connected with this tradition, but the source cannot be specified.[183]

Other writers specified a second version, according to which the female equestrian statue was not of Cloelia at all, but of Valeria, the daughter of the consul Publicola.[184] This affirmation must be connected with the account, mentioned by Plutarch, of Valeria's escape

---

[181] In *Mul. Virt.* 14 Plutarch expands slightly the notice on Lucretia that he had given in *Publ.* 1, as is natural in a work on virtue in women.

[182] Introduced by *enioi de phasi* in *Publ.* 19.2, by *eisi d' hoi legontes* in *Mul. Virt.* 14, 250 C.

[183] Valerius Maximus, grouped with other authorities, is named twice by Plutarch, in *Brutus* 53.4 and *Marcellus* 30.4, each time on the manner of the hero's death. Nothing suggests that he is Plutarch's source for this variant.

[184] *Publ.* 19.8: "a statue ... which some say is not of Cloelia but of Valeria." *Mul. Virt.* 14, 250 F: "an image of a woman ... which some say is of Cloelia, others of Valeria."

from the ambush which was set by Tarquin when the hostages were being returned to Porsenna. Although Dionysius refers to the ambush (5.33.3-4), Valeria's escape and her association with the equestrian statue is found elsewhere only in Pliny, ascribed to a certain Annius Fetialis.[185] The tale of Valeria must be considered a doublet of the well-established saga of Cloelia invented to magnify the Valerian *gens*, probably by the annalist Valerius Antias.[186] Plutarch in his narrative has combined this invention with the traditional account of Cloelia. In reporting Valeria's escape this could be done without challenging the traditional version, but where there was a contradiction Plutarch accepted the common ascription of the equestrian statue to Cloelia, and preserved the reference to Valeria as a variant.

It is not possible to define the sources of Plutarch's basic narrative. Livy's brief summary does not mention Valeria, Tarquin's ambush, or the horse given the heroine by Porsenna. Dionysius is far closer to Plutarch: he includes Valeria among the hostages and records the ambush and Porsenna's gift, although he omits Valeria's escape. Plutarch was certainly aware of Dionysius' account while writing this life as well as of the pro-Valerian source (Antias?) which contained the account of Valeria.[187] We have no way of telling whether Plutarch consulted other authors as well.

The equestrian statue connected with Cloelia stood on the Sacred

---

[185] Pliny *Naturalis historia* 34.29 (cf. H. Peter *Historicorum Romanorum Reliquiae* I², CCCXXIX). Nothing else is known of Fetialis: Pliny cites him in the same paragraph with Piso (consul 133 B.C.), but this need not mean they are contemporary, as suggested by Münzer, *Beiträge zur Quellenkritik der Naturgeschichte des Plinius* (Berlin 1897) 168-169. He is placed by P. von Rohden, *RE* s.v. Annius 43, I 2 (1894) 2265, in the early empire on the strength of a brick-stamp, *CIL* XV 796. Peter does not attempt to fix a date.

[186] Thus Peter, *Die Quellen* 50, Bocksch (above, n. 180) 170. Eduard Schwartz, *RE* s.v. Dionysius 113, V 1 (1905) 944, makes a well-founded objection to seeing Antias behind every mention of the Valerian *gens* in Roman history, but Antias remains the most likely source for the story of Valeria.

[187] The arguments for Plutarch's use of Dionysius in the *Coriolanus, Romulus, Camillus*, and *Pyrrhus* are concisely presented by Schwartz (above, n. 186) 943-945. W. Soltau, *Die Quellen Plutarchs in der Biographie des Valerius Publicola* (Progr. Zabern. 1905) rightly attacks the attempt of Peter and Bocksch to see Antias as Plutarch's unique source in the *Publicola*, but is quite unsuccessful in his attempt to demonstrate that Plutarch used Piso, Varro, and Antias through Dionysius and Juba.

Way near the temple of Jupiter Stator on the Velia.[188] Dionysius (5.35.2) explicitly states that he could no longer find the statue, and that it was reported to have been destroyed when some neighboring buildings burned down. Nevertheless, Seneca speaks of it in the present tense, and it is possible that it was re-erected.[189] However, the alternation of *stands—stood* in Plutarch's two versions is probably not significant. The Romans identified another bronze statue near the curia as Porsenna: Plutarch saw it and remarked its simple and archaic workmanship (*Publ.* 19.10). Horatius Cocles also was said to have had a statue, located first in the comitium, then moved to the Vulcanal (Gellius 4.5, Livy 2.10.12, Pliny *Naturalis historia* 34.22, 29, Plutarch *Publicola* 16.9). It is quite doubtful, however, that the statue of Cloelia was erected so early as tradition reported.[190]

Mulierum Virtutes 15: MICCA AND MEGISTO

The vicious tyranny and violent end of Aristotimus of Elis are dramatically recounted in this chapter. The account is by far the longest in the *Mulierum Virtutes*, and from its position at the middle of the book and at the end of the series concerning actions of groups of women it evidently was considered by Plutarch the most interesting story of this collection. In this account several women are brought to our attention, each of whom demonstrates in her own way female courage. The story is especially valuable for us because it preserves a

---

[188] Plut. *Publ.* 19.8: "an equestrian statue of her stands on the Sacred Way, where you go up to the Palatine," *Mul. Virt.* 14, 250 F: "There stood a statue on the sacred way," Livy 2.13.11: "in summa sacra via," Pliny *Naturalis historia* 34.29 "fuerit contra Jovis Statoris aedem in vestibulo Superbi domus." Cf. Servius, Seneca, and *De viris illustribus*, and S. B. Platner and T. Ashby, *Topographical Dictionary of Ancient Rome* (London 1929) 498, s.v. Statua Cloeliae.

[189] *Ad Marciam de consolatione* 16.2: "equestri insidens statuae in sacra via, celeberrimo loco, Cloelia exprobrat iuvenibus nostris..." See Platner and Ashby (above, n. 188).

[190] On the other hand, Schwegler's suggestion, *Römische Geschichte*[2] (Tübingen 1870) 185-187, followed by De Sanctis, *Storia dei Romani* I (Turin 1907) 448-449, that it was a statue of Venus Cluilia or Cluacina, seems hardly satisfactory. Even less so is the opinion of E. Pais, *Storia di Roma* I (Turin 1898) 479-482, that it was a statue of Venus Cloaca, later confused with a statue of a Valeria surmounting a bull in front of the Valerian house on the Sacred Way.

detailed narrative of a little-known event in Hellenistic history, the short-lived tyranny which Aristotimus, with the support of Antigonus Gonatas, held in Elis after the death of Pyrrhus. In addition to Plutarch there are preserved the far shorter but still useful accounts of Justin (26.1.4–10) and Pausanias (5.5.1, cf. 6.14.11).

Plutarch's narrative is composed of four incidents. First, he relates how Micca, an innocent maiden, was killed in the arms of her father when she refused to submit to the demands of Leukios, the captain of the tyrant's mercenaries. Then he gives a detailed narrative of Aristotimus' cruel treatment of the wives of the exiled patriots and of their courageous leader Megisto. The attempt of a group of prominent women, the Sixteen, to obtain mercy for the women only angered the tyrant more.[191] Finally, Plutarch continues, Hellanicus united the Elean patriots against the tyrant, caught him without his bodyguard, and killed him, aided by Cylon, Thrasybulus, and Lampis.[192] The citizens also wanted to abuse the tyrant's wife and children, but his wife hanged herself, and on the insistence of Megisto, the two young daughters were allowed to follow her example. Their untimely death is dramatized by Plutarch in a particularly moving passage.

Justin's epitome of Trogus does not mention the death of Micca or of Aristotimus' daughters, and yet it clearly shares a common source with Plutarch. At the beginning of his book 26 Justin speaks of the turmoil in the Peloponnesus following Pyrrhus' death,[193] during which Aristotimus was able to gain control of Elis. He tells the same

[191] The Sixteen were a Thyiad devoted to Dionysus and Hera, somewhat like that at Delphi, of which Plutarch's friend Clea was the leader (above, pp. 2, 79). See Nilsson, *Griechische Feste* 291–293 and L. Weniger, *Das Kollegium der sechzehn Frauen und der Dionysdienst in Elis* (Progr. Weimar, 1883). Plutarch also mentions the group in *Quaestiones Graecae* 36, 299 AB and *De Iside* 364 EF.

[192] For Cylon, see below. Thrasybulus was a soothsayer and democrat. He dedicated a statue to Pyrrhus at Olympia (Paus. 6.14.9) and gave advice to the Mantineans under attack by Agis of Sparta (Paus. 6.2.4, 8.10.5), and his statue was to be found at Olympia (Paus. 6.2.4). See Bernert, *RE* s.v. Thrasybulos 9, VI 1 A (1936) 576. He is perhaps the soothsayer who Plutarch says was consulted by Aristotimus before his death.

[193] He described Pyrrhus' death at the end of book 25 in a manner similar to that of Plutarch, *Pyrrhus* 34.

4+P.H.M.

story as Plutarch of the maltreatment of the wives of the exiles. According to him, however, Hellanicus, the leader of the conspiracy against the tyrant, had to threaten to betray his fellow conspirators to Aristotimus before they could be persuaded to attack the tyrant openly. After this incident, not found in Plutarch, the conspirators assassinated Aristotimus in the fifth month of his tyranny.

This tyranny is mentioned even more briefly by Pausanias in his short review of Elean history. He tells us that Aristotimus son of Demaretus son of Etymonus won the tyranny with the help of Antigonus, but that after six months he was overthrown by Chilon, Hellanicus, Lampis, and Cylon, of whom the last killed the tyrant at the altar of Zeus Soter, whither he had fled as a suppliant.

The versions of Plutarch and Justin must be from a common source, as is shown by the common details of the exiles' flight to Aetolia, their request for their families, Aristotimus' original promise to restore them, their subsequent maltreatment and imprisonment, and the description of the leader of the conspiracy, Hellanicus, as old and without children, and so less suspected. It is equally evident that this common source is Phylarchus.[194] Plutarch used Phylarchus in his account of the last campaign of Pyrrhus (*Pyrrhus* 27–34) which immediately preceded Aristotimus' tyranny, and also for the *Aratus* and *Agis and Cleomenes*, which follow. There is no doubt that he had read Phylarchus, and would have encountered there this account.[195] It has also been established that Trogus, whose work is epitomized by Justin, likewise used Phylarchus.[196]

---

[194] See Benedict Niese, *Geschichte der griechischen und makedonischen Staaten* II (Gotha 1899) 228 n. 1, W. W. Tarn, *Antigonos Gonatas* (London 1913) 280 n. 15, and Beloch, *Gr. Gesch.*[2] IV 1 (1925) 581 n. 1.

[195] See J. Kroymann, *RE* s.v. Phylarchos, suppl. 8 (1956) 476–477, 484–485, and Jacoby, *FGrHist* II C, Comm. to 81 (Phylarchus) pp. 133–134 and bibliography there cited. Two recent attempts to study Phylarchus from the evidence of Plutarch have been made by E. Gabba, "Studi su Filarco. Le biografie plutarchee di Agide e di Cleomene," *Athenaeum* 35 (1957) 3–55, 193–239 and T. W. Africa, *Phylarchus and the Spartan Revolution* (Los Angeles 1961).

[196] See Kroymann (above, n. 195) 482–483, and Jacoby (above, n. 195).

Phylarchus probably is also the ultimate source of Pausanias.[197] Certainty is not possible, for the notice of Pausanias is too brief, but the fact that he names three of the men mentioned by Plutarch is highly suggestive. Plutarch does not give Cylon credit for killing Aristotimus, although he plays an important part in his narrative. Pausanias' notice that Cylon was the actual tyrant-slayer may have been in Phylarchus, or added by Pausanias himself, who saw at Olympia a statue of Cylon erected by the Aetolian league because he had freed the Eleans from tyranny.[198]

Plutarch's account presents numerous features typical of Phylarchus' style, the most striking of which is the treatment of the memorable death scene of the daughters of Aristotimus. There the elder daughter allows her younger sister to die before herself, ties the noose about the girl's neck, and disposes her body, then hangs herself. This pathetic scene is remarkably close to two others from Phylarchus preserved by Plutarch. In *AgCl.* 20, when Amphares and the ephors had secretly killed Agis and immediately afterward his grandmother Archidamia. Agesistrata, his mother, was allowed to enter the prison to "visit Agis." She found her son's body stretched on the ground, and nearby her mother's still hanging. With her own hands she took down the body, disposed it decently beside that of her son, and then offered her own neck to the noose. Again, in *AgCl.* 59, after the death of Cleomenes, Ptolemy ordered his children, mother, and the attendant women to be executed. Cratesiclea, Cleomenes' mother, watched his

---

[197] Pausanias used Phylarchus elsewhere: see O. Regenbogen, *RE* s.v. Pausanias, suppl. 8 (1956) 1075, who derives Pausanias' account of Agis and Cleomenes from the source used by Plutarch.

[198] Paus. 6.14.11. A mid-third-century inscription at Delphi recording honors to Cyllon (sic) son of Cyllon of Elis (*SIG*[3] 423) was originally connected with the tyrant-slayer (thus Dittenberger), but is now assigned to his son; see Beloch *Gr. Gesch.*[2] IV 2 (1927) 406–407, R. Flacelière, *Les Aitoliens à Delphes* (Paris 1937) 194 and n. 5. The inscription is dated to the archonship of Callicles, but there were two archons of that name in this period, and the date of neither is established with certainty. See Flacelière, *ibid.*, Georges Daux, *Fouilles de Delphes* III, *Chronologie Delphique* (Paris 1943) 39, and E. Manni, *Athenaeum* 28 (1950) 90, 92. The Aetolians, who made the dedication at Olympia mentioned by Pausanias, were also in control of Delphi at this time.

children die before her eyes, then was herself killed. Among the women was the wife of Panteus, who silently and composedly laid out the dead as decently as possible, then when all were killed, drawing her clothes about her and allowing only the executioner to be present, submitted herself to the sword. The astounding similarity of treatment in these three accounts reveals the single hand of Phylarchus behind them all.

Phylarchus' well-known partiality to stories of women [199] is quite evident in *Mul. Virt.* 15 in the importance given the sufferings and deeds of Micca, Megisto, the Elean women, and the daughters of Aristotimus. Plutarch's story of the ambiguously interpreted omen, the eagle which dropped a tile on Aristotimus' house, is similar to that of the ambiguous dream which Pyrrhus had during the siege of Sparta.[200]

Plutarch's long narrative is only a part of Phylarchus' treatment of the tyranny at Elis. This account, which would have followed immediately upon the report of Pyrrhus' expedition against Sparta and his death at Argos, would have been an important part of Phylarchus' description of the condition of the Peloponnesus between Pyrrhus' death and the Chremonidean War. Phylarchus' anti-Macedonian bias, notable in his strong criticism of Aratus (*FGrHist* 81 F 52 = Plut. *Aratus* 38), is visible also in his reference to Antigonus' support of Aristotimus' cruel tyranny. It becomes clear also how differently Phylarchus fared in the hands of his excerptors. Plutarch was interested in virtues of women more than in the fall of the tyranny. Therefore one finds three stories of women, those of Micca, Megisto, and the daughters of Aristotimus, joined together by a historical account. Justin, on the other hand, mentions none of these women, and

---

[199] A list of his heroines would include Mysta, the concubine of Seleucus (*FGrHist* 81 F 30), Danae and Laodice (F 24), Daphne (F 32) and several known from Plutarch: Chilonis the wife of Cleonymus (*Pyrrhus* 26-28), and Chilonis the wife of Cleombrotus (*AgCl* 17), in addition to those already mentioned.

[200] Kroymann's doubts (*RE* s.v. Phylarchos [above, n. 195] 485) whether such dreams and omens were found in Phylarchus do not seem valid: compare *AgCl.* 28, the dream of the ephor, and *AgCl.* 60, the snake which defended the body of Cleomenes, both of which are in a Phylarchan context.

concentrates on political events of more interest to a historian. One could not know from Justin or Pausanias alone that their source was Phylarchus. It is only by comparison with the evidently Phylarchan account of Plutarch that their dependence on the historian becomes apparent. Yet they provide details, such as the timidity of the conspirators and the length of Aristotimus' tyranny, which are omitted by Plutarch.

Phylarchus furnishes useful evidence on the part Antigonus played in establishing tyrannies in the Peloponnesian cities. Pausanias is more explicit than Plutarch in crediting Antigonus with helping Aristotimus come to power. Tarn takes a mild view of the king, and doubts that Antigonus was active in establishing the tyranny,[201] although Polybius (2.41.10, cf. 9.29.6) ascribed to Antigonus a policy of planting tyrannies among the Greeks. Whatever Antigonus' role was in the beginning, however, he supported Aristotimus once he was in power, for Plutarch reports that Craterus attempted to help him. Nevertheless, Aristotimus' tyranny was not representative of those in the Peloponnesus at this time.[202] He shared with the notorious Apollodorus of Cassandreia the distinctive feature of oppressive tyranny, a barbarian bodyguard.[203] From the account of Phylarchus preserved in Plutarch we receive additional evidence of the indirect activity of the Aetolians against Antigonus, found in their reception of the Elean exiles and their support of the exiles' attempt to regain Elis from the tyrant favored by Antigonus. The honors granted to Cylon at Olympia and to his son at Delphi are consistent with this anti-Macedonian policy.[204]

---

[201] *Antigonos Gonatas* (London 1913) 278–281.
[202] Listed in Busolt-Swoboda, I 401 n. 4.
[203] See Diodorus 22.5.2. G. T. Griffith, *The Mercenaries of the Hellenistic World* (Cambridge 1935) 68, calls attention to the large number of Illyrians and Gauls serving as mercenaries in Greece at this time. Leukios, however, Aristotimus' captain, seems to be Italic (Lucius), cf. Niese (above, n. 194) II, 228, n. 3, Beloch, *Gr. Gesch.*² IV, 1, 581, and the Lucanian mercenaries in Athens ca. 300 B.C. (*IG* II² 1956), although the name was known in other regions: cf. *Leukios Thraix, lochagos* (203/2 B.C.) in *Berliner griechische Urkunden*, 1266, lines 40–41 and 45.
[204] See above, n. 198.

Mulierum Virtutes 16: PIERIA [205]

Some of the Ionians who came to Miletus with Neleus, the legendary leader of the Ionian migration, Plutarch informs us, quarreled with Neleus' sons, and went off to settle Myus, where they suffered much from the harassment of the Milesians. This war, however, was civil enough to permit the women from Myus to visit Miletus on feast-days. On one of these days, the most powerful of the sons of Neleus, Phrygius, fell in love with Pieria, a young girl from Myus, and offered her whatever she wished. "Make it so that I can come here often and accompanied by many others," said she. Phrygius, understanding her words, and much in love, stopped the war. Pieria became famous, so that even now (*achri nun*), Plutarch tells us, Milesian women pray that their husbands love them, as Phrygius loved Pieria.

Pieria's story is also told by Aristaenetus (*Epistles* 1.15)[206] and by Callimachus. The version of Aristaenetus is similar to Plutarch's, even to the tag ending preserving the Milesian saying, although it is rewritten in the artificial style favored by the later writer. Certain differences—he calls Phrygius the king of the city, rather than the most powerful, as in Plutarch—therefore do not indicate a different origin for the two versions. The argument of Richard Reizenstein's that Aristaenetus drew this story from the *Aitia* of Callimachus[207] has been confirmed by Pfeiffer, who discovered in some very fragmentary Callimachean material possible reference to the Pieria-Phrygius story.[208] Both Pfeiffer[209] and Jacoby[210] suggest that

[205] This is one of the stories from *Mulierum Virtutes* used by Polyaenus in his *Strategemata* (8.35). See Chapter II and especially p. 20.

[206] *Epistolographi Graeci* ed. E. Hercher pp. 146–147, *FGrHist* 496 F 6. Aristaenetus wrote love stories in the form of letters, in very rhetorical language, in the fifth century A.D. or soon after; see W. Schmid, *RE* s.v. Aristainetos 8, II 1 (1896) 851–852 and Schmid-Stählin II⁶ 2, 1048–49.

[207] *Index Lectionum in Academia Rostochiensi* 1892/93: "Inedita Poetarum Graecorum Fragmenta," pp. 15–16.

[208] *Callimachus*, ed. Rudolf Pfeiffer (Oxford 1949) frag. 80–83, pp. 87–91.

[209] Pfeiffer (above, n. 208), ad fr. 83, p. 91.

[210] Comm. to *FGrHist* 496 F 6. See Leandr(i)us, *FGrHist* 492, esp. F 18, for Callimachus' use of that writer. Jacoby suggests that Leandr(i)us is identical with Maeandrius, *FGrHist* 491.

Leandr(i)us, an author of *Milesiaka*, is the source of Callimachus here. Phrygius, the ruler of Miletus, is also mentioned at the end of a story by Parthenius.[211] In an account ascribed to Aristotle and the writers of *Milesiaka* we are told that Phobius, "one of the Neleids who was then ruling Miletus," became accursed and yielded the rule to Phrygius. Since it is probable that Aristotle also depended on *Milesiaka*, the ultimate source of all our information of Phrygius and Pieria can be traced to these local histories, although we cannot be sure that Callimachus and Aristotle depended on the same writer of *Milesiaka*; nor indeed can we be certain from the citation in Parthenius that Aristotle related the story of Pieria at all.[212] No indication of his source is given by Plutarch. *Milesiaka* are the ultimate source, as remarked by Jacoby,[213] and the number of details—such as the names of Pieria's father and mother and the name of the feast, the Neleis—suggests that it was taken directly from a Milesian writer. A peculiar characteristic of local historiography and of the Milesian tradition is preserved by Plutarch in his account of the war between Myus and Miletus. "Some of the Ionians who had come to Miletus quarreled with the sons of Neleus and going off to Myus they settled there." This settlement of Myus from Miletus is recorded nowhere else. In all the traditional accounts Myus is independent, one of the twelve cities of Ionia, founded at the time of the Ionian migration.[214] It is remarkable that there is no separate tradition for the foundation of Myus apart from the Ionian migration.[215] Myus was never a large city (it sent only three ships to the battle of Lade, Herodotus 6.8), nor is

---

[211] Parthenius 14 = *FGrHist* 496 F 1 (Collective citations from Milesian writers) and Aristotle fr. 556 Rose.

[212] On the problems of dating Leandr(i)us see Jacoby's introduction to *FGrHist* 491–492, where he tentatively suggests 330–300 B.C., rather late to be used by Aristotle.

[213] Comm. to *FGrHist* 496 F 6. He quite rightly refuses (Comm. to *FGrHist* 495, n. 6, p. 245) to connect this story (or *Mul. Virt.* 11 and 17) with Aristides of Miletus.

[214] See the references given by W. Ruge, *RE* s.v. Myus 2, XVI 2 (1935) 1431.

[215] See Wilamowitz, *SBBerlin*, 1906, 66, n. 3, and Michel B. Sakellariou, *La Migration grecque en Ionie* (Athens 1958) 76. According to this tradition Myus was founded by a son of Codrus: in Strabo 14, 633 by Cydrelus, a bastard; in Pausanias 7.2.10 by Cyaretus. A. E. Raubitschek has called to my attention that Cydrelus and Cyaretus are probably simply different readings of the same name.

any evidence of a tradition of local history preserved.[216] In the first part of the fourth century there was a land dispute between Myus and Miletus, referred to the Ionian cities for arbitration by the Persian satrap Struses, and resolved by him in favor of Miletus when the Myusians threw up their suit.[217] This implies that Myus was independent of Miletus, though weak. But by 228/7 B.C. the Milesians could order the Myusians to accept into their territory Cretan archers who had helped Miletus.[218] After this, Myus seems never to have been independent. In 201 it was awarded by Philip V to Magnesia,[219] although it was later recovered by the Milesians. Strabo reports (14, 636) that the city "now through lack of inhabitants had been united with (*sumpepolistai*) the Milesians." Pausanias (7.2.11) tells us that the city was deserted because of the stagnation of its harbor. It is evident that sometime between 388 and 228/7 B.C. Myus fell under the control of Miletus.[220] The story preserved by Plutarch of the settlement of Myus from Miletus, which has been traced to Milesian local historians, must be connected with this decline of Myus. This version, not otherwise found, is a pro-Milesian distortion of legendary history, supporting the claim of Miletus to Myusian territory. Whether it was created before or after the annexation of Myus cannot be determined, but its origin must fall in the fourth or third century, when Milesian historians, inflamed with patriotic zeal, were able to produce this account unknown to Herodotus,[221] Pherecydes,[222] or Hellanicus.[223] Unfortunately, the connection of Aristotle with the

[216] Jacoby, *FGrHist* III B omits the town completely.

[217] Tod, *GHI* II, 113 (= *SIG*³ 134). See Ruge, *RE* s.v. Myus 1431; Magie, *Roman Rule* II, 822, n. 9.

[218] *Milet* I 3, no. 33e, lines 12–13. See pp. 199–202, where Rehm defends his restorations and gives an account of Myusian-Milesian relations in this period.

[219] Polybius 16.24.9.

[220] Suggested dates for this annexation vary. Ruge, *RE* s.v. Myus 1433–34, is noncommital, but Rehm, *Milet* I 3, p. 201, states, "Möglich ist aber auch, dass Myus erst in den zweiten Hälfte des 3. Jahrhunderts v. Chr. in den Kämpfen, die sich ... zwischen Priene und Milet abgespielt haben ... unter Milet gekommen ist." He remarks that according to B. V. Head, *Historia Nummorum*² (Oxford 1911) 587, the last coins of Myus are from the fourth century.

[221] See Her. 1.142. [222] See Pherecydes, *FGrHist* 3 F 155.

[223] See Hellanicus, *FGrHist* 4 F 125 = 323 a F 23.

Phrygius story cannot give us a *terminus post quem* for this variant, since it is not known whether Aristotle mentioned the settlement of Myus, or even the war between Myus and Miletus.

The evidence concerning the feast of the Neleis at Miletus referred to by Plutarch is collected by Nilsson, who notes that according to Callimachus Neleus brought a statue of Artemis from Attica and established a cult to her at Miletus.[224]

Mulierum Virtutes 17: POLYCRITE [225]

This is another story of a Milesian war which is resolved by the love of a Milesian commander for an enemy girl. The Naxian writers (*hoi Naxiôn suggrapheis* = FGrHist 501 F 2) relate that Neaera, the wife of the Milesian Hypsicreon, ran away with Promedon, a Naxian, and took refuge on Naxos as a suppliant. The Naxians refused to yield her to Hypsicreon, and war ensued. Many Ionians helped the Milesians, but especially the Erythraeans, who were led by one Diognetus. Then, Plutarch tells us, the war which had begun by the depravity of a woman ended through another's virtue. A young Naxian prisoner, Polycrite, was loved by Diognetus and treated as his wife. Polycrite, when she saw the Milesians drunk and asleep after celebrating a feast, sent a message to her brothers in the city to attack the unprepared army. They did, and killed many of their opponents, though they spared Diognetus at Polycrite's request. Polycrite, however, expired from joy, and was buried at a tomb outside the gates, called the tomb of envy (*baskanou taphos*). Plutarch then adds the slightly different account of Aristotle (fr. 559 Rose), who reports that Polycrite was not taken prisoner, but that Diognetus loved her and yielded to her a piece of Milesian-held land, called the Delium. She in turn gave it to the Naxians. Thus the strength of the opponents was equalized, and the Naxians were able to make peace with the Milesians on their own terms.

---

[224] *Griechische Feste* 242–243. See Callimachus *in Dianam* (III) 225–227, *in Jovem* (I) 77–78, and scholia to the latter passage. Pfeiffer restores *Nêléidos* in fr. 80 line 18. The name Neleis for the feast is otherwise unknown.

[225] This is one of the stories from the *Mulierum Virtutes* used by Polyaenus in his *Strategemata* (8.36). See Chapter II and especially p. 20.

Unusual for Plutarch are the two references to sources for alternate versions of his story. Yet more information is provided by Parthenius, who in chapter 9 tells the story of Polycrite, and in chapter 18 that of Neaera and Hypsicreon. Parthenius' story of Polycrite, according to the lemma preserved in the manuscript, is taken from the first book of the *Naxiaka* of Andriscus (*FGrHist* 500 F 1), but was also written about by Theophrastus in the fourth book of his *Pros tous kairous*.[226] In his description of Polycrite's relation to Diognetus, Parthenius follows the version of Aristotle given by Plutarch; that is, the girl is not a captive, but a suppliant at the Delian temple, and Diognetus, enamored, offers to do whatever she wished. She asks for the tract of land, and he decides to give it to her. Together, they give it to the Naxians by the same trick described by the Naxian writers in Plutarch: Polycrite sends to her brothers (as before using an inscribed lead sheet hidden in a cake) to tell them that the Milesians have been celebrating a feast (here named the Thargelia) and are defenseless. In this version, however, Diognetus is killed in the battle. Further, Polycrite dies not from excess of joy as in the Naxian writers and also in Aristotle,[227] but suffocated by the presents heaped upon her by the Naxians.[228] She was buried "in the plain," and some say that Diognetus was buried with her.

The story of Neaera, Parthenius 18, is ascribed by the lemma to Theophrastus, the first book of the *Pros tous kairous*. The account is the same as that in Plutarch, although fuller and slightly more detailed, and need not be repeated here.[229]

---

[226] This fragment of Theophrastus is missing from Wimmer's collection, as is that given by Parthenius in c. 18.

[227] Gellius 3.15.1 (Arist. fr. 559 Rose): "Cognito repente insperato gaudio expirasse animam refert Aristoteles philosophus Polycritam, nobilem feminam Naxo insula."

[228] Recalling the story of Tarpeia, see Plutarch *Romulus* 17, *et al.*

[229] Note that according to Parthenius, Neaera "sat down as a suppliant at the hearth (*hestia*) in the prytaneum," but in Plutarch she simply "sat down as a suppliant of the hearth (*hestia*)," revealing the similarity and yet the opportunities for change of meaning which arise when a story is retold. *Hestia* is capitalized by Nachstädt in his text of Plutarch, incorrectly, if we may trust Parthenius. The confusion between the goddess Hestia and the common noun *hearth* is not present in the Greek.

It is most probable that all the stories stem from local Naxian tradition. The version ascribed to the Naxian writers in Plutarch attempts to explain the existence of a monument called the tomb of envy, as Jacoby noted.[230] Aristotle also reported this detail, as is shown by the fragment from Gellius. In Plutarch's narrative, therefore, we find two Naxian accounts: that ascribed to the "Naxian writers" and that which Aristotle took from a Naxian writer. Jacoby's suggestion that Plutarch's "Naxian writers" is really Andriscus, if Parthenius may be equated with Andriscus, is incorrect, for examination of Plutarch's story shows that the account of Parthenius has as much in common with the Aristotelian version as with that of the "Naxian writers." The Delium, Diognetus' offer, and Polycrite's bargain appear both in Aristotle and in Parthenius, but not in the version of the "Naxian writers." Thus if Parthenius equals Andriscus, neither of the accounts in Plutarch is from Andriscus, but from other Naxian writers. Theophrastus, whom the headings in Parthenius connect with both the Neaera and the Polycrite episode, must not have used Andriscus either, but probably followed Aristotle, who would have recorded the story in his *Constitution of the Naxians*.[231] The tradition about Neaera reveals no variants. The reference to Theophrastus may mean that Aristotle also narrated the story of Neaera. From the accounts of Plutarch and Parthenius we learn that there were at least three different Naxian versions of the story of Polycrite: that of Parthenius' source, Andriscus; that used by Aristotle; and that reported by Plutarch.

In a paper stressing the importance of Theophrastus' *Politika pros tous kairous* Ferdinand Dümmler argued that Plutarch drew upon this work of Theophrastus for his entire narrative.[232] Setting out from Henkel's opinion that the fourth book of Theophrastus contained stories of loves which caused or ended wars, among them Parthenius 9

---

[230] Comm. to *FGrHist* 500 F 1.
[231] The existence of which is attested by Athenaeus 8, 348 AC (Arist. fr. 558 Rose).
[232] "Zu den historischen Arbeiten der ältesten Peripatetiker," *RhMus* N.F. 42 (1887) 180–181 (= *Kleine Schriften* II [Leipzig 1901] 465–466). His conclusions are accepted by O. Regenbogen, *RE* s.v. Theophrastos, suppl. VII (1940) 1518.

and 18,[233] he considers more than unlikely the possibility that Plutarch actually went back to the Naxian tradition and added to it a variant which he had noted in Aristotle. On the other hand, he argues, Plutarch had devoted a special study to the work of Theophrastus which contained these stories (see the Lamprias catalogue 53: *Peri Theophrastou ⟨politikôn⟩ pros tous kairous*). Dümmler presumes that Theophrastus gave a Naxian version different from that of Aristotle and duly noted the differences between the two, and argues that this double notice would then have been taken over completely by Plutarch from Theophrastus.

Dümmler's argument is vitiated by two other citations in Plutarch from the Naxian writers. In the life of Theseus (20.8, *FGrHist* 501 F 1) he cites *Naxiôn tines* for a version of the Ariadne story. This may have been found in a religious or mythological work, or a biography of Theseus. Definitely historical, however, is the citation in *De Herodoti malignitate* 869 A (*FGrHist* 501 F 3). As part of his polemic against Herodotus, he gives the versions (all more favorable to the Naxians than that of Herodotus) of Hellanicus, Ephorus, and *hoi Naxiôn hôrographoi*. This correction, as others in this treatise against Herodotus, is backed by historical research on the part of Plutarch. Elsewhere in this work he also cites other local historians and, contrary to Dümmler, it is quite possible that in this case he himself saw this Naxian story, as he also had himself read Socrates of Argos (*Mul. Virt.* 4). Jacoby seems correct in not taking literally the plural citation of the Naxian writers: Plutarch probably only saw one.

Nor is there reason to believe that Plutarch did not use Aristotle directly. If Theophrastus were his source, he probably would have named him, as he does so often elsewhere in both the *Moralia* and the *Lives*. Although Plutarch had written a special study of the *Politika pros tous kairous*, he had also read and enjoyed the *Constitutions* of

---

[233] *Studien zur Geschichte der griechischen Lehre vom Staat* (Leipzig 1872) 23. Cf. Harpocration s.v. Aspasia (according to Theophrastus she is the cause of the Samian and Peloponnesian wars). Henkel emends the lemma of Parthenius 18 to "fourth book" (MS.: "first book"). The emendation is not noted in Martini's edition.

Aristotle.[234] The position upheld by various scholars that Plutarch did not use, or indeed never saw, Aristotle's *Constitutions* is untenable.[235]

The historical setting of the story of Polycrite has already been treated in the discussion of the Chian women (*Mul. Virt.* 3, above, pp. 42-43).

Mulierum Virtutes 18: LAMPSACE [236]

This chapter celebrates the heroine who gave Lampsacus its name, and describes the foundation of that city. Phobus, a Phocaean prince, was on business at Parium when he made friends with Mandron the king of the Bebrycians, who are called Pityoessians, and helped him in a war. Mandron offered him land if he wanted to lead colonists to Pityoessa, and when Phobus returned home he sent out his brother Blepsus with a group of Phocaean colonists. The colony thrived, so that the Bebrycians became envious and prepared to wipe out the Phocaeans while Mandron was absent. His daughter Lampsace learned of the plot, but could not dissuade the Bebrycians from this treachery, and so warned the Greeks. They, by a trick, were able to take the city and kill the barbarian men. They invited Mandron to return, but he thought it more prudent to go elsewhere with the wives and children of his citizens. Lampsace soon died of an illness, whereupon she was given heroic honors and the city named after her. Later it was decreed to sacrifice to her as a goddess, which the people of Lampsacus still do.

Plutarch identifies the source for this narrative in an aside at the beginning of his account. Phobus, he tells us, was the first to throw himself from the Leucadian Rocks into the sea "as Charon of Lampsacus

---

[234] See *Non posse suav.* 1093 C, quoted below p. 131.
[235] See below pp. 130-132.
[236] This is one of the stories from the *Mulierum Virtutes* used by Polyaenus in his *Strategemata* (8.37). See Chapter II and especially p. 23. Nachstädt calls the Phocaean prince *Phoxos*, as in Polyaenus, instead of *Phobos*, the reading of all the manuscripts of Plutarch.

has written."[237] Although Plutarch's citation narrowly taken refers only to this sentence, Charon would have narrated the foundation of Lampsacus and the origin of its name in his *Hôroi Lampsakênôn*, and without doubt his account is the source for Plutarch's whole chapter.

The narrative of Charon is fundamentally historical, with some novelistic elements. Charon is not describing the mythological foundation of the city, but the historical foundation dated by Eusebius in 654 B.C.[238] Phobus, a young Phocaean noble of the Codrid family[239] met Mandron while at Parium. This is in full accord with Eusebius, who records that Parium was founded some fifty years before Lampsacus, in 708/7 B.C.[240] Phobus, accepting Mandron's invitation, persuaded the Phocaeans to send out his brother Blepsus with a colony to Pityoessa. In addition to Charon's authoritative statement, Ephorus (*FGrHist* 70 F 46), Deiochus (*FGrHist* 471 F 3), and Mela (1.97) testify that Lampsacus was a Phocaean colony. The people of Lampsacus in Hellenistic times referred to the inhabitants of the Phocaean colony of Massilia as *hêmin adelphous* (*SIG*³ 591, line 26). In the face of this evidence, Strabo's statement that Lampsacus was a Milesian colony (13.1.19) is either incorrect or only half true. It is possible that some Milesians joined the Phocaeans in founding this

---

[237] *FGrHist* 262 F 7. Jacoby's full commentary on this fragment is very helpful and supersedes previous investigations, although he was not aware of the dependence of Polyaenus (8.37) upon Plutarch (see above, n. 236). I have not been able to see Eitrem, *Beitr. zur griech. Religionsgesch.* 3, 1920, 161, cited by Jacoby. Lionel Pearson discusses Charon in his *Early Ionian Historians* (Oxford, 1939) 139–151, summarizing this fragment on pp. 144–145.

[238] Eusebius' date is generally accepted as approximately accurate: see Beloch *Gr. Gesch.*² I 1, 256; F. Bilabel "Die ionische Kolonisation," *Philologus* Suppl. 14 (1921) 49–50; A. R. Burn, *The Lyric Age of Greece* (London 1960) 109 (but cf. p. 405). Carl Roebuck, *Ionian Trade and Colonization* (New York 1959) 113, prefers to revise Eusebius' date to 615 B.C.

[239] *Tou Kodridôn genous*. There is no reason to consider Phobus and his brother mythical (Jacoby, Comm. to *FGrHist* 262 F 7–8 p. 15, refers to "den ursprünglich mythischen charakter der brüder") although the names seem invented.

[240] Jacoby's opinion, Comm. to *FGrHist* 262 F 7–8 (p. 17) that "die lampsakenische chronik wird das höhere alter dieser stadt [Parium]... kaum anerkannt haben" seems based on the belief that Charon here treats the mythological foundation of Lampsacus.

colony in a territory dominated by Milesian settlements;[241] more probably Strabo's remark represents a Milesian distortion such as that noted with regard to the foundation of Myus (*Mul. Virt.* 16, see above, pp. 91-92). The initial invitation of the Bebrycian king and the later conflict between the Greeks and the natives seem to reflect actual history, although the story is partially expressed in novelistic terms and Plutarch has significantly compressed Charon's account. The historicity of Lampsace is dubious. Jacoby rightly observes that she was not a feminine hero-founder.[242] The cult of Lampsace presumably existed before the arrival of the Phocaeans, and the story of the maiden who aided the Greeks was invented to explain the name of the city.

This chapter of Plutarch is exceptionally valuable for our knowledge of Charon. It demonstrates that there was available in the time of Charon, more than two centuries after the event, a full and reasonably accurate account of the foundation of Lampsacus. Plutarch's reference to Phobus' trip to Parium, his help to Mandron, and his persuading of the Phocaeans reveals that Charon treated fully the Phocaean pre-history of the colonization of Lampsacus. There is no evidence, however, that Charon "hat ... von der *ktisis Iônias* sehr ausführlich gehandelt."[243] Rather, it is important to recognize that Charon treated the seventh-century foundation of Lampsacus as the real foundation of the city. Such a recognition would not preclude earlier mythical foundations or a connection, for example, of Pityoessa with the Trojan war.[244] Pindar's story of the Argonauts and Euphamos could exist side by side with Herodotus' history of Battus and the founding of Cyrene.

Charon reported more than Plutarch preserves concerning Mandron and the Bebrycians, probably describing the war in which

---

[241] See Jacoby, Comm. to *FGrHist* 262 F 7-8 (pp. 14-15).
[242] Comm. to *FGrHist* 262 F 7-8 (p. 14).
[243] Jacoby, Comm. to *FGrHist* 262 F 7-8 (p. 13).
[244] See Stephanus of Byzantium s.v. Lampsakos; Jacoby, Comm. to *FGrHist* 262 F 7-8 (p. 16).

Phobus aided them. Moreover, the last sentences of Plutarch's account mark a sharp abridgement of Charon's text, in which the relation of the colonists with Mandron would have been elaborated. As it is, the death of Lampsace awkwardly interrupts the report of the king's arrangements with the colonists.

When he wrote the *De Herodoti malignitate*, Plutarch had before him and quoted verbatim the *Persika* of Charon.[245] His direct use of this passage of the *Horoi* is not so certain, but since the dependence of Polyaenus on Plutarch has been established (see n. 236 above), there is no need to postulate with Jacoby an intermediate source used by both writers. In fact, Plutarch most likely read Charon himself and made this excerpt. Plutarch wrote a book *Foundings of Cities (Poleôn ktiseis*: Lamprias catalogue 195), which would have used local histories such as this. There would have been no better source for the foundation of Lampsacus than Charon.[246] Moreover, Plutarch's hand may be seen in the manner in which Charon was excerpted. The notice of Phobus' leap from the Leucadian Rocks was made by a writer who had read the full account of Charon, and wanted to mention this unique tradition. Plutarch would not have found such a story in a historical summary, and still less in an anthology, for it is completely independent of the foundation story.[247] Plutarch's preservation of the anecdote of Theagenes before the story of Timoclea (*Mul. Virt.* 24) is directly comparable to his treatment here. Similarly in the body of the narrative, Plutarch is primarily concerned with Lampsace, yet he narrates the history leading to the foundation of

---

[245] Jacoby, Comm. to *FGrHist* 262 F 9–10.

[246] There is no trace, for instance, of an Aristotelian constitution of Lampsacus. The notice of Deiochus (*FGrHist* 471 F 3) in his *Peri Kuzikou* would not have provided a full account of Lampsacus. Mela reports (1.97): "Lampsacum Phocaeis appellantibus nomen ex eo traxit, quod consulentibus in quasnam terras potissimum tenderent responsum erat, ubi primum fulsisset ibi sedem capessere." (Cf. also *Etymologicon Magnum* s.v. Lampsakos; Theophanes continuatus 6.20 [Corpus Scriptorum Historiae Byzantinae, Bonn 1838, p. 367]). This is not true local tradition, but an invention of which any learned Greek was capable. See Jacoby, Comm. to *FGrHist* 262 F 7–8 (p. 13).

[247] Since Plutarch refers to the story only parenthetically, it did not belong to the foundation narrative, as was argued by W. Aly, *Volksmärchen*, 218.

Lampsacus. These unimportant details would have been deleted by an intermediate source. Plutarch, however, because he had a complete narrative in front of him, briefly notes the principal events before Lampsace comes upon the scene. This desire to establish the circumstances of his story is a characteristic feature of Plutarch's method in the *Mulierum Virtutes*.[248] Plutarch's citation of Charon as well as his consistent use of local historians in this collection assures us that his source for this full account was Charon himself.[249]

Plutarch states, on the authority of Charon, that Phobus was the first to leap from the Leucadian Rocks.[250] We cannot presume that Phobus leaped from the rocks at Chalcedon,[251] or at Leuce on the gulf of Smyrna.[252] Plutarch's "first" is meaningful only if Charon spoke of the promontory of Leucas. Phobus, as all others who leapt from the promontory, must have been seeking a cure for love, although Plutarch does not expressly state his motive. The legend of this curative power for the leap from the Leucadian Rocks must therefore be at least as early as Charon.

Mulierum Virtutes 19: ARETAPHILA[253]

In this chapter Plutarch preserves for us a detailed account of an episode from the history of Cyrene in the time of Mithridates. In that period, we are told, a certain Nicocrates made himself tyrant of the city. One of his many despotic acts was to kill one Phaedimus and marry his wife Aretaphila. The citizens seemed powerless to oppose

---

[248] See *Mul. Virt.* 2, 3, 4, 8, 9, 14, 16, 20, 23, 25, 26.

[249] If Jacoby's hypothesis is correct, that the work *Peri Lampsakou* in two books is a Hellenistic abridgement of the *Hôroi Lampsakênôn* in four books (Comm. to *FGrHist* 262, p. 2), Plutarch may have used this shorter version. This would not detract from the value of his account.

[250] For the legend see Strabo 10, 452; Ptolemaius Chennus in Photius *Bibliotheca* 190, p. 153 A Bekker; Ovid *Heroides* 15.167–172; S. G. DeVries, *Epistula Sapphus ad Phaonem* (Berlin 1888) 101–103; Ulrich von Wilamowitz-Moellendorf, *Sappho und Simonides* (Berlin 1913) 25–33.

[251] Wilamowitz (above, n. 250) p. 29.

[252] Jacoby, Comm. to *FGrHist* 262 F 7–8 (p. 16).

[253] This is one of the stories from the *Mulierum Virtutes* used by Polyaenus in his *Strategemata* (8.38). See Chapter II and especially p. 24.

him, and so, imitating the daring of Thebe of Pherae,[254] Aretaphila began to prepare poisons to kill her tyrant husband. She was caught, but when tortured under the eye of Calbia, the tyrant's implacable mother, would admit only to brewing love potions. After she was released, the love-sick tyrant tried to win back her favors with large gifts. Aretaphila, however, conceived a new plan against him: she married her daughter to Nicocrates' brother Leander, and through her induced him to kill his brother. When Leander revealed himself equally a tyrant, Aretaphila stirred up a war with the Libyans, and bribed a Libyan ruler to capture Leander at a pretended peace conference. This plan was successful, the city was freed, and the citizens, having praised Aretaphila to the skies, burned Calbia alive and threw Leander in a sack into the sea. And Aretaphila returned to her weaving. Little wonder that Plutarch compares her with the ancient heroines.[255]

Apart from this rather extensive narrative, we have little information of Cyrene at this time. Ptolemy Apion in 96 B.C. had willed his small kingdom of Cyrene to Rome, and Rome had declared Cyrene free.[256] The two tyrants at Cyrene and Aretaphila's contrivances against them should be dated in this period of freedom, and more exactly, immediately before the winter of 87/86 B.C., as is clear from a notice in Plutarch's life of Lucullus. Lucullus was sent by Sulla in the winter of 87/86 to gather ships from Egypt and Libya. "Finding the people of Cyrene troubled by frequent tyrannies and wars, he

[254] A favorite example of feminine daring in the cause of justice. Her story is told by Plutarch, *Pelopidas* 35. Cf. also Plutarch, *De Herodoti malignitate* 856 A, Xenophon, *Hellenica* 6.4.35–37, Diodorus 16.14, Cicero, *De officiis* 2.7 (25), *De inventione* 2.49 (144), Valerius Maximus 9.13 ext. 3, Conon (*FGrHist* 26 F 1) 50. Theopompus' was the standard version of the story: see Plutarch, *Non posse suav.* 1093 C (*FGrHist* 115 F 337), quoted below, p. 113.

[255] 255 E: "Aretaphila displayed courage and activity rivalling that of the heroines."

[256] See Livy epitome 70: "Ptolemaeus Cyrenarum rex, cui cognomen Apionis fuit, mortuus heredem populum Romanum reliquit, et eius regni civitates senatus liberas esse iussit." Other references in Greenidge and Clay, *Sources for Roman History*[2] (Oxford 1960) 118. Cyrene was made a Roman province in 74 B.C. (Appian *Bellum Civile* 1.111). The history of Cyrene between 96–74 B.C. has recently been discussed at length by S. I. Oost, *CP* 58 (1963) 11–25, who relies heavily upon Plutarch.

took them in hand and settled their government."[257] The date agrees with Plutarch's "in the time of Mithridates." The tyrannies referred to in this passage are undoubtedly those of Nicocrates and Leander, and the wars would be the "Libyan war," stirred up by Aretaphila.[258]

Plutarch's source for this account is unknown. It would have been a history, detailed, and with a tendency to dramatize events. The history of Posidonius, which is cited by Plutarch three times in the *Marius* as well as frequently elsewhere, went down to at least 86 B.C. (*FGrHist* 87 F 37 = Plut. *Marius* 45.7). Posidonius gave a detailed account of Sulla's campaign in the East, and may well have also provided Plutarch with his information on events in Cyrene before the arrival of Lucullus.[259] Josephus cites Strabo in connection with Lucullus' visit to Cyrene.[260] Since Strabo is also quoted several times by Plutarch in lives of this period,[261] the story is possibly taken from him. However, although no known writer of *Kyrenaika* lived so late, there are many authors of histories of the Mithridatic period from whom Plutarch could have taken this story.

Despite its dramatic treatment, there is no reason to question the historical value of Plutarch's account. Plutarch no doubt encountered the story in the process of writing the lives from the early part of the civil wars. Although this vivid narrative had no place in any of these lives, he remembered it and included it in the *Mulierum Virtutes*.

Mulierum Virtutes 20: CAMMA[262]

In four consecutive stories Plutarch narrates the virtues of women

[257] Plutarch *Lucullus* 2.4; cf. Josephus *Antiquitates Judaicae* 14.114, who says that Lucullus was sent by Sulla to put down a revolt of the Jews. Oost (above, n. 256) 19, sees nothing contradictory in the two reports.
[258] See J. P. Thrige, *Res Cyrenensium*² (Hafniae 1828, reprinted Verbania 1940) 269, Oost (above, n. 256) 16–18.
[259] Jacoby, Comm. to *FGrHist* 87, II C p. 156, seems correct in refusing to identify the events narrated in Plutarch with the "war of the Cyrenaic (king) and Ptolemy" given by Suidas as the terminus of Posidonius' history (*FGrHist* 87 T 1).
[260] *Antiq. Jud.* 14.114 = *FGrHist* 91 F 7.
[261] *Sulla* 26 (*FGrHist* 91 F 8), *Lucullus* 28 (F 9), *Caesar* 63 (F 19).
[262] This is one of the stories taken from the *Mulierum Virtutes* used by Polyaenus in his *Strategemata* (8.39). See Chapter II and especially p. 23.

from Galatia. He consciously emphasizes their unity in his introductory sentences: the first begins abruptly, "There were in Galatia"; the second continues with "Galatia also gave us Stratonice and Chiomara..."; and the last story resumes once more, "But when Mithridates sent for sixty Galatians..."

The first of these stories, and the most dramatic, concerns Camma, the wife of the Galatian tetrarch Sinatus, who was loved also by another tetrarch, Sinorix. The latter, despairing of winning Camma while her husband lived, killed him, and after a short time wooed the widow, arguing that the murder was only a proof of his great love and no sign of wickedness. Though at first refusing, Camma finally let it be known that the marriage was agreeable to her. At the betrothal ceremony, she shared with him a potion which she had secretly poisoned, and when she saw that he had drunk it, cried out a prayer of thanksgiving to the goddess Artemis whose priestess she was, that she had been allowed to avenge her husband's murder.[263] Sinorix tried to shake off the poison by driving a chariot, but quickly succumbed, followed soon after by the joyful Camma.

The story is told also by Plutarch in *Amatorius* 22 (768 B-D). Comparison with the version of the *Amatorius* shows again Plutarch's free handling of historical anecdotes in his writings. In the *Amatorius* he is defending marital love. He argues that heterosexual love ennobles even the lowest type of person, and presents the devoted love of the courtesan Lais for Hippolochus the Thessalian as an example (c.21, 766 E-768 B). As for a noble woman, joined in love to a lawful husband, she would prefer to endure the embraces of bears or snakes

---

[263] W. M. Ramsay, *Historical Commentary on St. Paul's Epistle to the Galatians* (London 1899) 88, considers this sharing of a cup at marriage "part of an old Anatolian ritual," and notes that it is still part of Greek weddings. This contrary to Hendrick van Gelder, *Galatorum res in Graecia et Asia gestae* (Amsterdam 1888) 199, who thought it a Gallic custom. Ramsay remarks also that the goddess called by Plutarch Artemis must have been the Anatolian Bellona or Ma, whose ritual featured an annual procession of the goddess. This would have presented Camma vested as the goddess herself, suitable to provoke the admiration of which Plutarch speaks. F. Staehelin, *Geschichte der kleinasiatischen Galater* (Leipzig 1907) 46 n. 9, refers to the cults of Attis and the Great Mother and Zeus on Taunion also taken over by the Celts upon arrival in Galatia.

rather than the hand and bed of another man. His proof for this assertion is the story of Camma, who would not endure the advances of Sinorix, but preferred to kill both him and herself. The story in outline is the same in both versions, and they certainly come from a single original. Nevertheless, various differences appear. Because he is particularly interested in Camma's fidelity, Plutarch writes in the *Amatorius* that she was wooed after her husband's death "by many kings and dynasts." The version in the *Amatorius* is shorter, and leaves out such details as Camma's first refusal and the urgings of her friends and relatives. Markedly different is the prayer of the woman after Sinorix had taken the poison. It is addressed not to Artemis but to her dear husband, whom she was now joining in death, after having avenged his murder. The thought in both prayers is the same, triumphant fulfilment of a long-hidden desire for vengeance, but since Plutarch in the *Amatorius* stresses the woman's faithfulness, he presents a version which emphasizes how much Camma's love for her husband overrode every other thought.

The particular suitability of this version for the *Amatorius* suggests that the story was so adapted specifically for this dialogue. The account in the *Mulierum Virtutes*, on the other hand, would seem by its less specific focus closer to the version of Plutarch's source. This suggests that the latter account is also the earlier of the two. Both, however, seem to be written in the last decade of Plutarch's life.[264]

Before Pompey's reorganization of Asia Minor, each of the three Galatian tribes was ruled by four tetrarchs.[265] Among these men there existed a rather fluid balance of power, so that occasionally certain tetrarchs attempted to increase their influence at the expense of others.[266] Therefore Sinorix' murder of Sinatus probably had political

[264] See the evidence for the dates of the *Amatorius* and the *Mulierum Virtutes*, above, p. 2.
[265] On the Galatian tetrarchs see esp. Strabo 12, 566–567 and Magie, *Roman Rule* 372–374 and note 41 (with bibliography).
[266] Thus Livy (38.18–19) reports that three *reguli*, representing the three tribes of Galatia, opposed Gn. Manlius in 189 B.C., but that another *regulus*, Eposognatus, aided the Romans and attempted to persuade the other kings to submit to them. In 184 B.C. the Galatians fought Eumenes under the sole leadership of the tetrarch Ortiagon. See

motives as well as those presented by Plutarch, even though Plutarch omits all reference to that facet of the episode. The reader, however, may compare Sinorix' attempt to marry Camma with Plutarch's narrative of Eryxo (*Mul. Virt.* 25), in which the usurper Learchus tries to marry the widow of the king he murdered to strengthen his hold on the throne.

The Sinorix of this story is almost certainly the same as that named the father of Deiotarus I, tetrarch and king of Galatia, on the base of a statue dedicated to the latter by the Athenian people.[267] Since Deiotarus I was already tetrarch in 74 B.C.,[268] the murder of Sinatus and the death of Sinorix may be placed in the first quarter of the first century B.C. Unfortunately nothing else is known of Sinorix or the other figures in this episode.

Nachstädt notes the parallel drawn by Erwin Rohde with the story in Apuleius' *Metamorphoses* 8.1–4.[269] There Apuleius tells of a man who kills the husband of a woman he loves, courts the widow, and is blinded by her. Both stories, Rohde feels, go back "auf ein gemeinsames älteres Vorbild." That the story belongs to an old type is doubtless true. Plutarch's story, however, seems not to be fiction, but to depend on a historical source, as do the stories of the other Galatian women which follow.

Mulierum Virtutes 21: STRATONICE

This short chapter describes how Stratonice, the wife of Deiotarus, seeing her husband unhappy because she was not providing him with heirs to his kingdom, persuaded him to have children by a captive,

---

Magie, *Roman Rule* 21 and n. 59; Trogus, *Prologue* 32, now confirmed by an inscription from Telmessus, *Clara Rhodos* 2 (1932) 172–174, no. 3 = *RivFC* 60 (1932) 446–452: "Eumenes..., having fought against Prusias and Ortiagon and the Galatians and their allies..."

[267] *IG* II² 3429: *ho dêmos Dêiotaron Sinorigos Gal[at]ôn Tolis[t]obogiôn b[asilea]*.

[268] See Appian *Mithr.* 75 and Livy *Periochae* 94.

[269] *Der griechische Roman*³ (Leipzig 1914) 590. See also Walter Anderson, "Zu Apuleius' Novelle vom Tode der Charite," *Philologus* 68 (1909) 537–549, who tries to trace this story in other Indo-European traditions.

whom she herself selected, named Electra, and raised the resulting children as her own.

The story is not otherwise known. The Deiotarus concerned is not the most famous bearer of that name, Deiotarus I Philoromaios, as often supposed.[270] The wife of that king was named Berenice, as has been established by an inscription discovered at the tomb of his son.[271] The only known Deiotarus with which this anecdote may be connected is this same son, Deiotarus II Philopator, himself a king, coregent with his father.[272] It is said that the old king killed off all his sons but one to make the succession easier,[273] but his plan did not succeed, for the tomb inscription reveals that Deiotarus II died before his father. Stratonice's attempt to provide an heir for her husband was equally unsuccessful, for after the death of Deiotarus I the kingdom passed to his grandson Castor and not to any child of Deiotarus II. If Deiotarus II had children, they were not able to assert their rights as heirs. It is remarkable that Plutarch preserves even the name of the concubine Electra. Too little is known, however, about Plutarch's sources for activities in Asia Minor in this period (covered also in the lives of Lucullus, Pompey, and Brutus) to permit speculation as to the historian who provided him such detailed information.

[270] Deiotarus I, the son of Sinorix (see above, p. 106) fought as tetrarch against Mithridates in 74 B.C., was made king and sole tetrarch of the Tolistobogii, as well as ruler of much other territory, by Pompey, and by his death in 39 B.C. had gained control of the whole of Galatia. See Niese *RE* s.v. Deiotarus 2, IV 2 (1901) 2401–2403.

[271] See J. Coupry, *Revue archéologique* 6 (1935) 140–151: "King Deiotarus Philopator, tetrarch of the Galatian Tolistobogii and Trocmi, son of King Deiotarus Philoromaios, tetrarch of the Galatian Tolistobogii and Trocmi, and of Queen Berenice." Cf. Plutarch, *Adversus Coloten* 4, 1109 B, an anecdote about Berenice the wife of Deiotarus. I am indebted to Glen Bowersock of Harvard University for calling my attention to this inscription.

[272] See Cicero *Pro rege Deiotaro* 36, *Ad Atticum* 5.17.3, *Philippicae* 11.31, 33. An earlier Deiotarus, father of the Brogitarus established by Pompey as tetrarch of the Trocmi, would not have been a king. Deiotarus Philadelphos was king of Paphlagonia but is never identified as a Galatian. See Niese, *RE* s.v. Deiotarus 1 and 4, IV 2 (1901) 2401, 2404.

[273] Plutarch, *De Stoicorum repugnantiis* 32, 1049 C.

Mulierum Virtutes 22: CHIOMARA

Plutarch's third story of this set concerns Chiomara, the wife of the Galatian leader Ortiagon, who was captured by the Romans during the campaign of Gn. Manlius in 189 B.C. Plutarch tells us that she was prisoner of a centurion (*taxiarchos*) who first violated her and then let her be ransomed. When the Galatians had handed over the money agreed upon, Chiomara signed (*apo neumatos*) to one of them to kill the Roman, who was taking affectionate leave of her. He obeyed, and she picked up the cut-off head and carried it to her husband. Though amazed, he said only, "Wife, it is good to keep faith." "Yes," she replied, "but better that only one live who has known me." Plutarch adds that Polybius said that he had talked to Chiomara in Sardis and admired her sense and spirit.

The story of Chiomara was narrated by many Latin authors: Livy 38.24, Valerius Maximus 6.1, ext. 2, Florus 1.27, and [Aurelius Victor] *De viris illustribus* 55. Livy's story is the same as that of Plutarch, though fuller. In Livy, Chiomara is not named, and her husband is called Orgiagon. He reports at length the negotiations through various messengers for Chiomara's ransom, and that Chiomara gave the order in her own tongue (*lingua sua*) to kill the centurion while he was weighing out the gold brought in to him.

It has long been recognized that Livy depends upon Polybius for his account of the invasion of Galatia under Manlius.[274] That Plutarch also drew his account of Chiomara from Polybius is the natural conclusion from his references to him in the last sentence, and is confirmed by the similarity of his account with that of Livy.[275] His account could not derive from Livy, because Chiomara is not named by that author. The slight difference in the death of the centurion is not the effect of different sources, but of changes in phrasing natural in the retelling of such anecdotes.

---

[274] See Heinrich Nissen, *Kritische Untersuchungen über die Quellen... des Livius* (Berlin 1863) 203–205.
[275] The chapter is printed as a fragment of Polybius, 21.38.

"Mulierum Virtutes" 22: Chiomara

The account of Livy is the source for the other Latin versions of this story. Theodore Mommsen pointed out that they all reproduce the error found in Livy of writing Orgiagon for Ortiagon and that they all omit the name of the heroine, though it was given by Plutarch and therefore must have been in Polybius.[276]

According to Livy 38.18-27 and the fragments of Polybius 21.37-39 the consul Gn. Manlius Vulso after the Roman victory over Antiochus at Magnesia in 190 B.C. marched against Antiochus' Galatian allies.[277] Ortiagon was leader of the tribe of the Tolistobogii in this war (Livy 38.19.2), in which the Romans defeated the combined tribes of the Tolistobogii and the Trocmi in a great battle.

Polybius reports that he talked to Chiomara at Sardis. It is doubtful that Polybius took part in the Roman expedition of 190-189 and talked to Chiomara at that time as suggested by Mommsen.[278] It is unlikely that Chiomara should have been in Sardis willingly at any time: Sardis was a Pergamene stronghold, and her husband Ortiagon not only had fought against Pergamum in 190 with the other Galatians in Antiochus' force, and in 189 when Eumenes aided Manlius, but had led the Gauls to a new attack in conjunction with Prusias of Bithynia and others in 184.[279] He was defeated in this latter war by Eumenes and perhaps killed, for he is not heard of again. Chiomara's presence in Sardis is best explained by van Gelder's hypothesis that she was a captive (or perhaps hostage) after the defeat of her

---

[276] *Römische Forschungen* (Berlin 1879) 541 n. 38. The form Ortiagon is found in Plutarch, Suidas s.v. Ortiagon (= Polybius 22.21), Trogus *Prologue* 32, and Livy himself (in a different context) 38.19.2. This is the correct form: see the inscription from Telmessus, quoted in n. 266 above. Mommsen also remarks that the mistake was made in Livy's reading of the Greek text, caused by a confusion of tau and gamma. Boccaccio, who retells the story, *De mulieribus claris* 71, laments that no author has preserved the name of so famous a woman, since he did not use the *Mulierum Virtutes* of Plutarch, which alone has preserved the name, in composing his similar work.

[277] See Appian *Bellum Syricum* 42, Magie, *Roman Rule* p. 21 and n. 58 (p. 764).

[278] Mommsen (above, n. 276) 538-543, esp. 543, repeated by Elpidio Mioni, *Polibio* (Padova 1949) 4.

[279] See Trogus *Prologue* 32 and the Telmessus inscription quoted above, n. 266.

husband.[280] Polybius would have seen her during his travels to Asia Minor before 169.[281]

Mulierum Virtutes 23: WOMAN OF PERGAMUM

The concluding narrative in Plutarch's Galatian series is unusual in that the heroine, not Galatian but Pergamene, is not central to the account. Rather she seems a more or less stereotyped afterthought to the two stories of Galatian men in this chapter. While at Pergamum, Plutarch tells us, Mithridates had sixty of the Galatian nobles come to him as friends, but treated them insolently and tyrannically. Finally Eporedorix, the tetrarch of the Tosiopi, decided to kill him, and gained the support of the other Galatians. But the plot came to the king's ears, and he ordered them all to be executed, one by one. After giving the order, he recalled that there was one, particularly young and handsome, whom he wished to let live. It was late, but he sent a message to the executioner to spare him. The youth, called Bepolitanus, was saved by a strange stroke of fortune, for the executioner had admired his rich cloak, and wishing to preserve it clean and without bloodstain, was removing it with great care. At this time Mithridates' messenger arrived, and Bepolitanus was saved, paradoxically, by greed. But Eporedorix was executed, and his body thrown out unburied, and none dared to touch it, until a young Pergamene woman who had been known to Eporedorix tried to give it a proper burial. The king's men arrested her and took her to him, but he was struck by her young and innocent appearance, and hearing that love was the motive of her deed, he softened and allowed her to take and bury the body.

Mithridates VI Eupator massacred his Galatian allies, who seem to have been held in Pergamum more as hostages than friends, while holding court at Pergamum in 86 B.C.[282] It was only one of a number

---

[280] *Galatorum res*, 258.
[281] See Otto Cuntz, *Polybios und sein Werk* (Leipzig 1902) 76; K. Ziegler, *RE* s.v. Polybios, XXI 2 (1952) 1461.
[282] See Magie, *Roman Rule*, 223.

"Mulierum Virtutes" 23: Woman of Pergamum

of tyrannical acts against his allies and subjects which helped to weaken his new-found grasp on Asia Minor. Appian (*Mithr.* 46) mentions this slaughter, relating that not only the tetrarchs but their wives and children were slain, and their goods confiscated, because Mithridates feared that they would go over to Sulla. Mithridates then set up Eumachus, one of his generals, as satrap of Galatia, but he was at once expelled by the three tetrarchs who had been able to escape the slaughter. Bepolitanus was perhaps one of these.[283]

Plutarch's source for this story is not known. No other writer gives the narrative preserved by Plutarch: Appian treats the same event, but it is clear from his presentation and content that his version is founded on a tradition different from that of Plutarch. It is likely that Plutarch's source was a history, for in the preparation of his biographies of Sulla, Lucullus, and Pompey he had ample occasion to encounter a historical treatment of Mithridates' activities in Pergamum.

There is some difficulty with the names in this passage. Although Poredorax is the reading of the manuscripts, Eporedorix is a reasonable correction, and is accepted by Nachstädt. The form Poredorax is otherwise unattested, whereas Eporedorix is a Celtic name found in Caesar (*Bellum Gallicum* 7.39.1, 7.67.7) and in inscriptions from Gaul (*CIL* XIII 2728, 2805).[284] Plutarch tells us that Eporedorix was tetrarch of the Tosiopi. Most scholars have sought to emend this to names of known tribes.[285] The tetrarchs, however, were at this time rulers over clans, not tribes, and there is no reason to doubt that Tosiopi is a name of one of these twelve clans, as were also Voturi and Ambitouti (named by Pliny *Naturalis historia* 5.146).[286]

This triple narrative of Eporedorix, Bepolitanus, and the Pergamene woman forms a sort of bridge between the stories before and after it.

---

[283] See Ramsay, *Historical Commentary*, 97, n. 1.

[284] See Münzer, *RE* s.v. Eporedorix, VI 1 (1909) 250–251. Nevertheless, there is no need to assume that the names in Galatia and Gaul were exactly similar, and the manuscripts may preserve the correct form.

[285] That is, the Tolostoagii, Tectosagi or Tolistobogii: Nachstädt contents himself with writing Tosiopi with an obelisk.

[286] W. Ruge, *RE*, s.v. Tosiopoi, VI 2 A (1937) 1811, refers to some of those considering this reading corrupt.

On the one hand, the chief characters are Galatians, and at least one is a tetrarch, as were Sinatus, Sinorix, Deiotarus and Ortiagon. Nevertheless, the heroine is Pergamene and does not properly belong in the series of Camma, Stratonice, and Chiomara. Her courage, however, in defying Mithridates and the king's change of heart upon seeing her are quite similar to the courage of Timoclea and the respect of Alexander in *Mul. Virt.* 24 immediately following. Thus, as with the story of the Chian defense against Philip V in *Mul. Virt.* 3, this account is a connecting passage as well as an interesting narrative in its own right.

Mulierum Virtutes 24: TIMOCLEA [287]

In the midst of the ruins of Thebes, conquered and razed by Alexander, one woman's courage and high spirit proclaimed the mastery of virtue over fortune. Quite properly, therefore, Plutarch included the story of Timoclea in the *Mulierum Virtutes*. He evidently liked the story, for he refers to Timoclea twice elsewhere in the *Moralia*,[288] and in the *Alexander* (12) narrates a shorter version of the story told here.[289]

According to Plutarch's narrative, which is substantially the same in the two versions, Timoclea, a noblewoman of Thebes and sister of the general Theagenes who died at Chaeronea, suffered grievously at the hands of the leader of a band of Thracian soldiers.[290] Not content with violating her, he demanded her hidden valuables. She pretended to be resigned to his outrages, and led him to a well in which she said that she had placed her jewels and money. The soldier eagerly

[287] This is one of the stories from the *Mulierum Virtutes* used by Polyaenus in his *Strategemata* (8.40). See Chapter II and especially p. 21.

[288] *Conjugalia praecepta* 145 E and *Non posse suav.* 1093 C.

[289] Zonaras 4.9 summarizes *Alexander* 12. Jerome, *Adversus Jovinianum* 1.41 (Migne, *Patrologia latina* 23, 285 B) sketches the story briefly. He did not use Plutarch (see Ernst Bickel, *Diatribe in Senecae philosophi fragmenta* I [Leipzig 1915] 63), although his source must eventually be the same as that of Plutarch.

[290] Since it has been shown that Polyaenus' account is derived solely from Plutarch (see above, n. 287), there is no need to discuss the correctness of his calling the leader a hipparch (see Droysen, *Geschichte des Hellenismus*² I, 2, 394 and Jacoby, Comm. to *FGrHist* 139 F 2). It is either a mistake on the part of Polyaenus or a corruption of our text (that is, *hipparchos* from *ilarchos* = Plutarch's *érche . . . ilês*).

climbed down, and Timoclea and her handmaids threw stones down on him, killing him. The Macedonians brought her before Alexander for this, but when Alexander questioned her, she told him proudly that she was the sister of Theagenes, who fought at Chaeronea that the Greeks might not suffer as she had. "Indeed," said she to Alexander, "if you don't stop this, it would be better not to live another night." Alexander was amazed by her courage and sense, and he not only released her and her relatives, but ordered his generals to take precautions against any such outrage being repeated.

Although Plutarch does not mention a source either in the *Mulierum Virtutes* or the *Alexander*, a passage in the *Non posse suaviter vivi secundum Epicurum* (1093 C) makes it certain that his source is Aristobulus. In speaking of the joys of reading, Plutarch asks, "Who would be delighted more by spending the night with the most beautiful of women than by remaining awake with the account which Xenophon wrote about Panthea, or Aristobulus about Timoclea, or Theopompus about Thebe?" Aristobulus' account of Timoclea was undoubtedly exceptional, and there is no reason to doubt that it is the source of Plutarch's two versions.[291] The quoted passage also proves that Plutarch had read Aristobulus himself. In further support of Aristobulus' authorship of this account, Lionel Pearson points out that this story is appropriate to an author trying to show that Alexander's attack on Thebes was not "an act of wanton brutality," but that Alexander tried to maintain some discipline.[292] This is the first of a number of stories told by Plutarch in the *Alexander* showing the conqueror's generous attitude toward the women of the enemy.

---

[291] *Non posse suav.* 1093 C = FGrHist 139 F 2a (Aristobulus). Jacoby prints *Mul. Virt.* 24 as 139 F 2b, and only refers to *Alexander* 12 in the commentary. The attempts of Droysen (above, n. 290) and Fritz Wenger, *Die Alexander-Geschichte des Aristoboulos* (Diss. Wurzberg 1913) 5, to connect the story with Clitarchus because of its un-Aristobulian coloring are groundless. It is furthermore most unlikely that Plutarch could have used Clitarchus in any case: he cites him only twice, and in neither case directly; once in the great mass of citations on Alexander's encounter with the Amazons (*Alexander* 46, FGrHist 137 F 15), and again in a list of authorities for Themistocles' flight to Xerxes (*Themistocles* 27, FGrHist 137 F 33).
[292] *The Lost Histories of Alexander the Great* (n.p., 1960) 155.

"Mulierum Virtutes" 24: Timoclea

Thus far the two versions of Plutarch have been treated as one. Nevertheless they differ in detail, a consequence of the fact that the account in the *Alexander* is far shorter than its twin and has been made a part of the continuous narrative. In this abridged version Plutarch omits the anecdote of Theagenes[293] and the name of the Macedonian commander, Alexander.[294] The dramatic description of Timoclea's deception is sharply curtailed, and Timoclea is said to push her tormentor[295] into the well before she stoned him, without waiting for him to climb down. The scene in the garden in *Mul. Virt.* 24 is depicted in a high style foreign to Plutarch, which may be readily contrasted with that of *Alexander* 12. While in the *Alexander* Plutarch integrated the story and style of Aristobulus into the biography that he was writing, in *Mul. Virt.* 24 he preserved the fuller dimensions and the style of his original. The version of *Mul. Virt.* 24 thus is closer to the account of Aristobulus than that of *Alexander* 12, but it may not be argued that the *Mulierum Virtutes* must be earlier than the *Alexander*. In writing the *Alexander* Plutarch obviously used Aristobulus directly, for he cites him six times.[296] This means that he did not take the story of Timoclea from *Mulierum Virtutes*. Likewise he may have read Aristobulus and written the anecdote for this collection before composing the *Alexander*. Unfortunately these two

---

[293] When asked at Chaeronea how far he was chasing the enemy, Theagenes replied, "To Macedon!" The same anecdote is told of Stratocles, Polyaenus 4.2.2. Theagenes, a Theban general at Chaeronea, is known only from Plutarch, where he is associated with Timoclea, and from Dinarchus 1.74: "Theagenes was made leader of the phalanx, an unfortunate and bribetaking man, like this one (*scil.* Demosthenes)."

[294] Plutarch notes that the captain had the same name as his king, but not the same character, thus preparing the reader for the interview between Timoclea and Alexander. He refers to other namesakes of Alexander in *Alexander* 58 (a courageous soldier) and *De fortuna Alexandri* 334 A (the tyrant of Pherae). Cf. also Eustathius comm. to *Iliad* 17.720 ("like-named men, with like courage . . ."), who reports that Alexander wanted a worthless man who had his name either to change his name or change his character.

[295] He is here identified as a Thracian: an easy slip on a point which was of no importance to Plutarch's story. In *Mul. Virt.* 24, the Macedonian commands a band of Thracian soldiers.

[296] He also cites Aristobulus in *Demosthenes* 23 (*FGrHist* 139 F 3) and *De fortuna Alexandri* 327 F (F 4) and 341 C (F 46). I do not see the foundation for Jacoby's statement, Comm. to *FGrHist* 139, II D p. 509, "Plutarch kennt ihn, hat ihn aber kaum viel benutzt."

versions give no indication of the chronological relation of the works in which they appear.

Mulierum Virtutes 25: ERYXO[297]

The brief interlude of Learchus' tyranny in Cyrene, which Herodotus mentioned in a sentence, is reported in detail in this dramatic vignette of Plutarch. Herodotus' notice (4.160) occurs in the course of his history of the Battiad dynasty at Cyrene. Arcesilaus II, he tells us, quarreled with his brothers, who fled Cyrene and established themselves at Barce. When pursued by Arcesilaus they were able to inflict a stunning defeat upon him at Leukon. Herodotus continues:

> After this defeat his brother Learchus strangled Arcesilaus, who was sick and had taken a drug, and in turn the wife of Arcesilaus, called Eryxo, killed Learchus by deceit. Battus the child of Arcesilaus, who was lame and crooked-footed, then received his crown.

Herodotus then speaks of the reform of the Cyreniac constitution made by Demonax of Mantinea under Battus III the Lame (4.161).[298]

The account of Plutarch focuses upon Learchus' tyranny and his assassination by Eryxo and her brother. Arcesilaus II, Plutarch tells us, was overbearing even while his father, Battus II, was alive: after Battus' death, with the connivance of his friend Learchus, he became not a king but a tyrant. Learchus, however, was scheming to become tyrant himself. First he banished or murdered many of the nobles, laying the blame on Arcesilaus; then finally he poisoned the king, and became regent for the young heir. He attempted to confirm his position by marrying Eryxo, the widow of Arcesilaus, and adopting her son. She, by a ruse, persuaded him to come to her apartment unaccompanied, where he was slain by her eldest brother Polyarchus and two companions. The conspirators proclaimed young Battus

---

[297] This is one of the stories from the *Mulierum Virtutes* used by Polyaenus in his *Strategemata* (8.41). See Chapter II and especially pp. 21–22.

[298] Herodotus is the source of the account of Nicolaus of Damascus (*FGrHist* 90 F 50). See Jacoby's commentary. This story is not otherwise mentioned. Herodotus and Nicolaus use the form Learchus, Plutarch and Polyaenus Laarchus.

king (Battus III) and Polyarchus restored to the city its original form of government. Plutarch adds that the Egyptian troops of Learchus complained to Amasis, the king of Egypt, against Polyarchus and Eryxo, but that the latter were able to win the friendship of Amasis by a visit to Egypt, accompanied by Critola, their mother and the sister of Battus II.

Herodotus, who was tracing the history of the eight Battiad kings at Cyrene, had passed over in a few words Learchus' temporary interruption of this dynastic sequence. The different identifications of Learchus made by Herodotus and Plutarch must be viewed in this light. Herodotus reports immediately after his description of the *stasis* between the king and his brothers that Learchus murdered Arcesilaus. Thus, to him or his source, it was reasonable that Learchus be one of Arcesilaus' brothers. Plutarch's version, which ignores this conflict, identifies Learchus not as a brother but as a friend. Plutarch's version seems correct: he follows a Cyreniac account which reported the tyranny of Learchus in great detail. Herodotus' account is also drawn from a Cyreniac source,[299] but is both condensed and selective. The episode of Learchus is treated in a sentence, and Herodotus might easily have mistakenly assimilated Learchus' murder of Arcesilaus to the *stasis* of Arcesilaus' brothers. Nor does Herodotus' identification agree with the other material provided by Plutarch. If Learchus was only one of several brothers united against Arcesilaus, his assassination by Eryxo and Polyarchus would have solved nothing, for the faction would remain. Polyarchus' proclamation of Battus III king is reasonably only if he were the unchallenged claimant to the throne. The weight of probability therefore, supports Plutarch's account against that of Herodotus.[300]

The exiles mentioned by Plutarch were probably of the party of

---

[299] See Jacoby *RE* suppl. II (1913) 437 (s.v. Herodotos).

[300] This is also the conclusion of Jacoby, *Hermes* 60 (1925) 371–372 (*Abhandlungen zur griechischen Geschichtschreibung* [Leiden 1956] 171–172). The authority of Herodotus is respected by François Chamoux, *Cyrène sous la monarchie des Battiades* (Paris 1953) 138 n. 1, Santo Mazzarino, *Fra Oriente e Occidente* (Florence 1947) 359 n. 425, and H. Schaefer, *RhMus* 95 (1952) 165 n. 101.

Arcesilaus' brothers, and the enemies of both Arcesilaus and Learchus. Eryxo and Polyarchus were related to the royal family, for their mother Critola was the sister of Battus II. They seem to have supported the exiles by their opposition to Learchus: their proclaimed restoration of the ancestral constitution seems to have promised a reform, effected soon after by Demonax (see Her. 4.161) which would weaken the royal power after its abuse by Arcesilaus and his illegal successor Learchus.[301] Plutarch's reference to friendly relations with Egypt concurs with the report of Herodotus (2.181) that Amasis of Egypt married a Cyreniac woman. This friendship began after the defeat of an Egyptian force by Battus II in 570 B.C. (Her. 2.161, cf. 4.159). Learchus' use of Egyptian troops borrowed from Amasis is reasonable in this context, as is the presence of Critola the sister of Battus II on Eryxo's conciliatory mission to Egypt.[302]

Plutarch's ultimate source for this well-informed narrative must have been a Cyreniac local historian. Busolt suggested Acesandrus,[303] whom Plutarch quotes in the *Symposiaca* 675 AB (*FGrHist* 469 F 7). However, the fragments of Acesandrus refer only to the mythical period. Another possible source is Menecles of Barce (*FGrHist* 270), whose *Libukai historiai*, according to Jacoby, is "kein buch über Kyrene... sondern eine sammlung von vermutlich in sich geschlossen geschichten."[304] Although not himself properly a local historian, he would have drawn his stories from them. Menecles in his account of the trip of the first Battus to Delphi (*FGrHist* 270 F 6) differed considerably from Herodotus, as Plutarch's account does here. His story of Pheretime (*FGrHist* 270 F 5) is essentially the same as that of Herodotus (4.162–167), but is touched by the novelistic tone

---

[301] See Schaefer (above, n. 300). Schaefer suggests that Eryxo and Polyarchus represented a third faction, separate both from the exiles and Learchus. On the work of Demonax see Schaefer, pp. 166–170 and Busolt-Swoboda, I, 350.

[302] The attempt of Mazzarino (above, n. 300) 150–155, 313–317 to interpret these relations with Egypt as Cyreniac vassalage to Amasis is ill-founded. See Schaefer (above, n. 300) 157–158.

[303] *Gr. Gesch.*² I, 489 n. 2. Aristotle's *Constitution of the Cyrenians* (cf. fr. 528–531 Rose) probably mentioned Learchus, but his account would hardly have been so detailed.

[304] Comm. to *FGrHist* 270 F 5–6, p. 223.

notable also in Plutarch's story of Eryxo. Against this tentative identification is to be noted that Plutarch never cites Menecles.

Mulierum Virtutes 26: XENOCRITE

The history of yet another tyrant, Aristodemus *ho Malakos* of Italian Cumae in the fifth century, is narrated in this chapter. According to Plutarch, Aristodemus, after winning a name for himself fighting the barbarians, led a Cumaean expedition to aid Rome against the Etruscans and Tarquin. Upon his return, he seized power and showed himself a vicious and dissolute tyrant. He married Xenocrite, the daughter of an exile, without even asking her father's permission. However, resistance formed against him incited, among other things, by the outspoken reproach of an unnamed woman. Finally Xenocrite gave the revolutionaries a chance to catch him unarmed and kill him.

A longer and more detailed account of Aristodemus is preserved by Dionysius of Halicarnassus (*Roman Antiquities* 7.2-11, cf. 5.36), as well as a fragment concerning the tyrant from Diodorus (7.10). This short fragment calls the tyrant simply *Malakos*, and gives a typical picture of tyrannical activity. It is of no help in ascertaining the history of the tyrant or its tradition. Dionysius' story, on the other hand, is most interesting. Although Plutarch had without doubt read this account at some time,[305] his story is taken neither from him nor, as supposed by De Sanctis,[306] from a common source. They both remark certain features of Aristodemus' tyranny: his attempt, for example, to make the Cumaean youths effeminate (*Mul. Virt.* 26, 261 F and Dion. Hal. 7.9.4). Yet important elements of Plutarch's narrative are not found in Dionysius, and others contradict details of his accounts. Plutarch relates that Aristodemus seized power after corrupting the citizens in the army which he led to aid Rome, whereas in Dionysius the expedition in question was to Aricia, after peace

---

[305] Dionysius' narrative is in the middle of that part of his work (6.1-8.62) which forms the basis of Plutarch's narrative in the *Coriolanus*. See Schwartz, *RE* s.v. Dionysius 113, V 1 (1905) 943 and D. A. Russell, *Journal of Roman Studies* 53 (1963) 21-28.
[306] *Storia dei Romani* I (Turin 1907) 451 n. 1.

was concluded between Porsenna and the Romans.[307] Dionysius' narrative of the conspiracy is completely different from that of Plutarch. He tells us that the sons of the murdered aristocrats, whom Aristodemus had made shepherds, united with the Cumaean exiles in Capua led by Hippomedon and by a stratagem sneaked into the city and slew the tyrant and all his family, including his wife. In Plutarch, apart from the numerous other differences, Aristodemus' wife is a heroine, and after the assassination of her husband is honored with the priesthood of Demeter. Some similar elements in the two accounts, however, may be the result of Plutarch's reading of Dionysius. Thus, Plutarch's reference to the honors received by Aristodemus in the wars against the barbarians may have been prompted by Dionysius' account of the barbarian war (7.3-4).

The chronology of both accounts is difficult and reveals attempts to reconcile the different histories of Rome and Cumae.[308] Dionysius reports an extraordinary delay of twenty years between Aristodemus' first rise to fame in the war against the Etruscans (524 B.C.) and his seizure of power after raising the siege of Aricia. Plutarch's account is more vague, perhaps because it is not based upon an annalistic source. Nevertheless, his source partially shortened this disturbing gap by connecting Aristodemus' tyranny with the defense of Rome a few years before the battle at Aricia.

Certain special features of Plutarch's account may be noted. First, he comments on the tyrant's epithet *malakos*, rejecting the opinion of some (that is, Dionysius) that it is the Greek "gentle," and explains it as a barbarian word meaning a "mere boy" (*antipais*).[309] In the middle of the explanation another etymology is given: Aristodemus fought along with "the youths who were still wearing their hair long (these

[307] On Aristodemus' attitude toward the Etruscans, see M. Pallottino, *La parola del passato* 11 (1956), 81-88. There was a tradition that Tarquin in his old age fled to Aristodemus at Cumae: Dion. Hal. 6.21, 7.12, Livy 2.21.5, Cicero *Disputationes Tusculanae* 3.12.27.

[308] See Niese, *RE* s.v. Aristodemos 8, II 1 (1896) 922-923 and De Sanctis (above, n. 306).

[309] Plutarch thus also implicitly rejects the meaning "effeminate" which Dionysius reports as held by certain historians.

were called *korônistai*, from their long hair [*komê*], it seems)."[310] The interpretation of *malakos* would have been found in his source; the second etymology may be an addition of his own.

The importance of the two women in the downfall of Aristodemus is the distinctive characteristic of the narrative which attracted Plutarch. The role of Xenocrite in the assassination seems more or less typical, and was probably written by Plutarch's source in imitation of earlier accounts, such as that related of Thebe of Pherae.[311]

The sources for this history of Aristodemus cannot be established with any certainty. Timaeus is probably the source of Diodorus, and perhaps was used by Dionysius.[312] The tradition seems to have been confused, however, by other historians of Rome and Magna Graecia, as well as authors of *Kymaika* such as Hyperochus.[313]

Mulierum Virtutes 27: PYTHES' WIFE [314]

The Pythes of whom Plutarch speaks in this chapter is identical with the Pythius[315] who is the central figure in a well-known story of

---

[310] Athenaeus 8, 360 B gives another etymology of *korônistai* from Pamphilus of Alexandria.

[311] A famous tyrant-slayer celebrated by Theopompus (*FGrHist* 115 F 337) and many others; see above, n. 254.

[312] See Jacoby, Comm. to *FGrHist* 566 (Timaeus), III B pp. 527-529 and n. 30 (p. 313).

[313] Eduard Meyer, *Geschichte des Altertums* III² (1937) 750 n. 1, suggested that the accounts of Dionysius and Plutarch may ultimately derive from a chronicle such as Hyperochus. De Sanctis (above, n. 306) maintained that Hyperochus was clearly the source, and was followed by Jacques Heurgon, *Recherches sur l'histoire... de Capoue préromaine* (Paris 1942) 64. Cf. Hyperochus (*FGrHist* 576 F 1 = Athen. 12, 528) on the effeminate practices of the Cumeans, similar to those enforced by Aristodemus during his tyranny. The contradictions which have been remarked, however, show that the tradition is not so simple. In an article entitled "Griechische Nachrichten über Italien," *SBMunich* (1905) 59-132, W. Christ analyzes the various accounts (pp. 59-71) and concludes (p. 122) that they show the unmistakable tenor of Diocles of Peparethus: an author of whom we have only two fragments, the longer retold by Plutarch from Fabius Pictor (*FGrHist* 820 F 2 = *Romulus* 3).

[314] This title was added by Xylander; no break is indicated in the manuscripts. The first part of this chapter is one of the stories from the *Mulierum Virtutes* used by Polyaenus in his *Strategemata* (8.42). See Chapter II and especially pp. 20-21.

[315] The spelling of the name varies somewhat: *Puthês* (genitive *Putheô*) Plutarch; *Puthios* Herodotus; *Puthês* (genitive *Puthou*) Steph. Byz.; *Putheas* Schol. to Aristides; *Pythis* Pliny; *Pythius* Seneca. I shall use the form Pythes throughout.

Herodotus. By far the greater part of Plutarch's account, however, is completely independent of Herodotus, and indeed unique. Let us consider the version of Herodotus first.

Pythes, a fabulously wealthy Lydian of the time of Xerxes' invasion of Greece, is presented to us by the historian in two short but highly effective scenes (7.27-29, 38-39). In the first are described his wealth and favor with the king: he gives a feast for all the Persian troops; it is recalled that he gave Darius a golden plane tree and a golden vine; and he offers his enormous fortune to Xerxes for the war (the king allows him to keep his money and adds a gift of his own, to make the sum an even 4,000,000 staters). But in the second scene, Pythes asks Xerxes to spare his eldest son from the expedition against Greece, as a comfort to his old age. Xerxes is so enraged by this request that he orders the boy to be killed, cut in half and the two parts placed on either side of the road, and has the army march out to war between them.

The wealth of Pythes and the anger of Xerxes are frequently recalled in classical authors. Pliny (*Naturalis historia* 33.10 [47]) refers to the plane tree and vine, the dinner, and Pythes' request. Others mention only his great wealth,[316] the plane tree,[317] or Xerxes wrath.[318] All of these stories are derived from Herodotus.

The account of Plutarch treats perfunctorily, but in complete agreement with Herodotus, Pythes' hospitality to Xerxes, his request for the exemption of his son, and Xerxes' anger. However, the bulk of his narrative is devoted to two other stories not even suggested by Herodotus, stories which are more folk tale than history. According to the first story, Pythes was ruining his city by his desire for gold, forcing the citizens to work his mines to the exclusion of all else, even farming. His wise and kind wife, however, was moved by the distress

---

[316] Stephanus of Byzantium s.v. Pythopolis (whose source has calculated that the money offered by Pythes to Xerxes would equal about six darics per man); Suidas s.v. Apartian; Basil, *Sermo de legendis libris gentilium* 8 (Migne, *Patrologia Graeca* 31, 585c); Eustathius comm. to *Iliad.* 2.865; Tzetzes *Chiliades* 1.926-929.
[317] Scholiast to Aristides *Panathen.* 129, 8 (III, p. 147 Dindorf).
[318] Seneca *De ira* 3.16.4.

5*

of the people and formed a plan to make him aware of the senselessness of his passion. She had goldsmiths reproduce every kind of food in gold, and when Pythes sat down to eat she served him only these golden imitations. Thus she brought Pythes by hunger to realize his folly so that thereafter he required only a fifth of his subjects to work in the mines.[319]

In Plutarch's second tale Pythes' folly is complete renunciation of the world, a living death. The story is introduced by a summary of Herodotus' story of Xerxes' wrath to which Plutarch adds a significant detail: after Xerxes killed the one son, the other four fell in the expedition against Greece, so that Pythes was left childless. Discouraged with life, yet unwilling to die, Pythes retreated to a tomb in the middle of a river, where he lived cut off from mankind, fed from a boat floated down the river each day by his wife. He also entrusted the government of the city to her, and according to Plutarch, she administered it excellently.

It is readily apparent that the two folk-stories in Plutarch are quite independent of Herodotus' account. Not only is there no intimation of such stories in Herodotus, but even their tone of reproach of mortal folly is absent from his account. Yet the passage which connects the two episodes is obviously taken from Herodotus. By referring to the deaths of Pythes' other sons, Plutarch provides more effective motivation for the story following.

The first story of Pythes is very close to the theme of the well-known legend of Midas and the golden touch. It is not necessary to assume with W. Aly, however, that it is a rationalized version of that legend.[320] Herodotus knew a historical Midas, son of Gordias and king of Phrygia (1.14, 35, 45) and a tale of the wonderful Macedonian

---

[319] This story is retold in florid prose by the twelfth-century rhetor Nikephoros Basilikes (*Progymnasmata* 2.3 [Walz, *Rhetores Graeci* I, 430–432]). He does not give Pythes' name, but records his debt to Plutarch in the heading: "Story which also Plutarch tells in the parallel (lives)." The incorrect ascription is not surprising in a schoolbook of this kind. On Nikephoros see Krumbacher, *Byzantinische Literaturgeschichte*[2] (Munich 1897) 473–475.
[320] *Volksmärchen*, pp. 172–173.

rose garden of Midas where he caught Silenus (8.138), but no more. We first hear of Midas' gift of the golden touch in the time of Augustus from Conon (*FGrHist* 26 F 1, 1) and Ovid (*Metamorphoses* 11.85-145). Herodotus gives one fully developed tale of Pythes, but there may have been others. The wealth and culture of Lydia as well as of Phrygia encouraged the development of folk-legend about the figures of its leading men, and the account of Pythes found in Plutarch may have arisen independently alongside those in Herodotus concerning Pythes, Croesus, and Midas. That these tales would have common elements, or influence each other is only natural. Aly further suggests that the legend of Pythes was recorded by Xanthus of Lydia, remarking the obviously fictional and novelistic quality of some of his stories as well as the Ionic form of Pythes' name used by Plutarch. Especially interesting as an example of the moralistic folk tale of the type which Plutarch relates is Xanthus' anecdote of the gluttonous king: one night he ate his wife in his sleep, and awoke to find her hand, all that was left of her, still in his mouth (*FGrHist* 765 F 18). However, inasmuch as Plutarch never cites Xanthus, and considering the number of lost Ionian historians who may have given this story, the attempt to name Plutarch's source remains speculation. Plutarch's version of the story of Pythes' retreat to the tomb depends for its motivation on Herodotus' account of Pythes' treatment at the hands of Xerxes. Thus it is possible that here is given the account of an author, perhaps a local historian, who wrote after Herodotus and enlarged upon him, adding material from folk legend. It is also possible, however, that these stories were recorded without reference to Herodotus, and only later combined with his more famous account, either by Plutarch or by an earlier writer.

The amount of history contained in the narrative of Herodotus and Plutarch is uncertain. Aly treats Herodotus' account as a legend grown up after the Persian War, because the eclipse, which Herodotus says preceded Pythes' second encounter with Xerxes, must be dated in 478. However, the eclipse is not essential to the story of Pythes, and Herodotus may well have made the connection himself, after having been incorrectly informed that there was an eclipse at Sardis while Xerxes was there. There is no reason to doubt the historicity of Pythes, although in the absence of any confirmation by Herodotus we cannot be sure that he was the grandson of Croesus, as Stein and Macan argued in their commentaries to Herodotus 7.27. Plutarch's statement that Pythes was actually the ruler of a city, Pythopolis,[321] and owner of gold mines is quite possibly true.[322] The punishment of Pythes' son as given in Herodotus and followed by Plutarch, is perhaps a doublet of Darius' punishment of Oiobazos before he set off against Scythia (4.84).[323] It is a typical story of Persian tyrannical rule and may have no basis in fact.

[321] The name is implied in the name of the river Pythopolites, and affirmed by Stephanus of Byzantium s.v. Pythopolis.
[322] On the gold mines in Lydia, see Carl Roebuck, *Ionian Trade and Colonization* (New York 1959) 88-89; T. L. Shear, *CW* 17 (1924) 186-188.
[323] See Macan, Comm. to Herodotus 7.39.

IV
PLUTARCH'S INTEREST IN HISTORY

On the basis of the foregoing analysis of the *Mulierum Virtutes*, certain conclusions may be drawn concerning Plutarch's purpose, sources, and methods in this work and in his other historical writings, especially the *Parallel Lives*. In the introduction to his collection Plutarch clearly states his purpose—to give examples of virtue in women, with the special condition that he will avoid the best-known stories, unless the previous authors had omitted some detail worth hearing.[1]

The most remarkable effect of his resolve to avoid well-known stories is the complete absence from this collection of stories about Athens or Athenians, while Sparta is mentioned in only one story from its earliest period, just after the Dorian conquest (8, Tyrrhenian women). Plutarch must have felt that the histories of these two cities were too familiar to be repeated here. Similarly, he avoids Thucydides and Xenophon, two of the most famous Greek historians, and he does not relate stories from Herodotus, although several of his accounts are expansions or corrections of short notices in that author.[2] In fact, all the stories in the *Mulierum Virtutes* are taken from the works which no longer survive.[3] In selecting stories from Roman history his policy is the same: famous women such as Lucretia, Cornelia, and Porcia are remarkable for their absence. Moreover, none of Plutarch's stories may be dated later than the first half of the first century B.C., although he certainly knew many which occurred much later.[4]

---

[1] 243 D. [2] For Herodotus' relation to the *Mulierum Virtutes*, see below p. 136.
[3] Even the chapter from Polybius (22, Chiomara) is from a book now lost.
[4] E.g., the story of Empone, *Amatorius* 770 D–771 C, see above, Chapter I, n. 32.

Plutarch's expression, "those who have narrated the common, widespread stories" (*tous ta koina kai dedêmeumena pro hêmôn historêsantas*, 243 D) does not refer to earlier anthologists, as sometimes has been suggested, but to historians. Plutarch did not use an anthology in compiling this work; he himself points out that Clea was acquainted with the more famous tales, and she certainly would have had no need for a digest by him of an anthology. The anthology theory rested on the opinion that Polyaenus' *Strategemata* were independent of Plutarch's collection, and that both were derived from a common anthological source. The comparison of the two authors made in Chapter II, however, has demonstrated with certainty that Polyaenus is directly dependent upon Plutarch for eighteen of the nineteen stories of the *Strategemata* which are similar to anecdotes in the *Mulierum Virtutes*.[5] Thus collapses the only argument for an anthological source for Plutarch's collection. A detailed study of the individual stories, moreover, has revealed Plutarch's own hand at work throughout his collection. Not only is there no evidence for the anthology theory, but as has been shown, it runs counter to the evidence provided by the stories themselves. Of the twenty-seven stories here collected, eighteen are known only through Plutarch. The nine which are reported elsewhere conform completely to Plutarch's statement of intention, for they either treat uncommon and obscure incidents, or add new details to traditional accounts.

Thus the account of the Trojan women (*Mul. Virt.* 1) had been told in various forms as early as Hellanicus and Aristotle, yet for the Romans it was not the canonical version (it is not mentioned by Vergil or Livy), and to the Greeks it was remarkable because it connected a common story (the burning of the ships) with the founding of Rome.[6] In *Mul. Virt.* 2 (Phocian women) Plutarch added personal information to his account of an episode from the archaic history of

---

[5] See above, Chapter II.
[6] Note Plutarch's remark preceding another version of this story, *Quaestiones Romanae* 265 BC, to this effect.

Phocis, a region of little importance in Greek history—an episode which he narrated in much fuller form in his lost life of Daiphantus. Apart from Plutarch, our only source for this story is Pausanias, who was himself a notable collector of out-of-the-way anecdotes concerning local history and practices. The background of *Mul. Virt.* 4 (Argive women) is familiar from Herodotus, yet again Pausanias is our only other source for the story in Plutarch. Moreover, in *Mul. Virt.* 4 Plutarch added at least the citation of Socrates of Argos to the common account. The anecdotes of the Persian women (5), although not totally obscure (from Ctesias it found its way into Nicolaus of Damascus and Justin, and it was known also to Polyaenus), is hardly ordinary, and was enriched by Plutarch's reference to Ochus' miserliness and Alexander's liberality. In *Mul. Virt.* 8 (Tyrrhenian women) Plutarch does not give the account of Herodotus, but rather a historicized version (otherwise unknown) of his account, combined with an episode from Ephorus. The story of Cloelia (14) would have been familiar to Romans, but probably not to Plutarch's Greek readers. Moreover, Plutarch includes the story of Valeria, which is otherwise known to us only through a brief notice by the indefatigable elder Pliny. Callimachus gave an account of Pieria (16), Parthenius of Polycrite (17): both authors were famous for their efforts to search out unfamiliar stories. The fact that they narrate stories similar to those in Plutarch seems to corroborate the latter's statement that he collected uncommon anecdotes. Finally, although the story of Chiomara (22) was narrated by Polybius and after him by Livy, followed by other Romans, its setting in Galatia and its isolation from the main events of that period[7] justify its inclusion in Plutarch's collection. Thus even the few stories preserved in similar versions by other authors are seen to confirm fully Plutarch's affirmation in his introduction.

Thanks to Plutarch's express desire to assemble uncommon stories for this collection, the *Mulierum Virtutes* is especially valuable for

---

[7] Manlius led only a punitive expedition against Galatia, for Antiochus had already been defeated in the decisive battle of Magnesia the year before.

investigating his familiarity with Greek historical writing. In the past our estimates of Plutarch's first-hand reading have been subject to attacks of unrestrained skepticism.[8] More recently Plutarch has once more come to be recognized as one of the best-educated men of his time.[9] Let us review the authors who have been identified as sources for stories in the *Mulierum Virtutes* in the fuller context of Plutarch's complete works.

From the citations in the *Lives* it is certain that Plutarch used Ephorus for the biographies of the fifth and fourth centuries, most notably those of Pericles, Alcibiades, Lysander, Dion, and Pelopidas.[10] Our analysis of the *Mulierum Virtutes* reveals that the second part of *Mulierum Virtutes* 8 (Tyrrhenian women) on the colonization of Crete, is also taken from Ephorus, from the early books which treated the migrations after the Dorian invasion. This fact implies that Plutarch read large portions of Ephorus, if not the whole work, and not just those books treating the fifth and fourth centuries, an assumption which is confirmed by a suggestive anecdote related by Plutarch of a garrulous acquaintance at Chaeronea (*De garrulitate* 514 C = *FGrHist* 70 F 213). "Having read by chance two or three books of Ephorus, he wore out everybody and made every dinner unbearable by holding forth continually on the battle of Leuctra and its aftermath, and so won the nickname 'Epaminondas'." Plutarch is tolerantly amused: he himself knows Ephorus well.

The story of Micca and Megisto (15) is taken from another author

---

[8] See, e.g., Eduard Meyer, *Forschungen zur alten Geschichte* II (Halle 1899) 67: "Da—abgesehen von den nachher zu besprechenden Ausnahmen bei Nepos—auf der Hand leigt, dass sie (Nepos and Plutarch) Herodot, Thukydides, Xenophon nicht benutzt haben, und obwohl sich jetzt gezeigt hat, dass Plutarch die *pol.Ath.* des Aristoteles—und von der Schrift über den Staat der Lakedaemonier gilt natürlich dasselbe—nirgends zur Hand gehabt hat, sondern aus ihr nur das anführt, was er in seiner Vorlage fand, redet man immer noch von Ephoros und Theopomp u.a. als den Quellen des Plutarch."

[9] See Ziegler *RE* 914–928 and Theander, *BLund* 1950–1951, 1–86.

[10] See Theander, *BLund* 1950–1951, 62–63 and K. B. J. Herbert, *HSCP* 63 (1958) 510–513. The citations from *De Herodoti malignitate* 869 A and 855 F (*FGrHist* 70 F 187 and 189) and *Themistocles* 27 (F 190) demonstrate that Plutarch knew Ephorus' account of the Persian War.

whom Plutarch had used frequently in the *Lives*. Phylarchus is an important source in the *Pyrrhus*, *Aratus*, and *Agis and Cleomenes*.[11] The presence in the *Mulierum Virtutes* of this episode from Phylarchus, which falls immediately after Pyrrhus' fatal expedition to the Peloponnesus, described in Plutarch's biography, and before the events narrated in the *Aratus*, demonstrates that Plutarch had read Phylarchus' entire work, and not simply those passages which concerned the particular lives he was composing. Thus, when collecting the anecdotes for the *Mulierum Virtutes*, he was able to use this story from Phylarchus, which he had not had occasion to narrate in the *Lives*. Other quotations scattered throughout his writings further establish Plutarch's complete familiarity with Phylarchus, even for details not directly connected with the third century.[12]

The case of Polybius is similar. Plutarch's citations show that he drew upon Polybius in the *Marcellus*, *Aemilius Paulus*, *Cato Maior*, *Aratus*, *Agis and Cleomenes*, and *Philopoemen*.[13] His use of Polybius for the story of Chiomara (22) again proves that he did not restrict himself to those sections of history immediately useful for the *Lives*, but read the entire work. Further corroboration of this argument is furnished by his citation of Polybius 2.18.3 in *De Fortuna Romanorum* 325 F (on the retreat of the Gauls from Rome, a detail not mentioned in the *Camillus*) and of 36.16.11–12 in *An seni resp.* 791 F (on the age and virility of Masinissa).

Ctesias is cited ten times in the first twenty chapters of the *Artaxerxes*. The citations are usually accompanied by vehement criticisms of Ctesias as a historian, which reveal Plutarch's personal acquaintance with his work. Since Ctesias is an eyewitness source, Plutarch considers him more reliable for the reign of Artaxerxes than later writers

---

[11] See J. Kroymann, *RE* Suppl. 8 (1956) 484–485, s.v. Phylarchos, and Jacoby, *FGrHist* II C, p. 134.

[12] See *FGrHist* 81 F 74–79, odd facts reported in *Camillus* 19, *Demosthenes* 27, *Themistocles* 32, *De Alexandri fortuna* 342 D, *De Iside* 362 BC, and *Symposiaca* 680 D.

[13] See Theander, *BLund* 1950–1951, 52–53. Plutarch probably also drew from Polybius' life of Philopoemen. His lost lives of the two Scipios (Lamprias catalogue 7 and 28) would certainly have used material from Polybius; cf. the citation of 31.27 for the betrothal of Cornelia and Tiberius Gracchus, *Tiberius Gracchus* 4.

such as Dinon.[14] His distrust and the lack of suitable opportunity to quote him explain why Plutarch cites Ctesias only once apart from the *Artaxerxes*.[15] Nevertheless, the tale from Ctesias in *Mul. Virt.* 5 (Persian women) indicates that his reading in this author was not limited simply to the section on Artaxerxes. We know Ctesias was being read at the time of Plutarch: under Nero, Pamphile made an epitome of his work, and a papyrus fragment of his history discovered at Oxyrynchus (*POxy* 2330 = *FGrHist* 688 F 8b) was copied in the second century A.D. There is every reason to believe that Plutarch also read this author, whom Photius found interesting enough to read and epitomize even in the ninth century.

The story of Timoclea (24) is another version of the account in *Alexander* 12, but unlike the stories in *Mul. Virt.* 1 (Trojan women) and 14 (Valeria and Cloelia), which are derived from the respective *Lives*, it is taken directly from Plutarch's source for the anecdote, Aristobulus. It is evident from the numerous citations of Aristobulus in the *Alexander* that Plutarch had read his history. The story of Timoclea, which Plutarch found especially delightful,[16] he repeated in his collection of women's deeds in a form fuller and closer to the original than was possible in the biography.

Plutarch drew upon another writer whom some have attempted to disassociate from him.[17] Aristotle's *Politeiai*, and its companion *Nomima Barbarika*, were a mine of information on early Greece. In the *Politeiai* Aristotle treated the constitutional history of one hundred

---

[14] See *Artaxerxes* 1 (*FGrHist* 688 F 15a) and 6 (F 29a).

[15] The only other citation, *De sollertia animalium* 974 E (*FGrHist* 688 F 34b; on cows that count) is found also in Aelian, *De natura animalium* 7.1 and is probably not directly from Ctesias; see Jacoby *RE* s.v. Ktesias, XI 2 (1922) 2070.

[16] See *Non posse suav.* 1093 C, quoted above, p. 113.

[17] Wilamowitz stated the case against Plutarch's knowledge of the *Constitution of the Athenians* in *Aristoteles und Athen* (Berlin 1893) I 299–303, making much of the argument that there is no trace of its influence in the *Aristides*, *Cimon*, or *Pericles*. Eduard Meyer inferred from Plutarch's alleged ignorance of the *Constitution of the Athenians* (which surprised him) that Plutarch had not seen the Lacedaemonian constitution either (*Forschungen zur alten Geschichte* I [Halle 1892] 262 n. 1, cf. p. 238). Sandys in his second edition of the *Constitution of the Athenians* (London 1912) pp. xxxi–xxxiv voiced some doubts about this view, but seems to accept it.

and fifty-eight Greek cities, using material gathered by himself and his disciples. They were frequently quoted by scholiasts and lexicographers, notably Harpocration, to explain unusual customs or expressions. Yet useful though they were for the scholar, they had been written, as the exoteric Peripatetic books generally, for a wider public. The *Constitution of the Athenians* is remarkable for its compact and readable presentation of a mass of historical and constitutional information. Moreover, Aristotle was not averse to relieving his systematic treatment with anecdotes. The number of quotations preserved from the *Politeiai* is sufficient proof of their popularity even in Plutarch's day. Most important, however, Plutarch himself testifies to the pleasure to be had in reading them, and lists them in the first rank of Greek literature. There is a certain pleasure in learning even when it is painful, he tells us,

> but when history and the narration of great and noble deeds holds nothing harmful or painful, and moreover adds a forceful and pleasing diction, as do the *Hellenika* of Herodotus and the *Persika* of Xenophon and "whate'er Homer with godly knowledge prophesied," or the *Periodos* of Eudoxus, the *Foundations* and *Constitutions* (*ktiseis kai politeiai*) of Aristotle, or the *Lives of Men* of Aristoxenus, the delight is great, and pure and without regret as well. (*Non posse suav.* 1093 C.)

This testimonial Plutarch confirms in his writings: there are seven direct quotations of the *Constitution of the Athenians* alone, and another fifteen which have been reasonably ascribed to the remaining *Constitutions*, as well as many anonymous borrowings from Aristotelian material.[18] Plutarch's citations far outnumber those of other literary writers. The *Athenian* and *Lacedaemonian Constitutions*, of

---

[18] To Rose's collection may be added the citation *Lycurgus* 14, which refers to the *Constitution of the Lacedaemonians* rather than to *Politics* 1270 a 6. Plutarch cites the *LacPol* five other times in the *Lycurgus* (chaps 1, 5, 6, 28, 31 = fr. 533, 537, 536, 538, 534 Rose; compare also chap. 5 with fr. 535) but never cites the *Politics* elsewhere. The historical examples in the *Politics* were based on the same material as those of the *Politeiai*, if not on the *Politeiai* themselves. See Wilamowitz, *Aristoteles und Athen* (Berlin 1893) I, 359, H. Bloch, *HSCP* Suppl. 1 (1940) 356–357, and Felix Jacoby, *Atthis* (Oxford 1949) 210–212.

course, are quoted most frequently, but those of many other states are referred to, especially in the *Quaestiones Graecae*.[19] Plutarch's citation of Aristotle in his account of Polycrite (17), and his certain dependence on him for the story of the Trojan women (1), increase yet more the mass of evidence which proves his familiarity with and frequent use of Aristotle's collection.

Other writers used by Plutarch in the *Mulierum Virtutes* are cited in his short historical treatises although they were not important sources for the *Lives*. Thus Socrates of Argos, whom Plutarch gives as the authority for a detail in his account of the Argive women (4), is quoted several times for information on Greek cults in the *Quaestiones Graecae* and *Quaestiones Romanae*, as well as once in the *De Iside*. Plutarch took his account of Lampsace (18) from Charon of Lampsacus, whom he had quoted verbatim in the *De Herodoti malignitate*.[20]

Socrates and Charon were both local historians, to whom Plutarch referred for information about events not usually mentioned in more general histories. No doubt many other stories in this collection are derived from local historians. Plutarch cites the Naxian writers as a group as the source for one version of the story of Polycrite (17). The Naxians are also cited in *Theseus* 20.8 and *De Herodoti malignitate* 869 A–C. On other occasions Plutarch uses local historians anonymously: thus the analysis of *Mul. Virt.* 4 (Argive women) reveals Plutarch's familiarity with Argive local tradition, and is confirmed by his quotations of Socrates and his citation of the *Argolika* of Deinias in *Aratus* 29.4 (*FGrHist* 306 F 5).[21] Other accounts in the *Mulierum Virtutes* probably derived from local historians are those of the Chian women (3), the Melian women (7), the Milesian women (11), the Ceian women (12), Pieria (16, from a Milesian history),

---

[19] See Karl Giesen, "Plutarchs Quaestiones Graecae und Aristoteles' Politien," *Philologus* 60 (1901) 446–471 (who somewhat exaggerates Plutarch's debt to Aristotle) and W. R. Halliday, *The Greek Questions of Plutarch* (Oxford, 1928) 14–15.

[20] On the *De Herodoti malignitate*, see below, p. 136.

[21] Although Jacoby, Comm. to *FGrHist* 306 F 5 doubts that Plutarch knew Deinias directly.

Eryxo (25, from a Cyreniac history)[22] and Xenocrite (26, from a history of Italian Cumae).

This variety of authors[23] for a small collection of anecdotes is impressive evidence of Plutarch's broad historical reading. It is certain that Plutarch did not read through all these authors simply to gather material for the *Mulierum Virtutes*. On the contrary, this review of the authors used as sources in the *Mulierum Virtutes* leads us to one conclusion: that all Plutarch's historical works, the monumental corpus of biographies together with the several short treatises, share a common foundation formed by Plutarch's extended acquaintance with Greek and Roman history.

Further consideration of these works of Plutarch reveals additional proof for this conclusion. It has been shown that authors who were important sources for the *Lives*—Ephorus, Phylarchus, Polybius, Ctesias, Aristobulus, Aristotle—provided material also for the *Mulierum Virtutes*. The bond between the different works is still more explicit in certain cases, in which not only is an author used who was also used in the *Lives*, but the same story, or part of the same story, is narrated in both the *Mulierum Virtutes* and the *Lives*:

Mul. Virt. 1 (Trojan women): *Romulus* 1 (and *Quaestiones Romanae* 265 BC).

Mul. Virt. 2 (Phocian women): *Daiphantus* (now lost).

Mul. Virt. 5 (Persian women): *Alexander* 69.

Mul. Virt. 14 (Valeria and Cloelia): *Publicola* 18-19.

Mul. Virt. 24 (Timoclea): *Alexander* 12.

It is particularly interesting that of the five parallels listed here, only two seem to be completely dependent on the account in the *Lives*, *Mul. Virt.* 1 and 14. Two others, *Mul. Virt.* 5 and 24, are neither drawn from nor a source for the versions of the *Lives*. In these two cases

---

[22] The account of Aretaphila (19) may perhaps also be from a Cyreniac history.
[23] Still others who cannot be identified were the sources for the accounts of the Phocian women (2, 13), the anecdotes connected with Hannibal (6, Celtic women; 10, women of Salmantica), the Tyrrhenians in Sparta (8 pt. 1), Cloelia (14), the Galatian stories of Camma (20), Stratonice (21), and the woman of Pergamum (23), and the fables of Pythes (27).

Plutarch drew each version from the original account of his source, or rather from his memory of it, without consulting the version he himself had written earlier. The case of *Mul. Virt.* 2: *Daiphantus* is special, both because we do not possess the *Life* and because Plutarch expressly affirms the bond between the two versions. The account of the *Mulierum Virtutes* describes the role of the women in the events which he had treated in detail in the *Daiphantus*. Plutarch's statement makes it possible to gain some idea of the contents of the *Daiphantus* from the condensation of Phocian-Thessalian history in *Mul. Virt.* 2. Unfortunately we cannot be sure exactly how much difference there was between the treatment of the women's courageous resolution in the two versions.

Other stories in the *Mulierum Virtutes* are more loosely related to the *Lives*. The third episode of *Mul. Virt.* 3 (Chian women) describes the siege of Chios by Philip V in 201 B.C.; *Mul. Virt.* 22 (Chiomara) gives an anecdote from Polybius' account of the Roman expedition into Galatia in 189 B.C. Both stories belong to the period of the Roman wars with Philip V and Antiochus which played an important part in the *Cato Major*, *Flamininus*, and *Philopoemen*. The two episodes which Plutarch reports concerning Hannibal, *Mul. Virt.* 6 (Celtic women) and 10 (women of Salmantica), took place early in the second Punic war, which was also the setting of the *Fabius* and the *Marcellus* (and the *Scipio Africanus*, now lost). Again, the account of Aretaphila and Cyrene "at the time of the Mithridatic wars" in *Mul. Virt.* 19 and that of Mithridates' massacre of the Galatians in *Mul. Virt.* 23 belong to the period of the *Sulla* and the *Lucullus*. The reign of King Deiotarus, whose wife Stratonice is the heroine of *Mul. Virt.* 21, fell in the years treated in the *Brutus* and the lives of the other Romans of the mid-first century B.C. Finally, Plutarch's account of Xenocrite (26) was undoubtedly influenced by (though not derived from) the version of Dionysius of Halicarnassus which is imbedded in the latter's history of Coriolanus, the source of Plutarch's *Coriolanus*. These anecdotes that are thus drawn from the same periods as certain of the lives must be regarded as by-products, or additional fruits, of the investigations which Plutarch conducted preparatory to writing those biographies.

Besides the *Lives*, the *Mulierum Virtutes* has particularly close ties with three other short treatises. Although Plutarch's enthusiasm for history permeated all his writings,[24] in the *Quaestiones Graecae, Quaestiones Romanae*, and *De Herodoti malignitate* his full attention is devoted to historical problems. The *Parallel Lives* were concerned with the most famous leaders of Greece and Rome, and Plutarch's attention naturally concentrated upon the most glorious periods of the two peoples. In his lesser works, however, and in such isolated biographies as the *Daiphantus* or the *Aristomenes*, he could reveal his unfailing interest in other incidents from the past, his fascination with all facets of ancient Greece. That same gentle philosopher who preferred to remain in Chaeronea rather than enjoy the libraries and scholarly intercourse of Athens because "we live in a small town, and cling there lest it become smaller still" (*Demosthenes* 2), who served willingly in the humble offices of his community, remembering that Epaminondas had also taken these inglorious positions, enjoyed also discovering new details of the history and customs of Naxos and Samos, of Ithaca and Megara and Cyrene.

By proposing to avoid in the *Mulierum Virtutes* the well-known stories of women, Plutarch gained an opportunity to write of events far removed from the cities and the periods treated in the *Lives*, and established a sympathetic bond between this and his other minor historical works. Thus the *Quaestiones Graecae*, as the *Mulierum Virtutes*, mentions Sparta only once and avoids any consideration of Athenian history or custom, although some fifty-nine problems drawn from all Greece are considered. Of the authors shared by the two works Socrates of Argos and especially Aristotle have already been remarked. In addition, they share a single source for the slightly differing accounts in *Mul. Virt.* 8 (Tyrrhenian women) and

---

[24] Note that the versions of two of the stories from *Mulierum Virtutes* appear in the *De anima* (preserved in Gellius 15.10: *Mul. Virt.* 11, Milesian women) and the *Amatorius* (768 B-D: *Mul. Virt.* 20, Camma).

Quaestiones Graecae 296 B–D. Local historians and antiquarians must have been the source for many of the questions considered in this work.[25] Some of them undoubtedly were derived from Aristotle's *Constitutions*, but Plutarch's confrontation of Aristotle and the Naxian writers in *Mul. Virt.* 17 (Polycrite) shows that he also read the local historians themselves.

Roman historical and antiquarian writing was far less rich than Greek, and Plutarch's acquaintance with it less extensive, yet the *Quaestiones Romanae* makes apparent Plutarch's fascination with the peculiarities of Roman practice and the obscurities of Roman history. Many of his discussions are given in slightly different form in the Roman lives, especially the *Romulus* and *Numa*. Such is the case with the story of the Trojan women preserved in *Quaestiones Romanae* 265 BC. This account and that of *Romulus* 1 are derived independently from Aristotle; from *Romulus* 1 is derived the version of *Mul. Virt.* 1. The more or less independent treatment of the same problems in the *Quaestiones Romanae* and the *Lives* is another indication that Plutarch's general historical investigations were the source of both.

In his work *De Herodoti malignitate* Plutarch criticizes Herodotus for belittling the Greeks, especially in his account of the Persian wars. He corrects what he terms Herodotus' malicious errors from numerous epigrams and writers such as Charon of Lampsacus, Aristophanes of Boeotia, and the Naxian writers (*hoi Naxiôn hôrographoi*), besides well-known historians such as Hellanicus, Thucydides, and Ephorus. He especially attacks Herodotus' bias in favor of Athens, which he considers only a device to make light of the role played by the other states in the defense of Greece. To counteract this bias and record the actions of the other cities in the best possible light, the testimony of the local historians was invaluable. Similarly in the *Mulierum Virtutes* a number of stories from Herodotus are expanded and corrected, without, however, the scathing indictment of Herodotus found in the *De Herodoti malignitate*. Only in *Mul. Virt.* 4

[25] Note that Jacoby collects the sections on Samos (nos. 20, 54, 55, 56 and 57) in his *Anhang* to the local historians of Samos (*FGrHist* 545 F 3–7).

(Argive women) is Herodotus criticized by name. This account takes from Argive writers a notable expansion and express correction, in favor of Argos, of a story in Herodotus which Plutarch must have considered tendentious and pro-Spartan. Other stories in which Plutarch thus elaborates a brief notice in Herodotus are those of the Phocian women (2), Tyrrhenian women (8), Eryxo (25), and Pythes' wife (27).

A fourth historical work, now lost, the *Foundings of Cities* (*poleôn ktiseis*, Lamprias catalogue 195), probably contained accounts cognate to those in the *Mulierum Virtutes*. Plutarch tells stories connected with the founding of Rome (1, Trojan women), Leuconia (3, Chian women), Cryassa (7, Melian women), Lyttus (8, Tyrrhenian women), Myus (16, Pieria), and Lampsacus (18, Lampsace). These anecdotes would of necessity have been derived in great part from local historians, as the story of Lampsace is derived from Charon.

These briefly noted parallels between the *Mulierum Virtutes* and Plutarch's other historical works furnish additional proofs for the conclusion already drawn from our review of the authors used in this treatise—that Plutarch's various biographies and the shorter historical treatises rest upon the foundation of his exceptional familiarity with classical historical writing.

Two other observations are important for the proper evaluation of Plutarch's work by the historian. First, it is only natural that Plutarch's historical interest manifested itself not only in extensive reading, but also in a curiosity about monuments, places, festivals, or customs which recalled the past.[26] He enjoyed talking with his friends, and learned much from them. The story of the Phocian women, *Mul. Virt.* 2, is founded upon just such personal contact with the extant traces of the history he reported: a friend of his boasted to be a descendant of the hero Daiphantus, and Plutarch himself had visited Hyampolis (only some seven miles from Chaeronea), near which the famous battle with the Thessalians had been fought, and had watched

[26] A complete discussion of Plutarch's non-literary sources has not been written, but see C. Theander, *BLund*, 1950–1951, 2–32 and *Eranos* 57 (1959) 99–131.

the festival which, in his day, still recalled the victory. It was undoubtedly this personal acquaintance with Phocis and with these reminders of the past that inspired him to write the life of Daiphantus, an otherwise obscure Phocian hero. Certainly this contact has left its imprint on the anecdote in the *Mulierum Virtutes*.

Second, Plutarch's reliance upon his memory to store the wealth of material which he accumulated from his broad reading, discussions with friends, and personal observation must not be underestimated. Although he also took notes and made collections of anecdotes and other intriguing information,[27] his memory could have been the immediate source for the anecdotes of the *Mulierum Virtutes*, as for much of his other work.[28] Indeed, this was an essential difference between Plutarch and a modern historian: Plutarch did not write surrounded by his written authorities.[29] For Plutarch history was an account of past events and people, not a science. This attitude is discernible in the *Mulierum Virtutes*, in which Plutarch appears more as storyteller than historian.

Consider the incidental differences between two versions by Plutarch of the same story. In *Mul. Virt.* 14 he tells us that the companions of Cloelia tied their garments on their heads before swimming the Tiber: the version of *Publicola* 19 does not mention this, but does note that the river was curved and especially quiet where the girls swam across, a detail lacking in *Mul. Virt.* 14. We need not believe that Plutarch's source gave these details: such small bits of gratuitous information are the stock in trade of the storyteller who wishes to add charm to his anecdote and is not tied to a written text. Similar differences are noted in the other cases in which Plutarch tells the same

---

[27] See his references to his notes in *De tranquillitate animi* 464 F and *De cohibenda ira* 457 D, and the collections of *apophthegmata* (*Mor.* 172 A–242 D) probably made by him for his own use and later published.

[28] Note the revealing comment, *Pericles* 24.12, after he had added a brief notice of Cyrus' favorite courtesan, Aspasia, to his remarks on her more famous namesake: "These thoughts having come to mind while writing, it would perhaps have been unnatural to reject them and pass them by."

[29] See the observations on this score by A. W. Gomme, *Commentary on Thucydides* (Oxford 1945) I 84.

story twice. In *Mul. Virt.* 24 Timoclea allows her Macedonian assailant to climb down into the well before throwing stones upon him; in *Alexander* 12 he is a Thracian and she pushes him in. The difference reveals less a failure of memory (certainly not variant accounts in Plutarch's source!) than a lack of interest for what he regarded as irrelevant detail: Plutarch wished to recall the courage and intelligence of Timoclea, and incidental variations in his story did not concern him. An extreme example of this narrative freedom is found in his two accounts of Camma (*Mul. Virt.* 20 and *Amatorius* 768 B–D), in which he presents two quite different versions of Camma's prayer, but does not change the action or the moral of the story. In relating an anecdote Plutarch reshaped his source's account in accord with the context in which he wished to place it and his own remarkable narrative skill. He did not alter the essentials of the story, but he also did not intend its details to be scrutinized and compared with minute attention.

It follows that he did not hesitate to be selective in telling a story for a particular purpose, or to combine two sources to provide a more complete account. Thus for his story of Micca and Megisto (15) he chose to concentrate on the incidents in Phylarchus involving women and omitted important parts of Phylarchus' narrative which we know only through other authors. In the stories of the Argive women (4), Persian women (5), Tyrrhenian women (8), Valeria and Cloelia (14), and Polycrite (17), Plutarch conflated two or more sources into one account, a process facilitated by his dependence upon his memory as his immediate source.

In one instance, the account of the Trojan women (1), the basis of which is undoubtedly Aristotle, Plutarch in retelling the story here and in the *Romulus* modified an important feature and made the men Trojans to conform to opinions held in his own day.

This evidence of Plutarch's freedom in his treatment of his sources is especially important for the analysis of the historical accounts in the *Lives*. If Plutarch used more than one source for a short anecdote in the *Mulierum Virtutes*, he undoubtedly did the same in the *Lives*, and the determination of the source of any particular statement in the *Lives* becomes more difficult than has sometimes been believed. These conclusions also suggest that more effort should be made to understand Plutarch's own attitudes and interests, without supposing that he unfailingly reflects those of his source.

The examination of the anecdotes of the *Mulierum Virtutes* in relation to the *Lives* and the other historical treatises shows that Plutarch read many historical works entirely or in grand part, not just the particular sections which would be useful for a single life. Writers such as Ephorus, Aristotle, and Phylarchus, to name only a few, were important sources, and were supplemented by acquaintance with numerous local historians. Although his *Lives* often pass over events not immediately related to the statesman whose biography he is writing at that moment, he was quite familiar with the more general history of the period concerned, even with events in Salmantica or Galatia. Plutarch did not derive his information about these periods from predigested biographies or handbooks: he enjoyed history, he read historical works, and the knowledge thus acquired he poured out in his writings, in the *Mulierum Virtutes* as well as in the *Parallel Lives*. Although he was not primarily a historian, and certainly never a critical historian in the modern sense, Plutarch believed a man's character could be understood through his actions, and combined this moral interest with a deep love of his Hellenic past, so that he established himself as one of the great interpreters of classical antiquity. In the *Mulierum Virtutes* he is revealed as a true author and no compiler, for even in the shortest anecdotes, which offer so much less opportunity for the expression of a personal viewpoint than the *Lives*, Plutarch is seen to select, combine, abridge, and narrate anew his material in such a way that it becomes no longer another's, but his own. This personal re-creation of the classical past has made his own works themselves classics for succeeding generations.

BIBLIOGRAPHY

INDEX

BIBLIOGRAPHY

This is a selection of works which have been used in the preparation of this work. Bibliography for the individual stories will be found in the notes to the commentary on each story.

I. PLUTARCH

EDITIONS

Plutarch, *Opera Moralia*, ed. Daniel Wyttenbach, with notes (incomplete) and *index graecitatis*. 8 vols. Oxford 1795-1830; corr. rep. Leipzig, 1796-1834.
—— *Opera*, ed. T. Doehner and Fr. Dübner, with *index nominum et rerum*. 5 vols. Paris (Didot) 1841-1855.
—— *Moralia*, ed. G. N. Bernadakis. 7 vols. Leipzig (Teubner) 1888-1896.
—— *Lives*, Greek and English, trans. Bernadotte Perrin. 11 vols. London and New York (Loeb Classical Library) 1914-1926.
—— *Vitae*, ed. C. Lindskog and Konrat Ziegler, with indices. 4 vols. in 8. Leipzig (Teubner) 1914-1939.
—— —— —— re-edited Konrat Ziegler, vol. I, 1. Leipzig 1957; vol. I, 2. Leipzig 1959; vol. II, 1. Leipzig 1964; Third edition by Konrat Ziegler. vol. I, 1. Leipzig 1960.
—— *Roman Questions*, trans. and comm. H. J. Rose. Oxford 1924.
—— *Moralia*, ed. C. Hubert, W. Nachstädt, W. R. Paton, M. Pohlenz, W. Sieveking, J. B. Titchener, J. Wegehaupt, K. Ziegler. 6 vols. (vol. V, pt. 2, not yet published). Leipzig (Teubner) 1925– .
—— *Moralia*, Greek and English, ed. and trans. F. C. Babbitt, H. Cherniss, P. H. DeLacey, B. Einarson, H. N. Fowler, W. C. Helmbold, E. L. Minar, Jr., F. H. Sandbach. 11 vols. publ. of 15. London, New York, and Cambridge, Mass. (Loeb Classical Library) 1927– .
—— *Greek Questions*, ed. and comm. W. R. Halliday. Oxford 1928.
—— *Dialogue sur l'amour*, ed. R. Flacelière. (Annales de l'Université de Lyons 3e ser., Lettres, fasc. 21, Paris 1952).
—— *Vies*, ed. and trans. R. Flacelière, É. Chambry, M. Juneaux. Paris (Budé) vol. I, 1957; vol. II, 1961.
—— *Lives*, trans. by several hands (Dryden translation), 1683-1686, rev. by Arthur H. Clough, 1864.

Plutarch, *Morals*, trans. by several hands, cor. and rev. William W. Goodwin. 5 vols. Boston 1870.

SECONDARY WORKS

Dinse, M. *De libello Plutarchi gunaikôn aretai inscripto*, Berlin 1863.

Giesen, Karl. "Plutarchs Quaestiones Graecae und Aristoteles' Politien," *Philologus* 60 (1901) 446-471.

Gomme, A. W. *A Historical Commentary on Thucydides*, I-III. Oxford 1945-1956.

Hartman, J. J. *De Plutarcho scriptore et philosopho*. Leiden 1916.

Helmbold, William C. and O'Neil, Edward N. *Plutarch's Quotations* (Philological Monographs of the American Philological Association XIX, 1959).

Hirzel, Rudolf. *Der Dialog* II (Leipzig 1895) 124-237.

——— *Plutarch* (Das Erbe der Alten, IV). Leipzig 1912.

Macan, Reginald Walter. *Herodotos, the seventh, eighth, and ninth books*. II (London 1908) 84-93.

Meyer, Eduard. "Die Biographie Kimons," *Forschungen zur alten Geschichte* II (Halle 1899) 1-87.

Mittelhaus, Karl. *De Plutarchi praecepta gerendae reipublicae* (Diss. Berlin 1911).

Peter, Hermann. *Die Quellen Plutarchs in den Biographien der Römer*. Halle 1865.

Renoirte, Thérèse. *Les "Conseils politiques" de Plutarque*. Louvain 1951.

Schläpfer, Hans. *Plutarch und die klassischen Dichter*. Zürich 1950.

Schmid, Wilhelm and Stählin, Otto. *Geschichte der griechischen Litteratur*, II[6] 1 (Munich 1920) 485-534.

Theander, Carl. "Plutarchs Forschungen in Rom—Zur mündlichen Überlieferung als Quelle der Biographien," *Eranos* 57 (1959) 99-131.

——— "Plutarch und die Geschichte," *Bulletin de la Société Royale des Lettres de Lund*, 1950-1951, pp. 1-86.

Trench, Richard Chenevix. *Plutarch: His Life, His Parallel Lives, and His Morals*. London 1874.

Volkmann, Richard. *Leben, Schriften und Philosophie des Plutarch von Chaeronea*. 2 vols. Berlin 1869.

Ziegler, Konrat. *RE* s.v. Plutarchos 2, XXI 1(1951) 636-962. Published separately as *Plutarchos von Chaironeia*, Stuttgart 1949. (Cited as Ziegler, *RE*)

II. POLYAENUS

Polyaenus. *Strategemata*, ed. Eduard Wölfflin and Joannes Melber. Leipzig (Teubner) 1887.

Gutschmid, Alfred von. "De Aegyptiacis apud Polyaenum obviis eorumque fontibus," *Philologus* 11 (1856) 140-150 (*Kleine Schriften*, I [Leipzig 1889] 166-178).

Knott, Otto. "De fide et fontibus Polyaeni," *Commentationes philologae ienenses* 3 (1884) 49-96.

Lammert, Friedrich, *RE* s.v. *Strategemata*, IV 1 A (1931) 174-181.

—— *RE* s.v. Polyainos 8, XXI 2 (1952) 1432-1436.

Melber, J. "Über die Quellen und den Wert der Strategemensammlung Polyaens," *Jahrbücher für classische Philologie*, Suppl. Bd. 14 (1885) 417-688.

Schirmer, Adolf. *Über die Quellen des Polyaen*. Altenberg 1884.

III. GENERAL

Aly, Wolf. *Volksmärchen, Sage und Novelle bei Herodot und seinen Zeitgenossen*. Göttingen 1921.

Beloch, Julius. *Griechische Geschichte*^{2}. 4 vols. in 8. Strassburg, Berlin, Leipzig 1912-1927.

Bengston, Hermann. *Griechische Geschichte*^{2}. Munich 1960.

Bilabel, F. "Die ionische Kolonisation," *Philologus* Suppl. vol. XIV (1920) pt. 1.

Burn, A. R. *The Lyric Age of Greece*. London 1960.

Busolt, Georg. *Griechische Geschichte*^{2}. 2 vols. in 4. Gotha 1893-1904.

—— and Swoboda, Heinrich. *Griechische Staatskunde*^{3}. 2 vols. Munich 1920-1926.

Cambridge Ancient History, ed. J. B. Bury, S. A. Cook, F. E. Adcock, and M. P. Charlesworth.

De Sanctis, Gaetano. *Storia dei Romani*. Turin 1907- .

Dihle, Albrecht. *Studien zur griechischen Biographie, Abhandlungen Akademie Göttingen, Philosophische-historische Klasse*, 3. Folge, 37 (1956).

Fragmenta Historicorum Graecorum, ed. C. Müller. Paris 1841-1870.

Fragmente der griechischen Historiker, ed. Felix Jacoby. Berlin and Leiden 1923- .

Gelder, Henrick van. *Galatorum res in Graecia et Asia gestae*. Amsterdam 1888.

Höfer, Ulrich. *Konon: Text und Quellenuntersuchung*. Griefswald 1890.

Jacoby, Felix. *Atthis*. Oxford 1949.

—— *RE* s.v. Herodotos 7, suppl. 2 (1913) 205-520.

Kroymann, Jürgen. *RE* s.v. Phylarchos, suppl. 8 (1956) 471-489.

Leo, Friedrich. *Die griechische-römische Biographie*. Leipzig 1901.

Magie, David. *Roman Rule in Asia Minor*. 2 vols. Princeton 1950.

Meyer, Eduard. *Geschichte des Altertums*^{2}. Stuttgart 1937.

Nilsson, Martin. *Griechische Feste von religiöser Bedeutung.* Leipzig 1906 (unaltered reprint Darmstadt 1957).
Pearson, Lionel. *Early Ionian Historians.* Oxford 1939.
Ramsay, W. M. *Historical Commentary on St. Paul's Epistle to the Galatians.* London 1899.
Roebuck, Carl. *Ionian Trade and Colonization.* New York 1959.
Sakellariou, Michel B. *La Migration grecque en Ionie.* Athens 1959.
Tarn, W. W. *Hellenistic Civilisation*[3]. London 1952.

INDEX

The *Fragmente der Griechischen Historiker* are cited in the form 500 F 1 (not *FGrHist* 500 F 1).

Abydus: 35, 37
Academy: 4
Acarnanians: 35
Acesandrus: 117
    469 F 7: 117
Achaeans: 30–32
Achaemenids: 54
Achilles: 10
Aelian: *De nat. animal.* 7.1: 130
    Var. hist. 2.38: 77
Aeneas: 33
Aeschines: 39
    2.140: 37, 40
Aeschines the Socratic: 8
Aethilla: 34
Aetolia: 86
Aetolians: 87, 89
Africa: 75
Agamemnon: 3
Agesilaus: 10
Agesistrata: 87
Agis I of Sparta: 63
Agis IV of Sparta: 85, 87
Ajax: 10
Alcamenes: 62
Alcestis: 10
Alexander the Great: 35, 55–56, 112–114, 127
Alexander of Pherae: 114
Alexander (attacker of Timoclea): 114
Althaemenes of Argos: 60–61, 63
Amasis: 116–117
Amazons: 5, 11, 68–70, 113
Ambitouti: 111
Amisodarus: 69
Amphares: 87
Amphiclus: 42

Amphictyony of Delphi: 80
Amphissa: 79–80
Amyclae: 59, 63
Anaximenes of Lampsacus: 72 F 19: 54
Andriscus: 95
    500 F 1: 94
Annius Fetialis: 83
Anonymous: see *De incredibilibus, De mulieribus, De viris illustribus*
Anticlides: 140 F 5: 42
Antigonus Gonatas: 85–86, 88–89
Antiochus III, the great: 109, 127, 134
Antiochus Hierax: 11
Antipater the Stoic: 4
Antisthenes: 3
Antoninus Pius: 2
Apis: 73
Apollo: 2
Apollodorus of Cassandreia: 89
Apollonius of Aphrodisias or Letopolis (*FGrHist* 740): 58
Apollonius of Rhodes: 73
    Argonautica 1.1177 (and scholiast): 78
Apollonius the Stoic: 7
Apollonius of Tyre: 7
Appian: *Bell. Mac.* 4.1: 44. *Bell. Syr.* 42: 109. *Bell. Mithr.* 46: 111; 75: 106. *Bell. Civ.* 1.111: 102; 4.76–80: 35
Apuleius: *Metam.* 8.1–4: 106
Aratus (the general of Sicyon): 40, 88
Arbocala: 74
Arcesilaus II: 21, 115–117
Archidamia: 87
Aretaphila: 24, 101–103, 133–134
Argeia: 8
Argives: 46–49, 52
Argive writers: 50, 52–53, 132, 137

Index

Argolika: 48, 50
Argonauts: 28, 64, 99
Argos (the city): 44–48, 50–52, 88, 137
Argos (the hero): 46–47
Ariadne: 96
Ariamenes: 11
Aricia: 118–119
Aristaenetus: 90
    Epist. 1.15: 90
Aristides (governor on Ceos): 79
Aristides of Miletus: *Milesiaka*: 77, 91
Aristobulus: 113–114, 130, 133
    139 F 2a, F 2b: 113; F 3, 4, 46: 114
Aristodemus *ho Malakos*: 118–120
Aristomenes: 40, 62
Aristophanes: *Frogs* 970: 79
Aristophanes of Boeotia (*FGrHist* 379): 136
Aristotimus of Elis: 84–89
Aristotle: 31–33, 44, 96, 126, 132–133, 135–136, 139–140
    Ktiseis (*Foundations*): 131. *Nomima barbarika*: 31, 130. *Politeiai* (*Constitutions*, see also *Frags.*): 31, 33, 96–97, 130–131, 136. *Pol. Athen.*: 128, 130–131. *Pol. Laced.*: 128, 130–131. *Politics*: 131. 1259 b 1: 4; 1260 a 21: 3; 1260 a 21–24: 4; 1270 a 6: 131; 1271 b 28: 62; 1303 a 6: 49–50. *Fragment* 64 Rose: 4; F 485: 62; F 511, F 514: 78; F 528–531: 117; F 533–538: 131; F 556: 91–93; F 558: 95; F 559: 93–95; F 609 (=*FGrHist* 840 F 13): 30; F 610: 33; F 611,27: 78; F 611,28: 79; F 611, 43: 71; F 611, 44: 31; F 611, 58: 31
Aristoxenus: *Lives of Men*: 131
Arrian: *Anabasis* 1.24.4: 35
Artaxerxes II: 129–130
Artaxerxes III Ochus: see Ochus
Artemis: 38, 60, 93, 104–105
Artemisia: 3, 8
Artemon of Magnesia: 7
Asia Minor: 105, 107, 110–111
Aspasia (mistress of Pericles): 3, 67
Aspasia (courtesan of Cyrus): 138
Astapa: 35
Astyages: 26, 53–54
Athenaeus: *Deipn.* 6, 258 F–259 F: 42; 8, 348 AC: 95; 8, 360 B: 120; 9, 384 DE: 42; 10, 440 EF: 31; 12, 528: 120; 13, 563 E: 4; 13, 566 E: 79; 13, 593 AB: 10; 13, 610 D: 79
Athenians: 37, 58, 62, 67, 125
Athenopolis: 21
Athens: 62, 67, 79, 89, 125, 135–136
Atossa: 8
Attalus I: 44
Attalus II: 11
Attica: 65–66, 93
Attis: 104
Augustus: 123
Aurelius Victor: see *De viris illustribus*
Axiothea: 4

Banon: 22, 74–75
Barce: 115
Basil: *Sermo de leg. lib. gent.* 8: 121
Battus I: 99, 117
Battus II: 115–117
Battus III: 115–116
Bebrycians: 97–99
Bellerophon: 1, 28, 68–73
Bellona: 104
Bepolitanus: 110–111
Berenice: 107
Blepsus: 97–98
Boccaccio: *De mulieribus claris* 29: 64; 50: 81; 71: 109
Boeotia: 80
Bosphorus: 78
Bottiaeans: 62
Brauron: 60, 64–66, 68
Britomartis Chersonesus: 60
Brogitarus: 107
Brutus: 10, 35

Caesar, C. Julius: 9
    Bellum Gallicum 7.39.1, 7.67.7: 111
Calbia: 102
Callicles: 87
Callimachus: 90, 127
    Hymns I 77–78, III 225–227: 93. *Aitia*: 90. *Frag.* 80–83: 90–91; 80: 93
Camma: 2,6,11, 23, 26,28, 103–106, 112, 133, 139
Candia: 73
Caphene: 57

Capua: 119
Caria: 57-58
Carians: 57
Carthage: 75
Carthaginians: 56, 75
Carvilius: 78
Cassius Dio: 45.31.1: 81; 63.26.5: 69; 66.3,16: 6; Frag. 14.4 Melber: 81
Castor (King of Galatia): 107
Castor and Pollux: 64
Cato: 7, 10
Ceians: 79
Ceos: 78-79
Celts: 56, 104
Chaereas (*FGrHist* 177): 75
Chaeronea: 112-114, 128, 135, 137
Chalcedon: 101
Chalcis: 42-43
Charon of Carthage (*FHG* IV 360): 8
Charon of Lampsacus: 99-101, 132, 136-137
 Hôroi Lampsakênôn: 98, 100-101. *Peri Lampsakou:* 101. *Persika:* 100. 262 F 7: 24, 97-101
Chians: 41-42, 75, 79
Chian local history: 43
Chilon (of Elis): 86
Chilonis, wife of Cleombrotus: 88
Chilonis, wife of Cleonymus: 88
Chilonis, wife of Theopompus: 64
Chimaera: 68-72
Chimarrhus: 69-70
Chiomara: 28, 104, 108-109, 112, 125, 127, 129, 134
Chios: 41-44, 79, 134
Chremonidean War: 88
Cians: 78
Cicero: *Ad Atticum* 5.17.3: 107. *De invent.* 2.49(144): 102. *De off.* 2.7(25): 102. *De orat.* 2.11(44): 9. *Disp. Tusc.* 3.12.27: 119. *Phil.* 11.31,33: 107. *Pro rege Deiot.* 36: 107
Cios: 78
Claudia Quinta: 5, 6
Claudian: 18.447, 29.16-17: 80
Clea: 1-3,7,9,11, 79-80,85,126
Cleanthes: 4
Clement of Alexandria: *Protrep.* 2.27: 73. *Strom.* IV 8,59: 4

Cleobulina, daughter of Cleobulus: 5-6
Cleomenes I: 6, 45-49, 51
Cleomenes III: 87-88
Cleonae: 36
Cleonice: 7
Clitarchus: 113
 137 F 15, F 33: 113
Cloelia: 11, 18, 21, 80-84, 127, 130, 133, 138-139
Cnopus: 42-43
Codrus: 43, 91
Coelius Antipater: 74
Coins: *Guide to the Principal Coins of the Greeks*, Pl. I, no. 18: 69
Colones (Kolôneis): 41
Conon: 62, 67
 26 F 1, c.1: 123; c.36: 59-63; c.47: 60, 63; c. 50: 102
Constantinian excerpts: 46
Coriolanus: 81, 134
Cornelia, mother of the Gracchi: 6, 10-11, 125, 129
Cornelia, wife of Livius Drusus: 11
Cornelia, wife of Julius Caesar: 9
Corones: 41
Crataedas: 60
Craterus, general of Antigonus Gonatas: 89
Crates the Cynic: 4
Cratesiclea: 87
Cratesipolis: 21
Cretans: 61
Crete: 58-65, 67, 128
Critola: 116-117
Croesus: 123-124
Cryassa: 57-58, 137
Cryassos: 58
Ctesias: 8, 53-56, 127, 129-130, 133
 688 F 1b, 1c: 10. F 8b, 15a, 29a, 34b: 130. F 45 c. 20, F 45e: 71-72
Cuchulinn: 73
Cumae (in Italy): 118-119, 133
Cumeans: 120
Cumean history: 133
Cyaretus: 91
Cydrelus: 91
Cyllon: *see* Cylon
Cylon of Elis: 85-87, 89
Cyrenaic local history: 133

Index

Cyrene: 39, 99, 101–103, 115, 117, 134–135
Cyrus the Great: 35, 53–56
Cyrus the Younger: 138

Daiphantes: *see* Daiphantus
Daiphantus of Hyampolis: 35–40, 137
Danae: 88
Daphne: 88
Darius: 121, 124
De incredibilibus 8: 71
Deinias: 306 F 5: 132
Deiochus: 471 F 3: 98, 100
Deiotarus Philadelphos: 107
Deiotarus I Philoromaios: 106–107
Deiotarus II Philopator: 106–107, 112, 134
Deiotarus, father of Brogitarus: 107
Delium: 93, 95
Delphi: 1–3, 9, 43, 48, 79–80, 85, 87, 89, 117
Delphus: 58–61
Demaratus of Sparta: 45, 47, 51–52
Demaretus of Elis: 86
Demeter: 52, 119
Demonax of Mantinea: 115, 117
Demophilus: 79
Demosthenes: 114
De mulieribus: 8
    c. 1: 10
De viris illustribus 13: 81–82, 84; 55: 108
Dido: 8
Dinarchus: 1.74: 114
Dinon: 130
    690 F 21: 55
Diocles of Peparethus: 120
    820 F 2: 120
Diodorus Siculus: 1.85.3: 73; 2.4–20: 10; 7.10: 118, 120; 16.4: 102; 16.33.3: 80; 18.72.2: 78; 22.5.2: 89
Diogenes Laertius: 6.1.12: 3; 6.7.96–97, 17.1.33, 7.5.175: 4
Diognetus: 93–95
Dionysius of Halicarnassus: 83, 119–120, 134
    Rom. Ant. 1.72.2: 33; 1.72.3–4: 30–31; 5.21–35: 81, 83; 5.33: 81; 5.33.3–4: 83; 5.35.2: 84; 5.36: 118; 6.1–8.62: 118; 6.21: 119; 6.94.1: 81; 7.2–11: 118–120; 7.3–4: 119; 7.9.4: 118; 7.12: 119; 8.56: 49
Dionysus: 80, 85
Dorians: 59–60, 63, 68
Dracon: 70

Egypt: 22, 73, 102, 116–117
Elaphebolia: 36, 38
Eleans: 87
Electra: 107
Eleusis: 73
Elis: 79, 84–85, 87–89
Empone, wife of Sabinus: 6, 11, 125
Emporius Orator: p. 570 Helm: 80
Epaminondas: 128, 135
Ephorus: 37–38, 59–60, 62–65, 67–68, 96, 127–128, 133, 136, 140
    70 T 9: 79. 70 F 46: 98; F 93–96: 79; F 113: 63; F 117: 59, 62–63; F 149: 60–62, 64; F 187, 189, 190, 213: 128
Epicurus: 4
Epponina: *see* Empone
Eporedorix: 110–111
Eposognatus: 105
Eros: 6
Erythrae: 42–43
Erythraeans: 41–43, 93
Eryxo: 21–22, 106, 115–118, 133, 137
Etna, Mt.: 72
Etruscans: 118–119
Etymologicon Magnum: 58
    s.v. Lampsakos: 100
Etymonus: 86
Eudoxus: 131
Euhemerus: 69
Eumachus: 111
Eumenes II: 11, 105–106, 109
Eumetis: 6
Euphamos: 99
Euripides: 68
Eurysthenes: 60
Eusebius: 43, 98
Eustathius: Comm. to *Iliad* 2.865: 121; to 17.720: 114

Fabius Pictor (*FGrHist* 809): 120
Festus: s.v. Romam: 30–31
Flavia Clea: *see* Clea

Index

Florus: 1.10.7–8; 81–82; 1.27: 108
Frontinus: *Strateg.* 2.5.15: 41–42

Galatia: 44, 104–108, 111, 127, 134, 140
Galatians: 104–110, 112, 134
Galen: 10
Gaul: 6, 111
Gauls: 57, 89, 129
Gellius, Aulus: 3.15.1: 94–95; 4.3.2: 78; 4.5: 84; 15.10: 26, 76–77, 135; 17.21.44: 78
Gelon (of Phocis): 34, 39
Gordias: 122
Gorgias: *Frag. d. Vors.* 82 B 22: 3, 9
Gorgo: 5–6
Gortyn: 59–61
Gracchus, Tiberius: 129
Great Mother: *see* Magna Mater
Greece: 89, 121–122, 130, 135–136
Greeks: 33–36, 67, 89, 97, 99, 113, 126, 136

Hadrian: 2
Hannibal: 23, 56–57, 74–75, 133–134
Harpagus: 35, 72
Harpocration: 131
  s.v. Aspasia: 96
Hecataeus (*FGrHist* 1): 66, 69
Hellanicus: 8, 44, 48, 96, 126, 136
  4 F 4: 66; F 84: 33; F 125 = 323a F 23: 92
Hellanicus (of Elis): 85–86
Helmantica: *see* Salmantica
Helot War: 62–64
Hephaestopolis: 21
Hera: 85
Heraclea: 72
Heracles: 70, 72
Heraclidae: 59–60, 63
Heraclides Lembos: 31, 78–79
  Politeiai 15: 71; *see also* Aristotle, frag. 611
Heraclitus: *De incred.* 15: 70
Hermandica: *see* Salmantica
Herodorus: 69
Herodotus: vii, 8, 51, 66, 68, 78, 96, 99, 123–125, 127–128, 131, 136–137
  Hist. 1.14: 122; 1.18.3: 42; 1.35, 45: 122; 1.125.3: 54; 1.142: 92; 1.142.4: 42; 1.173: 71; 1.176: 35, 72; 2.102–110: 10; 2.161, 181: 117; 4.84: 124; 4.145–148: 63–65, 67–68; 4.145–146: 28; 4.146: 59; 4.159: 117; 4.160: 115–116; 4.161: 115, 117; 4.162–167: 117; 5.51: 6; 6.8: 91; 6.19: 47; 6.77.2: 47; 6.75.3–84.1: 45–51, 53; 6.138: 66; 7.27–29: 120–123; 7.27: 124; 7.38–39: 120–124; 7.239: 6; 8.27–28: 34, 36, 39; 8.27.2: 34, 40; 8.48: 60; 8.138: 123
Hesiod: 68
  Theogony 590–612: 3
Hestia: 94
Hierocles the Stoic: 4
Hieronymus of Cardia: 154 F 15: 52
Hipparchia: 4
Hippias of Erythrae: 421 F 1: 42–43
Hippoclus: 41, 43
Hippolochus of Thessaly: 104
Hippolytus: 8
Hippomedon: 119
Homer: 5, 131
  Iliad 2.824–827: 69; 6.156–195: 68; 16.328–329: 69; *Odyssey* 11.424–434: 3
Horatius Cocles: 80–82, 84
Hostius, L.: 78
Hyampolis: 36, 38, 40, 137
Hyperochus: 120
  576 F 1: 120
Hypsicreon: 93–94

Illyrians: 89
Imbros: 58–60, 62, 65–67
India: 72
Inscriptions:
  IG II² 1956: 89; II² 3429: 106; IX 90: 38
  SEG I 159: 2; IX 3: 39; XVIII 216: 9
  *SIG*³ 134 (= Tod *GHI* II, 113): 92; 423: 87; 591: 98
  Berl. Griech. Urkunden 1266: 89
  BCH 70 (1946) 254–259: 2
  Clara Rhodos 2 (1932) 172–174 no. 3 = *RivFC* 60 (1932) 446–452: 106, 109
  Hesperia 29 (1960) 198–223: 39
  Milet I, 3, no. 33e: 92; no. 41: 78
  Rev. Arch. 6 (1935) 140–151: 107
  Tod *GHI* II no. 204: 39

Inscriptions—*continued.*
    CIL XIII 2728, 2805: 111; XV 796: 83
Iobates: 69
Ion of Chios: 43
Ionia: 91
Ionians: 41–42, 69, 90–91, 93
Irene: 10
Isaras: 69
Isis: 2
Italy: 30, 56, 66
Ithaca: 135

Jerome: *Adv. Jovin.* 1.41: 112
Jews: 103
Josephus: *Ant. Jud.* 14.114: 103
Juba: 83
Julia (aunt of Julius Caesar): 9
Julius Caesar: *see* Caesar
Julius Civilis: 6
Julius Sabinus: 6
Jupiter Stator: 84
Justin: 127
    1.6.13–15: 53–55; Bks. 25–26: 85; 26.1.4–10: 85–86, 88–89
Juvenal: 8.265: 80

Keiai: 78
Kiai: 78
Kianos: 78
Kianis: 78
Koroneia: 41
Kymaika: 120

Laarchus: *see* Learchus
Lacedaemonians: 60, 62, 65. *See also* Spartans
Laconia: 58–60, 63–64, 68
Lactantius: *Div. inst.* 3.25: 4
Lade: 42, 48, 91
Lais: 104
Lampis: 85–86
Lampsace: 23, 58, 97, 99–101, 132, 137
Lampsacus: 97–101, 137
Laodice: 88
Latins: 30
Latium: 31
Leander: 102–103

Leandr(i)us: 91
    492 F 18: 90
Learchus: 21–22, 106, 115–117
Lelantine War: 42–43
Lemnians: 59–61, 63
Lemnos: 58–60, 62–68
Leo Diaconus: *Hist.* II 6: 73
Leon: 70
Leonidas: 6
Leontis: 8–9
Leucadian Rocks: 97, 100–101
Leucas: 101
Leuce: 101
Leuconia: 41–43, 137
Leuctra: 128
Leukios: 85, 89
Leukon: 115
Libya: 102
Libyans: 102
Livy: 33, 74, 108, 126–127
    2.9–14: 81, 83; 2.10.12: 84; 2.13.6–11: 81; 2.13.11: 84; 2.21.5: 119; 5.50.7: 9; 21.5: 75–76; 21.5.5: 74; 21.24: 56; 26.25.11–14: 35; 28.17: 75; 28.22.23: 35; 29.14: 6; 38.18–27: 109; 38.18–19: 105; 38.19.2: 109; 38.24: 108; *Epit.* 70: 102; *Epit.* 94: 106
Locris: 36
Lucius: 89
Lucius Verus, emperor: 13
Lucretia: 11, 82, 125
Lucullus: 102–103
Lyceas: 312 F 1: 52
Lycia: 68–69, 71–72
Lycians: 69–71
Lycophron: vs. 921: 33
Lycus: 72
Lyde: 8
Lydia: 123–124
Lydian: 121
Lysander: 67
Lyttians: 62
Lyttus: 58, 60–62, 137

Ma: 104
Macedonia: 13, 114
Macedonians: 113–114
Maeandrius (*FGrHist* 491): 90
Magna Graecia: 120

Index

Magna Mater: 6, 104
Magnesia: 92, 109, 127
Malakos: see Aristodemus ho Malakos
Mandron: 97–100
Manilius: 1.780: 80
Manlius Vulso, Gn.: 105, 108–109, 127
Mantineans: 85
Marcus Aurelius: 13
Mariandyni: 72
Masaesylian: 22, 75
Masinissa: 129
Massilia: 98
Matidia II (aunt of Antoninus Pius): 2
Maximus of Tyre: Diss. 37.5: 49
Medes: 26, 53, 55
Megara: 135
Megisto: 28, 84–85, 88, 128, 139
Mela: see Pomponius
Melanippus: 24, 28
Melians: 57
Melos: 57–60, 63–64, 68
Memmia Eurydice: 2
Menecles of Barce: 8, 117–118
    270 F 5, F 6: 117
Micca: 28, 84–85, 88, 128, 139
Midas: 122–123
Milesiaka: see Milesian local history
Milesians: 20, 46, 90, 92–94, 98, 132
Milesian writers: 496 F 1: 91; F 6: 90
Milesian local history: 76, 91–92
Miletus: 42–43, 48, 76, 78, 90–93
Miltiades: 67
Minyans: 28, 59, 64
Mithridates VI Eupator: 101, 103–104, 107, 110–112, 134
Mucius Scaevola: 80–82
Musonius Rufus: 4–5, 11
Mycale: 43
Myrsilus of Lesbos: 477 F 8–9: 66
Mysta: 88
Myus: 90–93, 99, 137
Myusians: 92

Naxian: 93–94
Naxian writers: 95, 132, 136
    501 F 1: 96; F 2: 93–95; F 3: 96
Naxos: 42, 93, 135
Nea Cryassa: 57–58
Neaera: 93–95

Neleids: 91
Neleis (feast): 91, 93
Neleus: 90–91, 93
Nepos, Cornelius: 128
Nero: 4, 130
Nestor: 10
Niceratus: 52
Nicocrates: 24, 101–103
Nicolaus of Damascus: 14, 54, 62, 67, 127
    90 F 28: 59; F 50: 115; F 66, c.36: 54; F 66, c.43–44: 53–55; F 99: 54; F 103k: 71
Nikephoros Basilikes: *Progymnasmata* 2.3: 122
Nitocris of Babylon: 8
Nitocris of Egypt: 8
Nymphaeus: 57
Nymphis: 432 F 4–5: 72; F 7: 71–73

Ochus: 55–56, 127
Odysseus: 10, 33
Oibares: 27, 54
Oiobazos: 124
Olympia: 85, 87, 89
Olympias: 10
Olympiodorus: *in Plat. Gorg.* XLIV 4: 69–70
Onomarchus: 80
Onomaris: 8
Oracula Sibyllina: 3.439–441, 4.112–113, 5.126–129: 69
Orgiagon: see Ortiagon
Ortiagon: 105–106, 108–109, 112
Osiris: 2
Ovid: *Heroides* 15. 167–172: 101; *Metam.* 11.85–145: 123
Oxyrynchus: 130

Palaephatus: *De incred.* 29: 70–71
Palatine: 84
Pamphile: 130
Pamphilus of Alexandria: 120
Pamphyliakon: 45
Pandarus: 69
Pandora: 3
Panteus: 88
Panthea: 113
Paphlagonia: 107

Papyri:
  Oxy. 2330: 130
  TAPA 72 (1941) 27–28: 41
Paradoxographus Vaticanus Rohdii: 57
Parium: 42–43, 97–99
Parnassus: 79–80
Paros: 42
Parthenius: 95, 127
  Narr. am. 9: 94–95; 14: 91; 18: 94–96
Parthian War: 13
Pasargadae: 1, 54–55
Paulus Orosius: 2.5.3: 81
Pausanias (Spartan general): 7
Pausanias: 127
  1.13.7–9, 1.13.8: 52; 2.20.8–10: 45–48, 51–52; 2.32.8: 71; 3.2.7, 4.19.4: 62; 5.5.1: 85–87, 89; 6.2.4, 6.14.9: 85; 6.14.11: 85, 87; 7.2.10: 91; 7.2.11: 92; 8.10.5: 85; 8.14.1–3: 70; 10.1.3–11: 34–40; 10.1.8: 35; 10.4.3: 79–80; 10.35.7: 38
Pegasus: 68–70
Pelasgians: 60, 63–68
Pelopidas: 10
Peloponnesus: 85, 88–89, 129
Peponilla: see Empone
Pergamum: 52, 109–111, 133
Pericles: 67
Persepolis: 55
Persians: 27, 34, 53–54
Persian War: 35, 123, 128
Phaedimus: 24, 28, 101
Phaedra: 8
Pherecydes: 3 F 155: 92
Pheretime: 8, 117
Philip V of Macedonia: 41, 44, 92, 112, 134
Philip of Theangela (FGrHist 741): 58
Philochorus: 328 F 99: 66; F 100: 59, 66; F 101: 66; F 104: 70
Philomelus: 80
Philonomus: 59, 63
Phobius: 91
Phobos: 24, 28, 97. See also Phobus
Phobus: 97–101. See also Phobos
Phocaeans: 97–100
Phocians: 34–39, 80
Phocian local history: 38
Phocis: 34, 36, 38–40, 127, 138

Photius: 130
  Bibl. cod. 161, 103 A Bekker: 7; 104 A: 8; 104 B: 7, 35; 105 A: 78; cod. 190, 153 A: 101; Lex. s.v. katêloiôsen: 37
Phoxos: 24, 28, 97. See also Phobus
Phrygia: 122–123
Phrygius: 90–91, 93
Phylarchus: 52, 86–89, 129, 133, 139–140
  81 F 24, F 30, F 32: 88; F 42: 79; F 52: 88; F 74–79: 129
Pieria: 20, 90–91, 127, 132, 137
Pindar: 68, 99
Piso (L. Calpurnius Piso Frugi): 83
Pityoessa: 97–99
Pityoessians: 97
Plataea: 39
Plato: 3
  Menex. 245 D: 67; Meno 73 AB: 3; Phaedrus: 6; Symp.: 6
Pliny the Elder: 127
  NH 5.146: 111; 33.137: 120–121; 34.22: 84; 34.29: 83–84
Plutarch:
  MORALIA: 5, 11, 96, 133
  Adv. Coloten 1109 B: 107
  Amatorius: 2, 6, 104–105
    766 E–768 B: 104; 768 B–D: 2, 6, 11, 26, 28, 104–105, 135, 139; 770 D–771 C: 6, 11, 125
  An seni resp. 791 F: 129
  Apophthegmata (Mor. 172 A–242 D): 138
  Apophth. reg.: 2
  Apophth. Lac.: 2, 50, 56
    223 AB 2, 3: 49; 223 BC 4, 5: 49; 241 B 4: 56
  Consol. ad ux.: 7
  De coh. ira 457 D: 138
  De fort. Alex. 327 F, 334 A, 341 C: 114; 342 D: 129
  De fort. Rom. 322 E–323 D: 10; 325 F: 129
  De frat. am. 488 D–489 F: 11
  De garr. 505 A–511 E: 11; 514 C: 128
  De Herodoti malig.: 100, 132, 135–136
    855 B: 51; 855 F: 128; 856 A: 102; 863 BC: 51; 869 A–C: 132; 869 A: 96, 128
  De Iside: 2, 3, 132
    351 E: 2; 355 C: 55; 360 B: 10;

Index

MORALIA—continued.
  362 BC: 129; 363 C: 55; 364 E: 2, 79; 364 EF: 85; 364 F: 53
  De primo frig. 953 CD: 79
  De sera num. vind. 558 A: 38
  De soll. anim. 974 E: 130
  De Stoic. repug. 1049 C: 107
  De tran. anim. 464 F: 138
  Mulierum Virtutes
    Introduction, 242 E: 3; 242 F: 1; 243 A: 9; 243 B–D: 9–10; 243 D: 11, 125–126. *Mul. Virt.* 1–15: 16. *Mul. Virt.* 1: 16, 23, 26, 30–34, 126, 130, 132–133, 136–137, 139. *Mul. Virt.* 2: 16, 21, 34–41, 101, 126, 133–134, 137; 244 B: 2, 35. *Mul. Virt.* 3: 16, 20, 41–44, 97, 101, 112, 132, 134, 137; 245 A: 75. *Mul. Virt.* 4: 15–17, 21, 24, 45–53, 96, 101, 127, 132, 136, 139. *Mul. Virt.* 5: 15, 26–27, 53–56, 73, 127, 130, 133, 139. *Mul. Virt.* 6: 16, 19, 56–57, 75, 133–134. *Mul. Virt.* 7: 16, 21, 57–58, 132, 137; 246 F: 75. *Mul. Virt.* 8: 16, 21, 26, 28, 58–68, 101, 125, 127–128, 133, 135, 137, 139; 247 E: 62. *Mul. Virt.* 9: 28, 56, 68–73, 101; 247 F: 69. *Mul. Virt.* 10: 16, 22–23, 41, 57, 74–76, 133–134. *Mul. Virt.* 11: 16, 20, 26, 76–77, 91, 132, 135. *Mul. Virt.* 12: 28, 77–79, 132. *Mul. Virt.* 13: 28, 79–80, 133. *Mul. Virt.* 14: 16, 18, 21, 25–26, 39, 80–84, 101, 127, 130, 133, 138–139; 250 C: 82; 250 F: 82, 84. *Mul. Virt.* 15: 28, 79, 84–89, 128, 139; 253 E: 1. *Mul. Virt.* 16–27: 16. *Mul. Virt.* 16: 20, 90–93, 99, 101, 127, 132, 137. *Mul. Virt.* 17: 20, 24, 42, 77, 91, 93–97, 127, 132, 136 139. *Mul. Virt.* 18: 23, 58, 97–101, 132, 137. *Mul. Virt.* 19: 24, 101–103, 134; 255 E: 102, 133. *Mul. Virt.* 20: 2, 6, 23, 26, 28, 101, 103–106, 133, 135, 139. *Mul. Virt.* 21: 16, 28, 106–107, 133–134. *Mul. Virt.* 22: 16, 28, 44, 108–110, 125, 127, 129, 134. *Mul. Virt.* 23: 16, 28, 101, 110–112, 133–134. *Mul. Virt.* 24: 10, 21, 24, 26, 100, 112–115, 130, 133, 139. *Mul. Virt.* 25: 21, 101, 106, 115–118, 133, 137. *Mul. Virt.* 26: 16, 28, 101, 118–120, 133–134; 261 F: 118.

  Mul. Virt. 27: 20, 120–124, 133, 137
  Non posse suav. 1093 C: 33, 97, 102, 112–113, 130–131; 1099 F: 38
  Praec. conj.: 5
    142 CD, 145 A: 6; 145 CD: 5; 145 E: 112
  Quaestiones Graecae: 33, 132, 135
    293 C–F: 79; 296 A (c. 20): 136; 296 B–D (c. 21): 26, 61–62, 136; 297 A (c. 25): 53; 299 A (c. 35): 62; 299 AB (c. 36): 85; 303 C–304 C (c. 54–57): 136
  Quaestiones Romanae: 31, 132, 135–136
    265 BC (c. 6): 26, 30–33, 126, 133, 136; 267 C: 78; 270 D–F (c. 26): 53; 277 A–C (c. 52): 53; 278 E: 78
  Sept. sap. conv. 148 C: 6
  Symposiaca: 38
    660 D: 38; 675 AB: 117; 680 D: 129; 731 D: 77
PARALLEL LIVES: 1, 5, 7, 9–11, 32, 40, 73, 96, 125, 128–129, 132–136, 139–140
  Aemilius Paulus: 129
  Agis and Cleom.: 86, 129
    17: 88; 20: 87; 28: 88; 59: 87; 60: 88
  Alcibiades: 128
  Alexander: 113–114, 130
    1: 11; 10.4: 10; 12: 10, 24, 26, 112–114, 130, 133, 139; 39.4–5: 10; 46: 113; 58: 114; 69: 55, 133
  Aratus: 40, 86, 129
    29.4: 132; 38: 88
  Aristides: 130
  Aristomenes (lost): 40, 135
  Artaxerxes: 54, 129–130
    1: 130; 6: 130
  Brutus: 107, 134
    13.2–6: 7, 10; 53: 54; 53.4–5: 10; 53.4: 82
  Caesar: 5.2–4: 9; 63: 103
  Camillus: 32, 83, 129
    8.3: 9; 19: 129; 22.4: 33
  Cato Maior: 129, 134
  Cimon: 130
    2: 11; 6.4–6: 7
  Coriolanus: 83, 118, 134
    10: 81; 38: 49
  Daiphantus (lost): 2, 35–37, 39–40, 127, 133–135, 138
  Demosthenes: 2: 135; 23: 114; 27: 129

PARALLEL LIVES—*continued*.
  Dion: 128
  Epaminondas (lost): 37
  Fabius: 32, 134
  Flamininus: 134
  Gaius Gracchus: 19: 10
  Tib. Gracchus: 1.4–5: 10; 4: 129
  Lucullus: 107, 111, 134
    2.4: 102–103; 28: 103
  Lycurgus: 32
    1, 5, 6, 14: 131; 15: 78; 28, 31: 131
  Lysander: 128
  Marcellus: 129, 134
    30.4: 82
  Marius: 103
    45.7: 103
  Nicias: 1: 11
  Numa: 32, 136
    25.11: 78
  Pelopidas: 128
    35: 102; 35.3–7: 7
  Pericles: 32, 128, 130
    2.5: 32; 24.12: 138
  Philopoemen: 37, 129, 134
  Pompey: 107, 111
    8: 11
  Publicola: 39, 83
    1, 16–18, 16.1: 82; 16.9: 84; 17.1.
    82; 18–19: 26, 81, 133; 18.1, 18.2: 82;
    19: 25, 81, 138; 19.2: 82; 19.8: 82, 84;
    19.10: 84
  Pyrrhus: 83, 129
    26–28: 88; 27–34: 86; 34: 52, 85
  Romulus: 31–32, 83, 136, 139
    1: 26, 30–33, 133, 136; 2.4–3.1: 73;
    3: 120; 15.7: 31; 17: 94; 22.5, 35.6: 78
  Scipio Afr. Major (lost): 129
  Scipio Afr. Minor (lost): 129, 134
  Sulla: 111, 134
    26: 103
  Themistocles: 32
    27: 113, 128; 32: 129
  Theseus: 32
    1: 32; 20.8: 96, 132
LOST WORKS
  De anima (*Mor.* VII, 20 Bern.): 26, 76–77, 135
  That a Woman Also Should Be Educated (*Mor.* VII, 125–127 Bern.): 6

Lamprias catalogue 7 (Scipio), 28 (Scipio), 35 (Daiphantus): see above among *Lives*. 53 (*Peri Theophrastou* ⟨*politikôn*⟩ *pros tous kairous*): 96. 195 (*Foundings of Cities*): 100, 137
Pollis: 58–61
Polyaenus: 12, 126–127
  Strategemata: 12–29, 126. 4.2.2: 114; 7.1–41: 15; 7.6.1–5, 7.6.1, 7.6.9: 54; 7.42–46: 15–16, 27; 7.45.1: 27; 7.45.2: 14–16, 26, 53–54; 7.47–50: 15–16, 27; 7.48: 16, 22–23, 27, 74–75; 7.49: 16, 21, 27–28, 58; 7.50: 16, 19–20, 27, 56; 8.1–24: 15; 8.25: 15; 8.25.2: 16, 23, 27, 30; 8.26–29: 15; 8.30–32: 15; 8.31: 16, 18, 21, 25–27, 80; 8.33–63: 15–16; 8.33: 15–18, 24, 27, 45, 49; 8.34: 64; 8.35–42: 14, 16, 90; 8.35: 20, 27; 8.36: 20, 24, 27, 93; 8.37: 23, 27–28, 97–98, 100; 8.38: 24, 27–28, 101; 8.39: 23, 27, 103; 8.40: 21, 24, 27, 112; 8.41: 21, 27, 115; 8.42: 20, 27, 120; 8.58: 21; 8.63: 16, 20, 27, 76; 8.64–71: 15; 8.64: 16, 21, 27, 57; 8.65: 16, 21, 27, 34, 40; 8.66: 16, 20, 27, 41; 8.68: 52; 8.71: 28, 64
Polyarchus: 22, 115–117
Polybius: 34, 44, 108–110, 125, 127, 129, 133–134
  2.18.3: 129; 2.41.10: 89; 3.14.1: 74; 3.14.3: 75–76; 3.20.5, 3.33.15: 75; 4.54: 62; 6. 11^a, 4: 31; 9.29.6: 89; 9.40.4–6: 35; 15. 21–23: 78; 16.21–22: 44; 16.24.9: 92; 16. 29–35: 35; 16.32.2: 37; 18.3: 78; 21.37–39: 109; 21.38: 108–109; 22.21: 109; 31.27: 129; 34.10: 56; 36.16.11–12: 129; *Life of Philopoemen:* 129
Polycrite: 20, 24, 93–95, 97, 127, 132, 136, 139
Polytecnus: 42
Pompeius Trogus: 85–86
  Prologue 32: 106, 109. See also Justin
Pompey: 105, 107
Pomponius Mela: 1.97: 98, 100
Popilia, mother of Catulus: 9
Porcia, wife of Brutus: 7, 10, 125
Poredorax: 111. *See* Eporedorix
Porsenna: 80–84, 119

Poseidon: 69–71
Posidonius: 103
　87 T 1, F 37: 103
Priene: 43, 92
Procles: 60
Promedon: 93
Proteus: 68
Prusias of Bithynia: 106, 109
Ptolemaius Chennus: 101
Ptolemy IV: 87
Ptolemy X: 103
Ptolemy Apion: 102
Ptolemy, son of Philadelphos: 10
Publicola: 82
Pyrenees: 56
Pyrrhus of Epirus: 52, 85–86, 88, 129
Pythes: 20–21, 120–124, 133, 137
Pythius: *see* Pythes
Pythopolis: 20–21, 124
Pythopolites (river): 21, 124

Rhodes: 60
Rhodogyne: 8
Rhoeus of Ambrossus: 35–36
Rhome: 23, 30–33
Rhone: 56
Roman history (Greek accounts): 840 F 13: 30
Romans: 81–82, 84, 105, 108–109, 119, 126–127, 134
Rome: 30–33, 78, 81–82, 102, 118–120, 126, 129, 135, 137

Sacred War: 80
Sacred Way: 81, 83–84
Salmantica: 1, 22, 57, 133–134, 140
Salmanticans: 41, 74–75
Samians: 44
Samian local historians: 545 F 3–7: 136
Samos: 44, 135
Sardis: 108–109, 124
Scholiast: to Aristides *Panathen.* 129.8: 120–121; to Homer, *Iliad* 6.181: 70–71; to Juvenal 8.264: 81; to Lycophron 17: 70
Scythia: 124
Seleucus II: 11, 88
Semiramis: 8–9
Semonides: Fr. 7 Diehl: 3

Seneca: *Ad Marciam de cons.* 16: 11; 16.2: 80, 84; *De ira* 3.16.4: 120–121
Sepeia: 18, 45–49, 51, 53
Servius Tullus: 10
Servius: to *Aeneid* 1.273: 31; to *Aeneid* 6.288: 71; to *Aeneid* 8.646: 81, 84
Sesostris: 10
Silenus (the god): 123
Silenus of Caleacte (*FGrHist* 175): 57, 74
Silius Italicus: 10.488–502, 13.828–830: 80
Sinatus: 104–106, 112
Sinorix: 23, 104–107, 112
Sixteen, the: 79, 85
Skiai: 78
Smyrna: 101
Socrates: 3–4, 67
Socrates of Argos: 18, 53, 96, 127, 132, 135
　310 F 2–5: 53; F 6: 45, 51–52
Solinus: *Coll.* 1.2: 31
Solymi: 68, 70
Sopater: 7, 35, 78
Sophists: 3
Sophocles: 68
　Frag. 270 Pear.: 66
Sosylus of Sparta: 74–75
　176 T 3, F 1: 75
Spain: 1, 56, 74
Sparta: 45, 48, 58, 61–64, 88, 125, 133, 135
Spartans: 28, 46, 49, 51, 59–60, 62–63
Stephanus of Byzantium: 58
　s.v. Cryassa: 58; s.v. Lampsakos: 99; s.v. Passargadae: 54; s.v. Phocis: 37; s.v. Pythopolis: 21, 120–121, 124
Stobaeus: 4
　II 31, 123: 5, 11; II 31, 126: 5; IV 22, 21–25: 4;　IV 23–24: 3;　IV 44, 83: 56
Stoicorum Vet. Frag.: I, fr. 247, III, fr. 253–254: 4
Stoics: 4, 6
Strabo: 62, 67
　Geogr. 7, fr. 44 M.: 70; 8.5.4(364): 59; 10.2.9(452): 101; 10.4.14(479): 60; 10.4.16(480): 61;　　10.4.17(481): 62; 10.4.18(481): 60; 12.5.1(566–567): 105; 13.1.7(585): 69; 13.1.14(588): 42;

Index

Strabo—*continued.*
13.1.19(589): 41, 98–99; 14.1.3(633): 43, 91; 14.1.10(636): 92; 15.3.7(730): 55; 15.3.8(730): 54. *Hist.:* 91 F 7, F 8, F 9, F 19: 103
Stratocles: 114
Stratonice: 28, 104, 106–107, 112, 133–134
Struses: 92
Suidas: 103
    s.v. Apartian: 121; s.v. Charon: 8; s.v. Kioi: 78; s.v. Ortiagon: 109; s.v. Polyainos: 13; s.v. Telesilla: 46
Sulla: 102–103, 111

Tacitus: *Hist.* 4.67: 6
Tagus river: 76
Tanaquil: 10
Tarpeia: 94
Tarquins: 80
Tarquin the Proud: 82–84, 118–119
Tatian: *Oratio ad Graecos* 33: 52
Taygetus: 64
Tectosagi: 111
Telmessus: 106, 109
Teles: 56
Telesilla: 17, 45–53
Tellias of Elis: 34–36
Thargelia (the heroine): 8
Thargelia (feast): 94
Theagenes: 100, 112–114
Theano, wife of Pythagoras: 5–6
Thebe of Pherae: 7, 102, 113, 120
Thebes: 112–113
Theiosso: 8
Themistocles: 39, 113
Theophanes continuatus: 6.20: 100
Theophrastus: *Nomoi* 77; ⟨*Politika*⟩ *pros tous kairous:* 77, 94–96
Theopompus: 113, 128
    115 F 337: 102, 120
Thera: 63–65
Theras: 64
Theseus: 8
Thespiae: 6
Thessalians: 34–37, 39–40, 137
Thrace: 70
Thracians: 31, 114, 139
Thrasybulus of Elis: 85

Thucydides: 125, 128, 136
    2.45.2: 3, 9; 4.109.4: 66; 5.84.2: 60; 8.24.3: 41
Thyiades: 79–80
Tiber: 6, 30–31, 138
Timaeus (*FGrHist* 566): 8, 120
Timoclea: 5, 10, 21, 26, 100, 112–114, 130, 133, 139
Timoxena: 6
Tolistobogii: 106–107, 109, 111
Tolostoagii: 111
Tomyris: 8
Tosiopi: 110–111
Triptolemus: 70
Trocmi: 107, 109
Troezen: 39, 71
Trogus, Pompeius: *see* Pompeius *and* Justin
Trojans: 30, 32, 69, 139
Troy: 30–32
Tyrrhenians: 8, 28, 31, 58–59, 62–67, 133
Tyrtaeus: 49
Tzetzes: 33
    Chiliades 1. 926–929: 121

Vaccaei: 74
Valeria: 21, 80, 82–84, 127, 130, 133, 139
Valerius Antias: 83
Valerius Maximus: 82
    3.2.2: 81–82; 4.6 ext. 3: 64; 6.1 ext. 2: 108; 9.13 ext. 3: 102
Valerius Publicola, M.: 82
Varro: 83
Velia: 84
Venus Cluilia, Cluacina, Cloaca: 84
Vergil: 33, 126
    Aeneid 8.651: 80
Vespasian: 6, 9
Voturi: 111
Vulcanal: 84

Xanthians: 35, 71
Xanthippe: 3
Xanthus (city): 35
Xanthus of Lydia: 123
    765 F 18: 123
Xenocrite: 28, 118, 120, 133–134
Xenophilus: 8

Xenophon: 113, 125, 128, 131
    Cyrop. 8.5.21: 55; *Hell.* 2.1.15: 67;
    6.4.35–37: 102; *Symp.* 2.9: 3
Xerxes: 11, 34, 40, 113, 121–124

Zacynthus: 72

Zarinaia: 8
Zeleia: 69
Zeleians: 69
Zeno: 4, 7
Zeus: 3. Z. Soter: 86. Z. on Taunion: 104
Zonaras: 4.9: 112; 8.6: 52

DATE DUE

PA 4368 .M7 S7 88-3412
Stadter, Philip A.
Plutarch's historical
 methods

PJC LEARNING RESOURCES CENTER

WITHDRAWN